DRYDEN'S HEROIC PLAYS

DRYDEN'S HEROIC PLAYS

Derek Hughes

University of Nebraska Press

Lincoln

PR
3427
H4
H8
1981

Library of Congress Cataloging in Publication Data

Hughes, Derek, 1944–
  Dryden's heroic plays.

  Based on the author's thesis, University of
Liverpool
  Includes bibliographical references and index.
  1. Dryden, John, 1631 – 1700—Criticism and
interpretation. 2. Heroes in literature. I. Title.
PR3427.H4H8 1980   821'.4   80–19109
ISBN 0–8032–2314–5

For Janice

Contents

Preface

Dryden's heroic plays are one of the most controversial areas of seventeenth-century drama, for there is no consensus about even the most elementary questions. Does Dryden endorse or reject his heroes' values? Are Almanzor and his like figures of flamboyant panache or extravagant absurdity? And, if they are absurd, are they intentionally so? So far, the heroic plays have received only limited and unsatisfactory studies, which have come to vastly divergent conclusions: that the plays are sustained celebrations of heroic idealism; that they trace the education of initially undisciplined heroes; that they are not about heroism at all, but are political tracts in disguise; or that they are extravaganzas of anti-heroic farce. The case for an anti-heroic reading, opened by D. W. Jefferson, has been most extensively and polemically stated by Bruce King, but his arguments have understandably failed to persuade since they lack organisation and rely too much on unverified, contentious assertion. Most critics, therefore, still (with the blessing of the California Dryden) see the heroic plays as largely uncritical celebrations of the ideal, though they disagree markedly about the plays' artistic value. I believe that Dryden's heroic plays have been unfortunate in two ways. No one has done anything like justice to their minutely integrated cohesion and sheer artistic intelligence. And, on the whole, their significance has been badly misrepresented, for they reveal profound scepticism about the utility and practicability of heroic endeavour. This is not to say, with King, that they are primarily farcical in character: Dryden does (like Ariosto) create episodes of anti-heroic comedy, but these make a very subordinate contribution to his serious, humane study of the disparity between divine aspiration and mortal reality.

The bulk of this book is devoted to extended analyses of the five heroic plays. My analyses are longer and more detailed than those which the plays have hitherto received, but I believe the length to be justified: in a field as controversial as this, one can take no common assumptions for granted; and the recent astonishing discrepancies of interpretation result from insufficiently close and at times factually inaccurate readings of the texts. Careful attention to the textual evidence is therefore imperative.

This book originates in a doctoral dissertation which I wrote some years ago at the University of Liverpool. My primary debt is therefore to my supervisor, Professor Kenneth Muir, who was generous both with advice and encouragement. Professor D. W. Jefferson was a helpful and complimentary external examiner. During the lengthy process of revision I have been particularly helped by advice from Professor Robert D. Hume of the Pennsylvania State University and Professor Claude Rawson of the University of Warwick. Many other colleagues at Warwick sustained me with friendly interest, as did colleagues in the English Department of Brock University, Ontario, in whose civilised and genial atmosphere this study was first conceived. Finally, I owe more than I can say to M. and Mme René Pertuzon.

I have deliberately chosen three inconsistencies of presentation, which I should perhaps here explain. In deciding whether or not to translate foreign quotations I have tried to help my readers without insulting their intelligence: accordingly, I have not translated passages in French but have translated my (infrequent) quotations from Greek, Latin, and Italian, except where the sense is self-evident or made clear in my text. At the cost of internal consistency, I have followed the conventions of each copy-text with regard to the abbreviation or non-abbreviation of speakers' names. And I refer to *Cassandra* and *Cleopatra* by their English titles, since I have used contemporary English translations of the French romances; but, after experimenting with *The Grand Cyrus*, I found it so unsatisfactory that I decided to retain the French title.

In giving page references to passages where consecutive pages are numbered identically, I distinguish the pages thus: 39 [1], 39 [2], and so on.

Derek Hughes
September 1979

Acknowledgements

The author and publishers wish to thank the following who have kindly given permission for the use of copyright material:

Cassell Ltd for extracts from *Pregnancy* by Gordon Bourne;

J. M. Dent & Sons Ltd and Elsevier-Dutton Publishing Co. Inc. for extracts from John Dryden's *Of Dramatic Poesy and Other Dramatic Essays,* edited by George Watson (1962), an Everyman's Library edition;

Gordian Press Inc. for extracts from *John Dryden, Dramatic Works* (6 volumes) edited by Montague Summers;

University of California Press for extracts from *The Works of John Dryden,* Volumes VIII, IX and X;

The University of Chicago Press for extracts from *John Dryden: Four Tragedies,* edited by L. A. Beaurline and Fredson Bowers.

Abbreviations

ELH   *Journal of English Literary History*
JEGP   *Journal of English and Germanic Philology*
MLN   *Modern Language Notes*
MLR   *Modern Language Review*
MP   *Modern Philology*
PMLA *Publications of the Modern Language Association*
PQ   *Philological Quarterly*
RES   *Review of English Studies*
SEL   *Studies in English Literature, 1500–1900*
SP   *Studies in Philology*

1 Dryden and the Idealisation of Man

1. THE "PERFECT PATTERN OF HEROIC VIRTUE"

"There are many wonders, and none is more wonderful than man," sings the Chorus in *Antigone*:[1] he has mastered the seas; with horse-drawn plough he vexes "the eldest of Gods, the unresting, imperishable Earth"; he traps or tames all species of animals; he has learned "speech, wind-swift thought", and the arts of civilisation; and, all-inventive, he has solved every intractable evil except death (ll. 334−64). As the tragedy takes its course, however, and the laws and contrivances of humanity prove to be blind and treacherous, the pride in man's glory proves to be cruelly deluded. "Both the future and the past demonstrate this law," sings the Chorus in its second stasimon: "when greatness enters the life of mortals, it enters with a curse" (ll. 611−14). The third stasimon ponders the irresistible frenzy of Eros, which draws "even the just mind into evil and destruction" (ll. 791−2); the fourth deals with inescapable destiny, imprisonment, madness, and blindness (ll. 944−87). In the end, we are left with Creon's "lead out of the way a futile man: . . . all that I touch goes awry, and an intolerable fate has descended on my head" (ll. 1339, 1346).

Here, in one of its greatest embodiments, is one of the most enduring subjects of tragic literature. Man, whose mind instinctively reaches for the infinite and seems to grasp the mastery of the world, is crushed into unbearable recognition of his blindness, impotence, and insignificance—or, more benignly, reborn into a knowledge of his frailty and fallibility. The tragedy of the earliest heroes, Gilgamesh and Achilles, lies in the disparity between their divine heritage and mortal destiny, the potential conferred by their immortal lineage and the annihilation which is the known condition and consequence of its fulfilment. Diversely, and with vastly differing degrees of pessimism or hope, each age recreates this pattern: it is to be seen in the tragedy of Chaucer's Troilus, who seeks the divine in the fatally human; in that of Marlowe's Faustus, who tires his brains "to get a Deity"[2] but squanders his soul in a career of pointless farce; in the terrible destruction of Lear's illusions; and in the experiences of Dryden's heroes.

Dryden's heroic plays neither celebrate the actions nor trace the education of exemplary supermen.[3] Nor are they the indiscriminate satires of Bruce King or the frigid moral tracts of Anne Barbeau.[4] Rather, they are humane, intelligent, and subtle studies of the disparity between Herculean aspiration and human reality. Of course, the reality is not one of unmixed, unintelligible desolation and loss: nowhere does a character equal the quiet vacancy of Creon's "all that I touch goes awry", and nowhere do we see the relentless operations of "an intolerable fate"; villains and secondary characters realise the fatal potential of human fallibility, and the heroes and heroines survive, though sometimes at the cost of the ideals they had represented. Indeed, Dryden's exposure of his heroes' illusions invites a disconcertingly wide range of responses. The psychological perplexity behind the heroic or Platonic mask is sensitively delineated, with great insight into the intricacies of self-deception and serious recognition of the dangers that ensue when weak characters rely on imaginary strength. But, demonstrably, there are also episodes. of comedy: one of Aureng-Zebe's quarrels with Indamora, for example, owes a large and obvious debt to one of Alceste's quarrels with Célimène in *Le Misanthrope*,[5] and the debt reveals the hero as a designedly comic figure. More than any writer since Chaucer, Dryden knew the narrowness of the division between tragic flaw and comic deficiency, and the ease with which one could suddenly modulate into the other. For this reason, the heroic plays have long seemed to present an aesthetic enigma. We are accustomed to the comic sub-plot, to the intelligently witty tragic hero or villain, even to occasional comedy at the principals' expense (as in *Antony and Cleopatra*). Nevertheless, the heroic plays can seem to invert all traditional dramatic order, for tragedy in its usual sense is acted out in a subsidiary level of the play and a counterpoint of unwitting comedy is provided not by the low characters of a subordinate plot but (on a few occasions) by the heroes and heroines in the full flight of their idealism. Interestingly, *Secret Love* and *Marriage à la Mode* do not share the aesthetic problems of the heroic plays, though they date from the same period and are similar in subject and source (both deriving from *Le Grand Cyrus*); where they differ is in having a separate, subordinate plot as a vehicle for comic commentary. The comic element in the heroic plays should not be overemphasised (as it is, greatly, by King), but comedy does intrude at some disconcerting moments, as in Berenice's ludicrous speeches from the scaffold.[6] Normally, I think, it is demonstrably deliberate. And normally, too, it has a quite specific and serious dramatic point.

The ideals that tantalise and delude Dryden's heroes are drawn principally from the French prose romances, from Caroline Platonic literature,[7] and from later developments of Caroline models, such as Davenant's *The Siege of Rhodes* and the plays of the Earl of Orrery. Dryden obviously knew and plundered the works of Corneille. H. F. Brooks has demonstrated extensive verbal reminiscence of Corneille in *Aureng-Zebe*,[8] and Corneille clearly influenced some of the most central and essential features of Dryden's dramatic symbolism: for example, Dryden imitates plays such as *Le Cid*, *Cinna*, and *Rodogune* by portraying characters who are caught up in a sustained, ritualised recreation of the past and of the identities of others;[9]

both *The Indian Emperour* and *Rodogune*, for instance, are concerned with characters who helplessly relive a past that they had sought to transcend. In studying Corneille, Dryden digested into his own creative personality those qualities of the older dramatist that were congenial to him. His use of romance and Platonic literature is quite different: what he rarely does with Corneille, and frequently does with the romance writers and Platonics, is to borrow whole episodes and turn them upside down, showing the impotence of romance idealism in a non-ideal world. For example, the love quadrangle of Montezuma, Orazia, Traxalla, and Zempoalla in *The Indian Queen* is based on that of Oroondates, Cassandra/Statira, Perdiccas, and Roxana in *Cassandra*;[10] Cortez' rivalry with Orbellan in *The Indian Emperour* on that of Arsaces/Artaxerxes and Arsacomes in the same romance (IV. iv. 23 – 8; V. 29 – 36); the Berenice – Maximin – Porphyrius triangle on that of Mariamne, Herod, and Tyridates in *Cleopatra*;[11] the conclusion of Part I of *The Conquest of Granada*, where Almahide saves Almanzor by agreeing to marry Boabdelin, is based on another episode from *Cassandra*, in which Parisatis saves Lysimachus by agreeing to marry Hephestion (II. ii. 221 – 3); the self-sacrificing idealism in which Almahide subsequently tries to school Almanzor is modelled on that of Orrery's Clorimun and his successors; and so on. In each case, however, Dryden's very human heroes fail to match the tinselly perfection of their ideal counterparts, as I shall show in some detail in subsequent chapters and in the Appendix.

Comparable allusion to Corneille is rare, though *The Indian Emperour* provides one example and, after the heroic play period, *All for Love* another. Like *Rodogune*, Alibech is loved by two royal brothers, and, like *Rodogune*, she stifles her true preference, offering herself to the brother who deserves her best;[12] but, unlike *Rodogune*, she fails to sustain her fierce resolution to the end. In his first meeting with Cleopatra, Antony too aspires to Cornelian heights, endeavouring to recreate the great scene in which Auguste confronts and accuses Cinna;[13] but, like Alibech, he proves incapable of sustaining his inflexible role. I do not, however, know of any other similarly allusive borrowings; indeed, allusive is perhaps too strong a term even in these cases. There is, of course, a considerable overlap between the ideals of Cornelian drama, French romance, and Platonic literature, and for this reason the aspirations of Dryden's heroes frequently match those of Corneille's; in fact, the universal diffusion of the ideals evoked in Dryden's plays provides the only credible motive for his unflagging concern with them. But, in almost every case of close, extended allusion or imitation, the reference is not to Corneille; and, indeed, Dryden's prefaces compare his characters not to Rodrigue or Chimène but to Artaban, Cassandra, Cleopatra, and Mandana.[14]

The French prose romances furnished the heroic plays with the majority of their character types. From La Calprenède's Artaban, Artaxerxes, and Mariamne Dryden derived at least in part the figures of the young Montezuma, Cortez, and Berenice. Almanzor's origins are more complex and less exclusively rooted in romance, since his ancestry embraces not only Artaban and Ponce de Leon, the hero of Georges de Scudéry's *Almahide*, but also Tasso's Rinaldo. Almahide's ancestry is also divided, since she is based on her Scudéry namesake, on La Calprenède's Parisatis, and on the Queen in Pérez de Hita's *Guerras Civiles de Granada*. Allusion to romance is, however, more sporadic in *Aureng-Zebe*, though Indamora is at times, in the play as in the Dedication, measured against Mandana, as Aureng-Zebe is against Cyrus. Moreover, the hero's ideals still evoke those of romance, and a character such as La Calprenède's Ariobarzanes, while not a model for Aureng-Zebe, provides a clear analogue to him. The romances also supplied the greater part of the code that Dryden's heroes seek to observe in war and love: in their valour, their jealous preservation of honour, their magnanimity to valiant foes, their instinctive support of the outnumbered, and their total dedication of their gifts to the service of love, the heroes aspire to conformity with the precepts of romance; similarly, heroines such as Berenice and Almahide mimic their romance counterparts in their attempts to refine their lovers' affections and to conform their own to the duties imposed by their forced marriages.

In some respects, however, Dryden's characters are still more ambitious— and unrealistic—in their idealism than their exemplars in the Scudérys and La Calprenède. In his Essay "Of Heroic Plays", prefixed to *The Conquest of Granada*, Dryden excoriates frigid paragons such as Cyrus and Oroondates, claiming for the irascible Almanzor the virtue of verisimilitude:

> You see how little these great authors [Homer and Tasso] did esteem the point of honour, so much magnified by the French, and so ridiculously aped by us. They made their heroes men of honour; but so as not to divest them quite of human passions and frailities [*sic*], they contented themselves to show you what men of great spirits would certainly do when they were provoked, not what they were obliged to do by the strict rules of moral virtue. For my own part I declare myself for Homer and Tasso, and am more in love with Achilles and Rinaldo than with Cyrus and Oroondates. I shall never subject my characters to the French standard, where love and honour are to be weighed by drams and scruples. (Watson, I. 164–5)

So far as it goes, Dryden's contrast between Almanzor and the romance paragons is accurate and illuminating. It does not, however, present the whole truth, for what Dryden does not say is what the hero Almanzor overtly *tries* to be in Part II is one far more ideal, far more impossibly virtuous, even than the tediously exemplary Cyrus or the still more exemplary Oroondates.

For all his humility and monumental scrupulosity, Cyrus is jealously possessive in his love for Mandana, correct in his behaviour towards rivals but resentful of their intrusion and unwilling to concede them the slightest solace. His possessiveness is shared by his associates, such as Aglatidas,[15] and is the rule throughout the romance: rarely do we see a love so spiritual that its votary can calmly see his loved one married to another, sublimating his passion into selfless service of the married pair.[16] Such sublimation, however, is the state to which Almahide tries to raise Almanzor, and which Almanzor frequently persuades himself that he has reached. Love in *Cassandra* does come closer to this ideal state. Both Oroondates and his friend Lysimachus see their mistresses (Statira and Parisatis) married to rivals (Alexander the Great and Hephestion) and both respond with self-denying magnanimity. Of the two, however, Lysimachus is the more extravagantly magnanimous: in his dealings with Statira Oroondates does take liberties beyond those permitted (I. vi. 163), but Lysimachus is schooled by Parisatis into an impeccable self-denial, consoling himself with the philosophical works of Callisthenes (II. ii. 228−9) and even offering to lay his head under Hephestion's foot (II. ii. 223). Such tame submissiveness clearly has no counterpart in *The Conquest of Granada*. Nevertheless, the triangle of Lysimachus, Parisatis, and Hephestion provides the source for that of Almanzor, Almahide, and Boabdelin, and Lysimachus' behaviour in part provides the ideal to which Almanzor is taught to aspire: the episode in which Almahide buys Almanzor's life by agreeing to marry Boabdelin (I. v. pp. 82−3) is based on a parallel episode in the Lysimachus story (II. ii. 221−3), and Almahide's subsequent attempts to educate Almanzor recall Parisatis' more successful efforts with her lover. When Dryden contrasts Almanzor and Oroondates, therefore, he is patently not telling the whole story: Almanzor certainly has human passions and frailties, but he reveals them in the course of an attempt to imitate a close friend of Oroondates—a friend even more punctilious and virtuous than Oroondates himself. The matter does not, however, end there, for Almanzor tries not only to imitate Lysimachus' virtues but to excel him in those few areas where he retains a tincture of human weakness. Even Lysimachus has a residue of humanity in that he is consumed by an inextinguishable sorrow during his life of virtuous resignation (II. ii. 226−9), and in this respect he is of far frailer stuff than the ideal lovers of English Platonic literature. The absolute, inhuman perfection of such lovers is the goal to which Almahide and, under her influence, Almanzor aspire. To understand Almahide and her kind most fully, therefore, we must turn to the idealisation of human relationships that dominated Caroline court literature and survived into the Restoration period.

The beings who populate Platonic literature are ones who have seemingly escaped the expulsion from Eden. Retaining, or recovering, a perfect subordination of will to reason, they cultivate a love untainted with bodily desire (a smokeless and unfuelled flame)[17] and satisfied with telepathic contemplation of the partner's mind or soul.[18] Carlell's Arviragus and Philicia engage in an "intelligence" of "soules",[19] Suckling's Aglaura and Thersames "Have mingled soules more than two meeting brooks" (IV. iv.

123), and Glapthorne's *Argalus* avows undiminished love to the alarmingly disfigured Parthenia, protesting, ."'twas thy excellent minde/That I admir'd."[20] The fundamental doctrines of Platonism are well summed up in the Song of Sunesis and Thelema (Reason and Will) at the end of Davenant's *The Temple of Love*:

> *Sunesis.*
> Come melt thy soul in mine, that when unite,
> We may become one virtuous appetite.
> *Thelema.*
> First breathe thine into me, thine is the part
> More heavenly, and doth more adorn the heart.
> *Both.*
> Thus mix'd, our love will ever be discreet,
>   And all our thoughts and actions pure,
> When perfect Will, and strengthened Reason meet,
>   Then Love's created to endure.   (p. 303)

Dreams of such incorporeal love haunt several of Dryden's heroines. In *Tyrannick Love*, for example, Berenice claims that her love for Porphyrius has been a communion of spirit in which the body has had no part:

> In death I'le owne a Love to him so pure;
> As will the test of Heav'n it self endure:
> A Love so chast, as Conscience could not chide;
> But cherisht it, and kept it by its side:
> A Love which never knew a hot desire,
> But flam'd as harmless as a lambent fire:
> A Love which pure from Soul to Soul might pass,
> As light transmitted through a Crystal glass: (V. 453−60)

Here, however, the Platonic dream is immediately exposed as a naïve fantasy. The speech misrepresents the real sexual conflict that Berenice has experienced, and it is soon startlingly and emphatically contradicted. Wondering what will happen when, after death, she and Porphyrius really do meet Soul to Soul rather than face to face, she fears that they will not recognise each other "when bodies are not there" (v. 491) and longs to be able to hang an identity tag on her soul. For all her claims to communion of spirit, she knows Porphyrius only in the flesh.

Since love was inspired by essential qualities of soul rather than accidents of the flesh, the mingling of identities with a virtuous woman was capable of ennobling an imperfect or evil lover: the ignoble Guimantes in *Arviragus and Philicia* is transformed by striving for oneness with the object of his love (II. II. sig. [E10ᵛ]), and the tyrant Misander in William Cartwright's *The Siege* is similarly redeemed (III. 1275−407).[21] Romance heroes, of course, are also elevated by their mistresses' influence, but the transformation of the Platonic lover differs from that of his romance counterpart in the mystic nature of its processes and the calm transcendence of bodily passions that it confers; such are the transformations that, with many un-Platonic set-backs, Almahide attempts to achieve in Almanzor, and Indamora in Morat. Since love was a meeting of matched souls, moreover, it could be portrayed as realising a divinely ordained symmetry: Cupid is no longer a blind boy but a precise mathematician,[22] calculating unions very different from, say, the whimsically irrational attachments of *A Midsummer Night's Dream*. The Matchless Orinda, for example, declares that she and her dearest Antenor

> were born to love, brought to agree
> By the impressions of Divine decree.[23]

Paradoxically, however, the Platonics could also regard the objects of affection as easily interchangeable: since love was excited by virtue of soul, people of equal virtue were equally lovable; similarly, since love was the product of reason, it could easily be vanquished or diverted when reason so demanded. The tragic potentialities of passion unconquered and unrequited were repeatedly dispersed in facile, last-minute changes of affection that ensured a minimum of heart-ache and a maximum pairing of characters. Lovers for whom no partner could be found benefited no less from the rational ordering of the affections, instantly banishing thwarted desires and variously adopting the wars, their sword, or glory as a mistress.[24] For example, at the end of Davenant's *Love and Honour* the heroine, Evandra, is faced with the problem of choosing between two equally worthy suitors, Leonell and Alvaro. The problem, however, is quickly and painlessly solved: deciding to conform her will to her father's choice, Evandra instantly summons up love for Leonell:

> Alvaro's virtues, sir, and yours, have both
> An equal claim. Persons I ne'er admir'd
> So much to make a difference in my choice;
> Therefore my father's promise, and my love,
> Have made me yours.[25]

Rejected, Alvaro shows that he too has total control over his passions:

> To Evandra, gladness be still renew'd,
> Who since I see so worthily bestow'd,
> My love is quieted in everlasting rest.   (v. p. 184)

He proves his point by contentedly marrying Leonell's sister, whom, we now learn, he had promised (and forgotten) to marry five years earlier.[26] A third suitor, Prospero, is left unmatched but returns to the wars with perfect equanimity. Even these displays of imperturbable reason, however, do not represent the pinnacle of Platonic virtue. Still more improbably, spouses or fiancé(e)s could take a rationally unpossessive view of their partner's Platonic relationship with another; sunlight, after all, is not diminished by being shared. In William Cartwright's *The Royall Slave*, for example, King Arsamnes quickly suppresses jealous suspicion and acquiesces in Queen Atossa's Platonic communion with the virtuous Cratander. Needless to say, interlopers were no less complaisant towards established partners.[27] Indeed, magnanimous lovers could often rise to complete disregard of self, preferring to deserve rather than to possess, and even striving to further the loved one's union with a more favoured rival.[28]

The spiritualisation of love was paralleled by that of friendship, which similarly became a perfect mingling of souls and identities. The conventional ideal is well represented in Antony's (misconceived) analysis of his relationship with Dollabella:

> I was his Soul; he liv'd not but in me:
> We were so clos'd within each other's brests,
> The rivets were not found that join'd us first.
> That does not reach us yet: we were so mixt,
> As meeting streams, both to our selves were lost;
> We were one mass; we could not give or take,
> But from the same; for he was I, I he.   (III. 91—7)[29]

The shared identity of friends provided a further means for the tearless fifth act re-alignment of affections. Throughout the second part of *Arvirus and Philicia*, for example, the Danish Queen obdurately impedes the match of hero and heroine because of her own love for Arviragus. At the end of Act v, however, she repentantly declares that she will herself join the lovers in marriage, only to disturb the unexpected felicity by announcing that she too will marry Arviragus; nevertheless, good humour is immediately restored when she reveals that she is to marry Arviragus not in his own person but in that of his friend and *alter ego*, Guiderius—who has, conveniently, transferred his own affections from Philicia to the Queen (II. v. sigs. [G10v– G11]). Love is once again confined to contemplation of the spirit, and tragic passions are once again exorcised with a contrived and ludicrous ease. The idealisation of friendship also provided further opportunities for self-denying magnanimity: as the ideal lover could further the loved one's courtship of a more favoured rival, so ideal friends, finding themselves in love with the same woman, could strive to advance each other's cause, even to the point of wooing the loved one on the rival's behalf.[30] This, the most improbable feat of all, was also one of the most common. It was, of course, a favourite subject of Orrery,[31] but it had become a wearisome cliché long before Orrery appropriated it.

In their easy control and selfless transcendence of passion the Platonic lovers and ideal friends provide examples which Dryden's irresolute and fallible characters deludedly try to imitate. In marrying Boabdelin, for example, Almahide persuades herself that she can, like Evandra, direct her passions at the call of reason, achieving a total conformity between inclination and duty: "But know, that when my person I resign'd," she tells her husband, "I was too noble not to give my mind" (II. I. p. 101). Similarly, she imagines that Almanzor can subdue his passions and pursue a life of selfless, unrewarded service, deserving a love that he can never possess. She imagines, too, that she can equal Atossa and her kind by accommodating both husband and Platonic lover in a placid and virtuous triangle that is free from all misunderstanding. In all these assumptions, however, she overestimates both her own capacities and those of her two partners. Berenice in *Tyrannick Love* flatters herself with similar self-deception. Two of Dryden's heroines—Valeria in *Tyrannick Love* and Amalthea in *Marriage à la Mode*— do rise to imitation of Platonic paragons, each helping the loved one to the mistress of his choice.[32] Nevertheless, Dryden destroys the stereotyped pattern in evoking it, for the heroines' self-sacrifice earns them no release from passion: Valeria is driven to suicide by anguished and unextinguishable love, and Amalthea arrives not at tranquil renunciation but at a painful acceptance of sterile, undeserved solitude. Dryden similarly evokes, and rejects, the expedient that had so successfully assuaged tormenting passions in *Arviragus and Philicia*. At the end of *The Indian Queen* Montezuma offers himself to Zempoalla as a surrogate for the dead Acacis, hoping that he can, like Guiderius, provide a complete embodiment of his friend's identity: "O that you wou'd believe / *Acacis* lives in me, and cease to grieve," he pleads.[33] Zempoalla's passions, however, are not to be assuaged or diverted with such outrageous ease, and find peace only in death. The Platonic paragons belong to an unfallen world in which passion, firmly subjugated to reason, is controlled with a facility that precludes tragedy. When Dryden conjures up the Elysian mirage, however, he uses it merely as a deceptive prelude to the triumph of unruly passion. Indeed, he habitually tempers the felicity of his endings by showing a character in the Caroline mould—an Acacis, Valeria, or Melesinda—driven to death by indomitable and hopeless passion. Against the Eden of the Platonics he set all the sad variety of an impaired and imperfect world.

In all the respects outlined above the Platonic lovers greatly outshine their Scudéry and La Calprenède counterparts. Love in the romances is certainly idealised, but it is rarely the placid servant of imperturbable reason,[34] and unrequited love is surmounted with ease only when the love is not deeply rooted.[35] Out of duty to parents or pique against lovers, heroines do marry partners whom they have not hitherto loved, but as a rule they continue not to love them, lacking the Platonic heroine's facility in harmonising inclination with duty.[36] A few heroines, such as Parisatis and Statira, do come close to the Platonic pattern, but even they retain a modicum of humanity: they follow the path of virtue with ease and they conjure up some affection for their husbands, but they cannot banish distress at losing their first, true love. As a result, placid *ménages à trois* such as that of Atossa are rare: virtue and propriety may be inviolably preserved, but inner discontent will nevertheless remain. Heroic romance does boast a few lovers capable of magnanimous acts of renunciation,[37] but they are by no means the stock figures that they are in Platonic tradition. Absurd and impossible as the romance characters are, they are far less so than those of Carlell, Cartwright, Davenant, and Orrery.

In reworking material from heroic romance, then, Dryden consistently makes two contrary kinds of modification. The ideals which his characters pursue are far more demanding even than those of the romance hero, but the characters who pursue the ideals are normally far more fallible than those of romance: Almanzor and Almahide, for example, outstrip Lysimachus and Parisatis in the extent both of their aspirations and their flaws. Whereas romance and Platonic literature celebrate the attainment of the ideal, Dryden's heroic plays portray the inevitable disparity between ideal aspiration and mundane reality. Sometimes, he can portray the disparity merely by showing a romance figure in pursuit of a Platonic ideal. For example, Berenice's perplexity and misery are no greater than those of many a romance heroine in a loveless marriage (though she is markedly weaker than her chief exemplar, Mariamne). Where she differs from the romance heroine is in her refusal to recognise her perplexity, her self-deluding claims to a perfection that she does not possess; she is distinguished from the romance heroine not by her emotional vulnerability but by the Platonic self-deception with which she disguises her pain. Dryden alters the significance of the romance heroine's vulnerability by altering the context in which it is viewed.

Similarly, the heroic plays are less comfortably anodyne than the romances not because their deaths are more numerous but because the deaths are given a different emphasis and significance. Like the heroic plays, *Le Grand Cyrus* ends in a mixture of tragedy and felicity: Cyrus' two chief rivals, the Kings of Pontus and Assyria, are released by death from the miseries of unrequited love (IX. i. 7, iii. 128), and the ideal couple of Spitridates and Araminta, failing to find happiness, are united only in death (X. ii. 165, iii. 206). The deaths of Cyrus' rivals, however, merely provide an easy tidying of loose ends; those of Spitridates and Araminta a meaningless variation of emotional sensation. Dryden, by contrast, makes his deaths a significant and essential part of an integrated dramatic design. Death in the romances, for example, does not follow and negate expectation of a Platonic mastery of passion. In the heroic plays it does: Acacis, for instance, had at first seemed to exemplify the supremacy of reason over passion. Furthermore, the endings of the heroic plays create a sense of moral imbalance absent from those of romance. In *Cyrus* the worthiest suitor has won and the less worthy have conveniently been released from their misery; the deaths of Acacis and Valeria, like the bleak loneliness of Amalthea, do not leave us with the same sense of comfortable order. Moreover, such deaths complete symbolic patterns which contradict the most basic assumptions of romance. The deaths of Spitridates and Araminta provide an isolated tragedy, an isolated contrast with the happiness of Cyrus and Mandana; they do not convey a tragic generalisation about the vanity of passion and the self-destructiveness of the passionate life. The deaths of Dryden's characters, however, convey exactly such a generalisation. Each of his plays suggests that dedication to passion is enslavement to mortality, that all who seek divinity in the pursuit of passion are, by a tragic paradox, merely strengthening their bondage to change and death. Deaths such as that of Acacis exemplify the self-annihilation which each of the heroic dreamers has unwittingly courted. The romance writers and Platonics portray an impossible transcendence of humanity; Dryden examines the path to imaginary divinity and finds it to be a path only to death. Here lies his most profound difference from the escapist writers with whom he has so often been confounded; and here is the heroic plays' closest link with earlier forms of tragedy. When, after the death of Patroclus, Achilles returns to battle, he is set apart from humanity by all the trappings of divinity: he wears divine armour, shines with divine fire, and feeds on the food of the Olympians. But the price of his brief divinity is to be death at the hands of an effeminate coward. In his line of martial super-heroes Dryden recreates and varies the paradox archetypally embodied in Achilles.

II. THE IMPERFECT HERO

There is a commonplace objection to those who suggest that Dryden portrays his heroes with conscious scepticism and irony: namely, that Dryden nowhere gives explicit warrant for their views. This objection is not entirely true; what is true is that our interpretation of the secondary evidence—principally the criticism—is necessarily determined by our interpretation of the plays themselves. In my opinion the Preface to *The Conquest of Granada* ("Of Heroic Plays: An Essay" [1672]) permits us to see Almanzor as a flawed and self-deluding character; others take a different view. Clearer judgements upon heroism appear in *The State of Innocence* (1674) and the Dedication of *Aureng-Zebe* (1675), but these works are of debatable relevance, since they postdate "Of Heroic Plays" by just sufficiently long for the pro-heroic critic to postulate an intervening change of mind. Nevertheless, they deserve to be considered, for they were written while Dryden was still involved with the heroic play, and they display the two complementary beliefs that were to inform his discussions of the heroic for the remainder of his life: a belief in the viciousness of heroic manslaughter and the impracticability of romance idealism. When it is attainable, heroic aspiration is perverse; when admirable, it is unattainable.

Were Dryden the celebrant of Almanzoresque prowess, *Paradise Lost* would be a surprising work for him to dramatise, since Milton repudiates the epic celebration of fallen belligerence. And Dryden retains Milton's rejection of heroic tradition, merely introducing a change of focus appropriate to the change of medium; for, when Raphael shows Adam the future consequences of the Fall, he makes him the first spectator of a heroic play, a witness of the carnage caused by misguided heroism:

> See yon' mad fools who, for some trivial Right,
> For love, or for mistaken honour fight:
> See those, more mad, who throw their lives away
> In needless wars; the Stakes which Monarchs lay,
> When for each others Provinces they play.[38]

In the Dedication of *Aureng-Zebe*, by contrast, Dryden raises different but complementary questions about the utility of heroic endeavour, dwelling not on the perversely but the unattainably ideal. He has, he stresses, created characters of realistic frailty rather than romantic perfection: "I confess, I have onely represented a practicable Virtue, mix'd with the frailties and imperfections of humane life. I have made my *Heroine* fearful of death, which neither *Cassandra* nor *Cleopatra* would have been; and they themselves [the ladies of the audience], I doubt it not, would have outdone Romance in that particular."[39] Then, affecting to qualify the dogmatism of his assertions, he expands his statement into a Montaignesque generalisation about the helpless capriciousness of man and the folly of his grandiose pretensions:

> Yet, after all, I will not be too positive. *Homo sum, humani à me nihil alienum puto.* As I am a Man, I must be changeable: and sometimes the gravest of us all are so, even upon ridiculous accidents. Our minds are perpetually wrought on by the temperament of our Bodies, which makes me suspect: they are nearer alli'd, than either our Philosophers or School-Divines will allow them to be. I have observ'd, says *Montaign*, that when the Body is out of Order, its Companion is seldom at his ease. An ill Dream, or a Cloudy day, has power to change this wretched Creature, who is so proud of a reasonable Soul, and make him think what he thought not yesterday.[40]

Both *The State of Innocence* and the *Aureng-Zebe* Dedication reveal sentiments that were to recur throughout the later criticism, in reflections on the vanity of human pretensions and the viciousness of the Homeric hero.[41] But, the traditionalist will argue, Dryden's attitude towards the heroic ideal changed profoundly in the immediate aftermath of *The Conquest of Granada*. And, since the chief evidence for Dryden's earlier hero-worship is drawn from the texts of the heroic plays, we are back where we started.

In fact, the theory of a rapid disenchantment with heroic subjects in

1672—4 is hard to sustain. As early as the Preface to *Secret Love* (1668) Dryden had been preoccupied with justification of the manifestly flawed hero, defending the emotionally perplexed and politically disloyal Philocles by enquiring of his "over-wise censors: who told them I intended him a perfect character, or indeed what necessity was there he should be so, the variety of images being one great beauty of a play?" (Watson, 1. 106). Here, as in the *Aureng-Zebe* Dedication, Dryden counters expectations of romantic perfection by defending the representation of human frailty—as he was to do again in "Of Heroic Plays". More interesting, however, is the fact that the judgements of *The State of Innocence* are anticipated in *The Conquest of Granada* itself, where Almanzor is subjected to celestial censure similar in authority and sentiment to that of Raphael; for the ghost of Almanzor's mother roundly rebukes him for perverse love and perverse honour, for pursuing an adulterous passion and defending a false religion:

Yet bred in errors thou dost mis-imploy
That strength Heav'n gave thee, and its flock destroy. . . .
Heaven does not now thy Ignorance reprove;
But warns thee from known Crimes of lawless Love.
That Crime thou know'st, and knowing, dost not shun,
Shall an unknown, and greater Crime pull on:
But, if thus warn'd, thou leav'st this cursed place,
Then shalt thou know the Author of thy Race.   (II. IV. p. 140)

In *The Conquest of Granada*, indeed, Dryden adopts the striking course of portraying a hero whose deeds of valour are without exception performed for the wrong side, and whose one act of Christian piety is one of submission, of surrender to his father.

We cannot base a reading of the heroic plays on the secondary evidence; of the evidence cited above, only that of the Ghost's speech is conclusively relevant (and, I think, clearly inimical to the pro-heroic case). I would simply stress that, should the plays themselves seem to invite suspicion of their heroes, Dryden's explicit judgements do not forbid it: the Ghost's verdicts encourage suspicion, and we need not see a changed attitude towards heroism in the comments of 1674 onwards. Nor do we have to ignore the Dedication and Preface of *The Conquest of Granada*, which on the whole are of great interest and pertinence. Their chief, and very instructive, burden is to reject the romance paragon and to defend the flawed hero by appeal to the practice of Homer and Tasso, and only occasionally are they slightly discrepant with the text of the play: one discrepancy occurs in the Dedication, where Dryden concedes Almanzor's flaws, likens them to those of Achilles and Rinaldo, but then minimises their importance, terming them "moles and dimples which hinder not a face from being beautifull; though that beauty be not regular" (pp. 17—18); in "Of Heroic Plays", similarly, he cites Achilles' and Rinaldo's willingness to kill their kings as evidence that they were not "*quite*" divested "of human passions and frailities" (p. 164;

italics added). The emphasis which Dryden here gives to heroic imperfection is not that of the Ghost's speeches nor, as we shall see, of *The Conquest of Granada* as a whole; nor does it really make sense of the appeal to Tasso's practice. What Dryden is doing here is what he demonstrably does on other occasions: namely, to try to satisfy as many parties as possible, justifying the flawed hero while permitting the admiration of romance addicts should they wish to bestow it.[42] Elsewhere in "Of Heroic Plays", for example, he roundly denounces and repudiates paragons of the French type only to seek the best of both worlds by claiming that he has, nevertheless, provided some: "Yet where I have designed the patterns of exact virtues, such as in this play are the parts of Almahide, of Ozmyn, and Benzayda, I may safely challenge the best of theirs" (p. 165). Such fence-sitting briefly enters into the discussion of Almanzor; but, for the most part, Dryden is concerned to make his hero not morally attractive but aesthetically respectable.

Early in the essay, Dryden cites *The Siege of Rhodes* as the first heroic play, declares that its aim was "to introduce the examples of moral virtue writ in verse" (pp. 157–8), identifies several of its weaknesses, including insufficient "variety of characters" (p. 158), and suggests that he found in *Orlando Furioso* something of what *The Siege of Rhodes* lacked. When he comes to the chief object of the essay, the defence of Almanzor, he develops these preliminary points, returning to epic precedent and elaborating the distinctior. between a morally exemplary and dramatically interesting set of characters. Replying to the charge that Almanzor "is no perfect pattern of heroic virtue" (p. 163), he traces his hero's ancestry:

> The first image I had of him was from the Achilles of Homer, the next from Tasso's Rinaldo (who was a copy of the former), and the third from the Artaban of Monsieur Calprenède (who has imitated both). The original of these (Achilles) is taken by Homer for his hero; and is described by him as one who in strength and courage surpassed the rest of the Grecian army; but, withal, of so fiery a temper, and so impatient of an injury, even from his King and General, that when his mistress was to be forced from him by the command of Agamemnon, he not only disobeyed it, but returned him an answer full of contumely, and in the most opprobrious words he could imagine. . . .
>
> Tasso's chief character, Rinaldo, was a man of the same temper; for when he had slain Gernando in his heat of passion, he not only refused to be judged by Godfrey, his general, but threatened that if he came to seize him, he would right himself by arms upon him. . . .
>
> You see how little these great authors did esteem the point of honour, so much magnified by the French, and so ridiculously aped by us. They made their heroes men of honour; but so as not to divest them quite of human passions and frailities, they contented themselves to show you what men of great spirits would certainly do when they were provoked, not what they were obliged to do by the strict rules of moral virtue. For my own

part I declare myself for Homer and Tasso, and am more in love with Achilles and Rinaldo than with Cyrus and Oroondates. (pp. 163, 164– 5)

As I have already said, we should in reading this passage remember that Almanzor spends much of his time attempting to be a greater paragon even than Cyrus and Oroondates; Dryden's comments not only alert us to Almanzor's passions and frailties but point to a disparity between his frailties and his pretensions. Yet most critics have not even read this passage as testimony to Almanzor's human weaknesses, believing the gist of Dryden's argument to be that Almanzor's actions are worthy of approbation even if they are not strictly, technically, and pedantically virtuous. Robert D. Hume states a common view when he suggests that Dryden is defending Almanzor "as a pattern of heroic virtue by comparing him with Achilles"[43] (whereas Dryden is actually citing a hero whose heroism was distinctly less than virtuous); John Heath Stubbs regards the citation of Achilles as evidence that Almanzor is a figure of "natural virtue";[44] and Eugene M. Waith and Michael W. Alssid both arbitrarily assume that Dryden's view of Homer and Tasso approximated to that of Sir Philip Sidney, who praised Achilles and Rinaldo (and even Turnus and Tydeus) as types of "magnanimity and justice".[45]

Epics, however, are not necessarily stocked with exemplary or near-exemplary characters. *Orlando Furioso* mingles heroic splendour with flagrant anti-heroic bathos,[46] and Rinaldo is until late in *Gerusalemme Liberata* a very seriously flawed character; indeed, the most extended analysis of his flaws, delivered by a hermit, is very similar in content to the Ghost's criticism of Almanzor. Achilles was certainly interpreted as an exemplary character, but by no means universally so. Rather, his character was as diversely debated as that of Almanzor, so that by invoking him Dryden was not so much settling the debate about his own hero as diverting it to another: if, for whatever reason, his readers admire Achilles, they cannot consistently condemn Almanzor; but the verdicts on Achilles that Dryden cites—of Horace and even Agamemnon—permit us to temper poetic approbation with moral doubts.

Achilles' career is no more morally worthy of imitation than are those of Lear, Othello, or Coriolanus, for he is a tragic character whose rage leads him increasingly to abandon the *mores* of heroic society and of humanity itself, until, with his desecration of Hector's corpse, he is condemned by the gods in council for abandoning "shame" and knowing "savage thoughts, like a lion" (*Iliad* XXIV. 44, 41); only in his great encounter with the bereaved Priam, under the shadow of his own impending death, does he readopt and transfigure the conventions that contain the chaos of human existence. Extreme both in savagery and magnanimity, he has been a problem case since the beginning of literary criticism, and the problems were particularly evident in the sixteenth and seventeenth centuries, where belief both in the instructive function of poetry and in the primacy of the epic as a

genre made the morality of classical epics a very live issue. In the production
of new epics, imitation of ancient models could be used to measure the old,
inadequate order against the greater order of Christianity, as in *Gerusalemme
Liberata*, *Annus Mirabilis*, and *Paradise Lost*; indeed, the conquest of Granada
formed the subject for one epic of Christian heroism.[47] But the reading of
Homer could pose problems: if, as many theorists asserted, the epic should
provide princes with patterns for imitation, how can the portrayal of
Achilles be justified?[48] There were three principal courses: to deny Achilles'
flaws, to regard him as an inexcusable monster, or (least frequently) to
concede his flaws and justify them on artistic and didactic grounds. So
problematic was Achilles, in fact, that we sometimes find the same critic
adopting contrary approaches in different works.

   The main lines of the debate, however, had already been laid down in
antiquity. The attack on Achilles was initiated in Book III of Plato's *Republic*,
where, condemning the corrupting influence of poetry, Socrates censures
Achilles' vituperations against Agamemnon, his desecration of his enemy's
corpse, his human sacrifice at the tomb of Patroclus, and even his ransoming
of Hector's body.[49] A brief comment in Aristotle's *Poetics* is textually
corrupt, and in the Renaissance was used to prove anything from Achilles'
virtue to his unrelieved vice.[50] The most frequently used authority,
however, was Horace, who discusses Achilles and the *Iliad* in the *Ars Poetica*
and the Epistle to Lollius Maximus (*Epistles* I. ii), and in both reconciles the
didactic function of poetry with the portrayal of gravely flawed characters.
In a famous passage in the *Ars Poetica*, cited in Dryden's defence of
Almanzor, Horace argues the virtues of verisimilitude, urging that tra-
ditional characters should be portrayed with their traditional qualities and
vices: Medea should be indomitable and savage, Ixion treacherous, and
Achilles restless, wrathful, inflexible, and fierce, declaring himself to be
above laws and claiming that all must yield to force:

> scriptor honoratum si forte reponis Achillem,
> inpiger, iracundus, inexorabilis, acer
> iura sibi neget nata, nihil non arroget armis.
> sit Medea ferox invictaque, flebilis Ino,
> perfidus Ixion, Io vaga, tristis Orestes.[51]

In this Epistle to Lollius Maximus, furthermore, Horace sets forth the lessons
to be learned from Homer, who teaches us better than any orator "quid sit
pulchrum, quid turpe, quid utile, quid non" (l. 3).[52] For Horace, the
Odyssey provides a study of human virtue, the *Iliad* one of human vice,
depicting "stultorum regum et populorum . . . aestus" (l. 8).[53] Whatever
madness the kings engage in, the Achaeans · suffer; and both Tro-
jans and Greeks are equally embroiled in sedition, guile, crime, lust, and
wrath:

quidquid delirant reges, plectuntur Achivi.
seditione, dolis, scelere atque libidine et ira
Iliacos intra muros peccatur et extra. (ll. 14 – 16)

Plato and Horace thus pass similar moral judgements on the events of the
Iliad but draw contrary conclusions from their judgements: Plato believes
that the *Iliad*, like most poetry, is a thing of corrupting beauty that must be
banished from the commonwealth; Horace, on the other hand, claims for
Homer's portrayal of human savagery and vice the merits of verisimilitude
and instructiveness. Plutarch also justified Achilles as a designedly repre-
hensible character,[54] and his account may have had some influence on Le
Bossu, but it was Plato and Horace who were repeatedly echoed in
sixteenth- and seventeenth-century criticism.

Simple condemnation of Achilles can be found in Paolo Beni's
Comparatione di Homero, Virgilio, e Torquato, Pierre Le Moyne's "Traité du
Poëme Héroïque" (sigs. o iiijʳ – o vᵛ), Pierre Mambrun's *De Cultura Animi*,
Rapin's *La Comparaison d'Homère et de Virgile*, and by implication in
Davenant's Preface to *Gondibert* (p. 43);[55] of these writers, Beni and Rapin
cite Horace in confirmation of Achilles' grave flaws, and Beni, Le Moyne,
and Mambrun carp at the morality even of Virgil's characters. Praise of
Achilles can be found, for example, in Trissino's *Poetica*, Sidney's *Apology*,
and, confusingly, in Mambrun's *De Epico Carmine* (p. 437) and Rapin's
Réflexions sur la Poétique d'Aristote (p. 124).[56] The most balanced discussion
of Achilles, however, is provided by Tasso in his *Discourses on the Heroic
Poem*, a work that is of especial interest in revealing how the creator of
Rinaldo viewed the original of his hero. Tasso does at first entertain the idea
that Achilles may have been intended as an exemplary hero (II. pp. 29 – 30,
40). In Book III, however, he elaborately corroborates "Plato's objections to
his avarice and cruelty" (pp. 93 – 8), but departs from Plato in defending the
portrayal of a vicious hero. Homer, he reflects, did not lack perfection of
moral habit, "since he creates in Nestor the image of perfect virtue"
(pp. 98 – 9). But Nestor, perfect in moral habit, is not perfect in age, and
Tasso now blends Aristotle and Horace in the proposition that a poet should
attribute to his characters qualities appropriate to their age, circumstances,
and fame: the furious Turnus, for instance, aptly exemplifies the moral habit
of a young man (p. 100). And so Homer's portrayal of the vicious Achilles
can be justified, and Tasso concludes his examination by invoking the
authority of Horace: "That is why Horace did not think Homer erred in
describing Achilles thus: 'If haply, when you write, you bring to the stage
the honouring of Achilles, let him be impatient, passionate, ruthless, fierce;
let him claim that laws are not for him, let him ever make appeal to the
sword'" (p. 105).

Tasso's treatment of the Achilles figure in *Gerusalemme Liberata* is
consistent with his analysis in the *Discourses*. In his poem Tasso creates two
imitations of Achilles, one a pagan and one a Christian, one vicious and one

flawed. Argante, the proud, boastful, and violent pagan, is first characterised
in a close translation of Horace's famous description of Achilles:

> Impaziente, inessorabil, fèro,
> Ne l'arme infaticabile ed invitto,
> D'ogni Dio sprezzatore, e che ripone
> Ne la spada sua legge e sua ragione.[57]

Here, the Achillean hero is simply to be condemned. Rinaldo, however, is a
more complex figure, a flawed character with a potential for great good; but
his potential is realised only when he outgrows his resemblance to Achilles.
The reader who examines "Of Heroic Plays" without knowing its frame of
reference may imagine that Rinaldo is a figure whose heroic energy exempts
him from the normal rules of morality, as a great composer might use
parallel fifths to good effect. But this is simply not the case. Rinaldo's flaws
are clearly stated and, like those of Achilles (and Almanzor), provoke
unequivocal divine censure: his quarrel with Goffredo condemns him to
isolation from the Christian cause, as a result of which he becomes deludedly
enslaved to the pagan enchantress Armida (as Almanzor, I shall argue,
becomes psychologically enslaved to Lyndaraxa); in a divinely sent vision,
Goffredo is told that Rinaldo has been led into "errore" by "soverchio d'ira"
(XIV. 17);[58] a hermit reproves Rinaldo for his sins (as the Ghost reproves
Almanzor), urging that his strength is only properly used in fighting the foes
of Christ (XVII. 59–63); and, before he can return to his true calling, he has to
be purged of his sins, for the world and the flesh have so infected him with
their darkness that the Nile, the Ganges, and the Ocean would not suffice to
cleanse him (XVIII. 8). Rinaldo, like Almanzor, is a hero whose flaws divert
his energies into the service of a perverse cause. By no stretch of the
imagination can his example be used to prove Almanzor a "perfect pattern
of heroic virtue".

Tasso's discussion of Achilles displays an intelligence and discrimination
equalled by no other epic theorist that I have read. His closest rival is René Le
Bossu, who published his *Traité du Poëme Epique* in 1675, three years after
Dryden published "Of Heroic Plays". Le Bossu defends the *Iliad* by foisting
a rigidly didactic purpose on it, elaborating Horace by claiming that it shows
the evils of political discord and the advantages of political unity.[59] Such an
interpretation, of course, vastly impoverishes the poem, but it does enable Le
Bossu to see Achilles as both morally flawed and poetically excellent, and to
give an account of him which is, if not accurate, at least more recognisable
than that of Sidney. In Book II he cites Achilles as proof that the epic hero
need not be a figure of exemplary virtue, arguing that Homer, Aristotle, and
Horace "n'ont assurément jamais prétendu que l'Achilles . . . fut un
modéle de vertu" (II. xvii. p. 263), and he develops his interpretation of
Achilles in Book IV, in a chapter entitled "Si un Héros Poëtique doit être
honnête-homme" (II. v. pp. 36–46). Making a distinction "entre un Héros
en Morale, & un Héros en Poësie", he asserts that Achilles and Mezentius

(a significant pairing) have as much "bonté Poëtique" as Ulysses and Aeneas, and that "ces deux hommes cruels & injustes sont des Héros Poëtiques aussi réguliers que ces deux Princes si justes, si sages & si bons" (IV. v. p. 37); the rest of the chapter continues in much the same vein, with copious citation of Horace. Dryden seized on Le Bossu's theories as soon as they were published, and in "The Grounds of Criticism" (1679) saw nothing incongruous about applying his analysis of the *Iliad* to *The Conquest of Granada* (Watson, I. 248). Throughout the later criticism, moreover, he consistently follows Le Bossu, seeing Achilles as at once poetically excellent and morally vitiated—though in the Preface to *Examen Poeticum* (1693) he does suggest that Homer failed to make his own evaluation of Achilles sufficiently clear.[60] Le Bossu's work was not, of course, available to Dryden when he wrote *The Conquest of Granada*; the interpretation of *The Conquest* in "The Grounds of Criticism" is Procrustean; and the criticism of the eighties and nineties cannot safely be applied to the heroic plays. But Dryden's quickness to seize on Le Bossu is interesting, and Le Bossu's view of Achilles is largely a variant of that contained in two works that he does cite: the *Ars Poetica* and *Gerusalemme Liberata*.

Achilles, then, is a controversial character, and his appearance in "Of Heroic Plays" cannot be taken as necessary evidence of Almanzor's irreproachability. Dryden clearly does not share the views of Beni, Le Moyne, and their like. Neither, however, does he share the views of Sidney, for Sidney cites Achilles as a type of "magnanimity and justice" whereas Dryden cites him as a type of choleric lawlessness. Dryden's selection of precedent and authority constitutes an aesthetic defence of the markedly flawed hero and elaborates his earlier defence of Philocles: he has been charged with failing to provide a "perfect pattern of heroic virtue" and he replies that the example of Homer and Tasso frees him from the obligation to provide one. Even Artaban has to be led away from his immature impulsiveness by the gentle guidance of Elisa, but Dryden does not dwell upon him, instead enumerating the flaws of the more extensively imperfect Rinaldo and Achilles: Minerva, he reminds us, had to prevent Achilles' "insolence" from proceeding to the slaughter of Agamemnon; and, he adds, Agamemnon's attack on Achilles' arrogance gives a good assessment of his nature:

Agamemnon gives his character thus to Nestor:

ἀλλ᾽ ὅδ᾽ ἀνὴρ ἐθέλει περὶ πάντων ἔμμεναι ἄλλων,
πάντων μὲν κρατέειν ἐθέλει, πάντεσσι δ᾽ ἀνάσσειν.[61]

and Horace gives the same description of him in his *Art of Poetry* (p. 164).

Even when Dryden has the opportunity for moral defence of Almanzor, he does not seem terribly interested in it. Commenting on the hero's free-and-easy treatment of his royal employer, he observes quite rightly that

Almanzor "is not born their subject whom he serves, and . . . is injured by them to a very high degree" (p. 165). But he does not press on with the moral line, returning instead to Achilles' and Rinaldo's clearly reprehensible treatment of their kings: "He threatens them, and speaks insolently of soverign [*sic*] power; but so do Achilles and Rinaldo, who were subjects and soldiers to Agamemnon and Godfrey of Bulloigne" (p. 165). The defence by literary precedent here counteracts the moral defence.

Having justified Almanzor's poetic pedigree by citing the precedents of Achilles and Rinaldo, Dryden contrasts him, in a passage already discussed, with pedantically scrupulous characters such as Cyrus and Oroondates. Here his position is identical with that espoused in the Dedication of *Aureng-Zebe* and subsequent critical works, where he rejects the idealisation and deification of man, arguing that human life is necessarily attended by "frailties and imperfections"; for here too he repudiates the impossibly ideal devotees of "the strict rules of moral virtue", arguing the merits of the realistic hero who has not been falsely purged of "human passions and frailities" (pp. 164 – 5). This passage gives still greater warrant for a sceptical view of Almanzor's claims when we remember that his passions and frailties repeatedly thwart him in what are, demonstrably, attempts to excel and imitate the very kind of paragon here disparaged. Moreover, the remainder of the essay provides further hints of a disparity between Almanzor's frailties and his pretensions. Once more stressing the verisimilitude of Almanzor's character and the soundness of his pedigree, Dryden defends the extravagance of his language by citing the example of Jonson's Cethegus:

> He talks extravagantly in his passion; but, if I would take the pains to quote an hundred passages of Ben Jonson's Cethegus, I could easily show you that the rhodomontades of Almanzor are neither so irrational as his, nor so impossible to be put in execution; for Cethegus threatens to destroy nature, and to raise a new one out of it; . . . and a thousand other things as extravagant he says, but performs not one action in the play. (p. 165)

Dryden's citation of Cethegus shows how little he equated literary precedent with moral norm. Moreover, the citation is of a character whose bombastic vaunts, as Dryden admits, are absurdly divorced from reality, and Dryden only claims that Almanzor's "rhodomontades" (a clearly pejorative term)[62] differ from Cethegus' in the degree of their absurd impracticability: "they are not *so* irrational as his, nor *so* impossible to be put in execution" (italics added). But there is a disparity between Almanzor's boasts and his actions, as Dryden implicitly concedes in his next paragraph.

The remainder of the essay is intended to vindicate the practicability of Almanzor's actions, and during the course of it Dryden makes the obvious but significant point that Almanzor is far from invincible; indeed, he makes a very frank confession of his hero's ultimate impotence: "in the first part, he is made a prisoner [twice]; and, in the last, defeated, and not able to preserve the city from being taken" (p. 166). In repudiating Cyrus and Oroondates in favour of the frail and passionate mortal, Dryden had implicitly conceded the spuriousness of some of his hero's pretensions, since Almanzor repeatedly aspires to outstrip Oroondates in his transcendence of passion. In asserting Almanzor's vulnerability, similarly, Dryden identifies a weakness unseen by the hero himself: Almanzor's claims to omnipotence are even more strident than his claims to Platonic selflessness, and they are no less at odds with the facts, some of which Dryden here brings to our attention. Almanzor's boasts are not "so impossible to be put in execution" as Cethegus', but there is a demonstrable gap between promise and performance, which the essay encourages us to discover. The text of *The Conquest of Granada* reveals, I believe, a dangerously flawed hero whose extravagant illusions are consistently contradicted by the realities of life and the frailties of his own nature. "Of Heroic Plays" is by no means as inimical to such a view of Almanzor as is often assumed. Nevertheless, the only certain guides to the meaning of the heroic plays are the texts of the plays themselves.

2 The Indian Queen

Even sympathetic critics of Dryden's heroic plays are prepared to concede that their characters are portrayed without psychological subtlety or, indeed, plausibility.[1] King, admitting the plays' "distorted representation of human nature", sees their characters as vehicles for satire against modish intellectual cults (*Dryden's Major Plays*, p. 2), and Miss Barbeau treats them as mere personifications of abstract ideas: "Dryden's characters", she writes, "are ideas of human nature; each one is a rational construct, a walking set of attitudes. Clearly, Dryden does not attempt to create the kind of multifaceted and subtly shaded individual Shakespeare creates" (*Intellectual Design of Dryden's Heroic Plays*, p. 4). She later quotes with approval Chase's assertion that each character is "the exponent and champion of a single phase, a single idea".[2] In some ways, certainly, the characters of the first three heroic plays are clumsily drawn: many characters are drawn from few prototypes; they change according to the arbitrary decision of the puppeteer rather than the logic of their own natures; and they are disappointingly transparent, for not until *The Conquest of Granada* could Dryden hint that his creatures have dimensions unknown to themselves and incompletely revealed in their self-analysis and self-justification. Nevertheless, the case has been overstated and wrongly stated, for the plays are populated neither by the heroic stereotypes of traditional criticism nor by the walking attitudes of recent exegesis. On the contrary, Dryden's characters are creatures of endlessly and subtly shifting caprice, irresolution, and idiosyncrasy, certainly casting themselves in stereotyped roles such as Miss Barbeau describes but repeatedly proving too erratic and imperfect to sustain their chosen parts. Repeatedly, also, the roles themselves reveal unexpected complexities and take the characters in unforeseen directions. Critics have seen only the initial schematism of role and have missed the intricate and ironic shifts of character by means of which the schematism is subsequently invalidated. For example, to invoke a notion inimical to dramatic subtlety, Acacis and Orazia seem at first to be the "norms" of *The Indian Queen* (1664);[3] gradually, however, the vagaries of irrationality, egocentricity, and passion render them too weak, too largely and perplexedly human, to uphold their facile exemplary roles. For the first three acts of *The Indian Queen* Miss Barbeau's analysis is reasonably accurate, but with the last two acts it becomes regrettably Procrustean; and the last two acts are those which most closely anticipate Dryden's unaided efforts in the genre of the heroic play.

1. THE QUEST FOR DIVINITY

With the *partial* exception of Acacis and Orazia, the characters of *The Indian Queen* are plainly dominated by passion and dedicated to its gratification. Unstable, neglectful of the obligations imposed by civilised society, they aspire to the condition of the gods, seeking an absolute freedom that will secure unrestricted scope for the desires; each, like Lyndaraxa in *The Conquest of Granada*, longs "To be that one, to live without controul" (I. II. p. 42). Zempoalla, obviously, is a creature of turbulent passions, their violence emphasised by images of elemental upheaval, of floods and conflagrations, [4] and Montezuma's passions, similarly turbulent, are characterised with similar images: of storms, flames, and raging water. [5] In Traxalla and Zempoalla, as Miss Barbeau has noted (pp. 64–6), passion manifests itself in a craving for untrammelled power and liberty: urged by love and ambition, they have combined to overthrow their lawful ruler, and they are both strident in their demands for freedom and self-sufficiency, Traxalla longing "to grant himself, all he dares wish" (II. ii. 44) and Zempoalla craving the

> power to which the Gods their worship owe,
> Which, uncontroul'd, makes all things just below.   (III. i. 159–60)

Angered by Montezuma's love for Orazia, the Ynca too claims divine self-sufficiency, rejecting the hero's "feeble aid" and attributing Montezuma's victory against the Mexicans to his own invincible "Fortunes" (I. i. 55, 53). His services scorned, Montezuma similarly claims absolute freedom, repudiating all notion of a "Bond" with the Ynca (I. i. 75) and defecting to the enemy in search of boundless self-gratification. Against these characters, and in particular against Montezuma, are at first set the figures of Orazia and Acacis, the former opposing egocentricity with altruism, the latter opposing the hero's "wilde distempers" (I. i. 66) and anarchic freedom with the voice of civilised reason and with ideas of social obligation, of "honor" and "obedience" (I. i. 74, 76).

The chief action of the play concerns the development of Montezuma. Reared in the state of nature (V. i. 237–51), he for a long time clings to its principles, unable to comprehend the constraints that human society necessarily imposes on individual action. His passions thwarted by the Ynca's opposition, he seeks more compliant allies, captures and deposes the imagined oppressor of his desires, and boasts that he transcends the restrictive hierarchical order of society, claiming a divine prerogative "To despise Scepters, and dispose of Kings" (II. i. 28). Soon, however, he discovers that his new allies offer him no more freedom than his old. He had captured Orazia and her father in the deluded hope that conquest would further his love, but he quickly finds that he has subdued them not for himself but for a tyrannical power implacably intent on their deaths. When first commanded to surrender his prisoners to his superiors, he replies with his characteristic claim to total freedom, now clearly arrogating divine power to himself:[6]

> Stay your bold hands from reaching at what's mine,
> If any title springs from victory;
> You safer may attempt to rob a shrine,
> And hope forgiveness from the Deity.   (II. i. 61 – 4)

This speech, however, marks the end of Montezuma's illusory freedom, for dreams of absolute liberty are soon to be destroyed by political realities: the prisoners are more efficiently protected by Acacis' social authority than by Montezuma's individualistic power (II. i. 87 – 9); soon, nevertheless, they are seized; and soon Montezuma himself is imprisoned and in danger of death. On losing possession of his prisoners, Montezuma falls into bewilderment at the disintegration of his illusions:

> Can there be Gods to see, and suffer this?
> Or does mankinde make his own fate or bliss;
> While every good and bad happens by chance,
> Not from their orders, but their ignorance?   (II. iii. 48 – 51)

In asserting his claim to the prisoners, Montezuma had spoken with confidence in his divine invincibility; now, his own godhead discredited, he abandons all faith in the divine. He has lost his solipsistic belief in his divinity, but he can still only see the universe in his own image: if he cannot be a god, then gods do not exist. His lawless pursuit of self-gratification has been a career of blind self-absorption; he must now learn to value and comprehend lives and minds independent of his own, and the rest of the play traces his erratic, imperfect attempts to escape from the prison of his passions and enter into the experiences and sufferings of others. In Act v he achieves a single success, brief and quickly reversed.

II. ENSLAVEMENT TO PASSION

The pursuit of passion, of course, cannot confer divinity. In each of Dryden's tragedies deluded and passionate mortals seek apotheosis and find only mental chaos, enslavement, and death. Indeed, as Berenice and St Catharine recognise in *Tyrannick Love*, the pursuit of passion *is* the pursuit of death:

> *Ber.* Yet a few days, and those which now appear
> In youth and beauty like the blooming year,
> In life's swift Scene shall change; and cares shall come,
> And heavy age, and death's relentless doom.
> *S. Cath.* Yet man, by pleasures seeks that Fate which he would shun;
> And, suck'd in by the stream, does to the Whirl-pool run.
>
> (IV. 413 – 18)

To paraphrase: transience and decay are essential principles of man's earthly nature; those who hope to transcend them by abandonment to sensual passion merely strengthen their bondage to mortality, hastening what they would avoid.

Here, in its most compact and explicit form, is the rationale of Dryden's criticism of the heroic life. Like *All for Love*, the heroic plays are filled with passionate characters, godlike in aspiration, whose efforts to transcend sublunary change merely entangle them in the mortality which they fear. Such self-destruction is an inevitable consequence of the nature of passion: to allow passion to control reason is to allow desire for temporal, transient goods to blind the faculties which can perceive the changeless goods of eternity; and to expect true happiness from sublunary things is to expect the eternal from the transitory, to place deluded faith in a realm vitiated by mortality. For these reasons, St Catharine's assertion of the fatality of pleasure proceeds appropriately from Berenice's discourse on mutability.

Dryden's tragedies trace the careers of characters who, by a deadly paradox, seek immortality by enslaving themselves to decay. His traditionally Christian view that passion is the servant of mortality is most obviously and strikingly revealed in his habit of portraying sexual desire as inseparable from fascination with death. Satan, the first being whose quest for divinity enslaved him to change, finds that he both lusts for Eve's body and longs to destroy it:

> I could (so variously my passions move)
> Enjoy and blast her in the act of love.[7]

And, as soon as Adam and Eve have followed his example, seeking apotheosis and finding decay, their lusts too begin to bear the taint of mortality; once man has become the prey of passion and death, orgasm and annihilation become closely associated experiences, death seeming to be an orgasmic draining of life:

> *Adam.* If [death] will come, let us to joyes make hast;
> Then let him seize us when our pleasure's past.
> We'll take up all before; and death shall find
> We have drain'd life, and left a void behind.   (v. p. 454)[8]

Adam's confused and morbid lusts are those of all Dryden's slaves of mutability. For example, Nourmahal's proposed murder of Aureng-Zebe is to be a clearly erotic experience (III. 335–7), and even Ozmyn in *The Conquest of Granada* anticipates sexual pleasure in a death inflicted by his mistress:

> To his commands I joyn my own request,
> All wounds from you are welcome to my brest.   (I. IV. p. 67)

> Let me kiss yours [*sc.* hands], when you my wound begin;
> Then, easie Death will slide with pleasure in.   (I. IV. p. 69)

In the second example the insertion of the sword is to be an obviously coital
experience, with the lovers' sexual roles startlingly reversed.

The conjunction of apparent opposites created by the sex – death imagery
is repeated in many of Dryden's most characteristic and striking images of
mutability. At the beginning of *All for Love*, for example, Serapion describes
the devastation and death caused by the very floods that are the sole source of
Egypt's abundant fertility (I. 1 – 15). Similarly, the day of the tragedy is at
once Antony's birthday and death-day. Generation and corruption become
inextricably linked in their causes, and the process of fruition is seen merely
as a subordinate stage in the larger process of dissolution; working at the
heart of all earthly growth is the principle of mortality.[9] As copulation
merges with death, so generation merges with decay; the workings of the
passionate life reflect those of the mutable world to which it is enslaved.

Dryden's entire critique of the life of passion is already adumbrated in *The
Indian Queen*: here, as in later plays, passion deludes its devotees with the
prospect of immutable and all-powerful divinity, but in reality brings
helpless instability, servitude, and death. As in *The Indian Emperour* and
Tyrannick Love, the play's principal concerns are extensively set forth in the
incantation scene, which is dominated by the themes of mutability and
mortality, and which portrays the creatures of passion as prisoners of the
physical world and the physical body:

> *Poor Mortals that are clog'd with Earth below*
>   *Sink under Love and Care,*
>   *While we that dwell in Air*
> *Such heavy Passions never know.*
>   *Why then shou'd Mortals be*
>   *Unwilling to be free*
>   *From Blood, that sullen Cloud,*
> *Which shining Souls does shroud?*
>   *Then they'l shew bright,*
>   *And like us light,*
> *When Leaving Bodies with their Care,*
>   *They slide to us and Air.*   (III. ii. 119 – 30)

The cloud image (l. 125) echoes the storm imagery that throughout the play
denotes passionate excess.

Imprisonment in the physical body is also imprisonment in the sublunary
world of discordant elements, whose shifting combinations were held to
cause the ceaseless, inexorable change of earthly things.[10] Ismeron summons
the deities who "*see what men are doom'd to do; / Where Elements in discord
dwell*" (III. ii. 67–8), and identifies imprisonment in the body with

enslavement to the realm of shifting elements, giving their mixture and strife total control over the body and the passions:

There all th' informing Elements repair,
Swift Messengers of Water, Fire, and Air,
To give account of Actions whence they came,
And how they govern every mortal frame;
How from their various mixture, or their strife,
Are known the Calms and Tempests of our life.   (I. ii. 52-7)

The turmoil of the elements is here the cause of the storms of passion (just as it is the cause of the storms and other natural upheavals of the external world), so that the fluctuations of passion mimic the fluctuations of the sublunary realm which is their province;[11] to yield to passion is to abandon oneself to the mutable sphere of discordant elements, and, for this reason, pursuit of passion is pursuit of death.

All the characters of *The Indian Queen* are "*clog'd with Earth*" (III. ii. 119), subject to arbitrary and irresistible emotional change, enslaved and often destroyed by their desires. Proudly seeking to establish their self-sufficiency, the Ynca and Montezuma embark on courses that lead swiftly to bondage and the threat of death. Having deposed his monarch to enthrone his mistress, Traxalla finds that he must submit to the power that he has created, vainly pleading former services and urging an inexorable Zempoalla to spare Orazia and execute Montezuma.[12] Zempoalla herself is destroyed by her passion for power, preferring the self-assertion of suicide to the impotence of life (v. i. 272-96), and by her passion for Montezuma, unable to kill him when she knows that clemency cannot gain his love and must ensure her own overthrow (v. i. 207). More than anyone else, she acts out the self-enslavement and self-destruction elucidated in the incantation scene, providing a quintessential example of the deathward impulse that each character, to some degree, mimics and recreates. The fatality of her passions is best illustrated through the medium of her vow to sacrifice the prisoners taken in battle, which she swears in her opening scene (i. ii. 50-5). Originally intended to avenge her son's supposed death, the vow ultimately produces the very bereavement it was to have assuaged, since her insistence on the sacrifice ultimately drives Acacis to suicide (v. i. 92-179); the cause of the vow becomes its effect, and the words of mistaken anguish that precede it—"O my *Acacis*" (I. ii. 1)—are repeated with tragic fitness when it claims its first victim (v. i. 144). Zempoalla's own fate proceeds from her vow with equal nicety and irony: although initially moved by vengefulness, she soon begins to use the vow as a means of furthering her love for Montezuma, hoping by its means to rid herself of Orazia's rivalry; but the intended instrument of love eventually becomes the instrument of death, since Zempoalla fails to slaughter the prisoners and pays the penalty that she had proposed for failure (I. ii. 83), herself becoming the sacrificial victim. Her maternal love destroys her son; her sexual love and love of power destroy her.

The fatality of Zempoalla's passions is anticipated in the imagery that throughout the play portrays their violence. Repeatedly, she is associated with the motif of the raging flame, which denotes both the savage voracity of her passions and the barbaric rites of sacrifice that they demand. The flames of sacrifice are an expression of the flames of her mind, and her savage gods are merely deifications of her savage passions:

> I'le kindle other Flames, since I must burn,
> And all their Temples into ashes turn. . . .
> Loves flames into the Strangers brest convey, . . .
> Make him but burn for me in flames like mine,
> Victims shall bleed, and feasted Altars shine.
>   (III. ii. 141−2, 146, 149−50)[13]

In falling victim to her vow, Zempoalla falls victim only to her own passions, to the wild and tormenting flames that have gradually consumed her throughout the play.[14]

The destructiveness of passion, however, is not only suicidal in nature. Adam sees the orgasm as self-annihilation, Satan as destruction of the sexual partner, and *The Indian Queen* affords examples of Satanic as well as Adamic love: "Next to possess," declares Zempoalla, " 'tis pleasure to destroy" (III. ii. 16). In her blending of eroticism and violence she is followed by Traxalla, who boasts, "I will prove / Those joyes in vengeance, which I want in love" (IV. ii. 108−9). Remarkably, however, the capacity of love to destroy the beloved is most extensively exemplified by the hero and heroine. At the beginning of Act IV Montezuma and Orazia are each protected by the villainous lover from the villainous rival, and each is asked to repay protection with love (IV. i. 30−122). Dryden here imitates the plight of Oroondates and Cassandra towards the end of *Cassandra* (v. v. 45−8: see Appendix, pp. 158−60), but characteristically multiplies the frailties of his borrowed characters; for, whereas La Calprenède's lovers ultimately cannot demand each other's deaths, Dryden's are both possessively insistent that the partner die rather than favour the rival. Surprisingly, moreover, the first of the pair to feel the destructive jealousy is Orazia, hitherto Montezuma's mentor in virtue:

> *Oraz.* Forgive my Passion, I had rather see
> You dead, than kind to anything but me.
>   *Mont.* O my *Orazia*!
> To what new joys and knowledg am I brought!
> Are deaths hard lessons by a Woman taught?   (IV. i. 65−9)

Orazia's fatal possessiveness is plainly a lapse from her seemingly exemplary

role, for at the beginning of the act, before Zempoalla entered and when
Traxalla posed the only threat to Montezuma, the heroine had been nobly
concerned for her lover's life:

> *Mont.* When I am dead *Orazia* may forgive;
> She never must, if I dare wish to live.
>   *Oraz.* Hold, hold——O *Montezuma*, can you be
> So careless of your self, but more of me?
> Though you have brought me to this misery,
> I blush to say I cannot see you die.
>   *Mont.* Can my approaching Fate such pity move?
> The Gods and you at once forgive and love.   (IV. i. 17—24)

Orazia here brings about an important step in Montezuma's education,
confronting the originally egocentric hero with an outward-going concern
for others that extends to spontaneous pardon for extreme wrongs—a
human reflection of divine attributes (l. 24). The instructress, however,
proves to be less ideal than her precepts, attaining divine magnanimity
only to plummet into very human selfishness: her saintly concern for
Montezuma's life is emphatically cancelled by her destructive jealousy, so
that the "rational construct" (Barbeau, *Intellectual Design of Dryden's Heroic
Plays*, p. 4) suddenly becomes human, unable to sustain her stereotyped
part.[15]
    Acacis, parallel to Orazia in his seemingly stereotyped virtue, is parallel
also in his lapses from excellence, similarly yielding to the fatal demands of
passion: at first he seems to be a figure of Caroline perfection, an ideal friend
and an embodiment of pure reason; by the end of the play insurmountable
passion has driven him to seek his friend's death (IV. ii. 12—44) and to
contrive his own (v. i. 143). In their fatal jealousy both Orazia and Acacis
reveal a flaw in the façade of conventional perfection, an indelible kinship
with the turbulent and destructive villains; all characters are ruled by passion
and, consequently, by change and mortality. Orazia's descent from divinity
to humanity illustrates a pattern that is to dominate the latter part of the play,
as characters increasingly reveal a caprice and complexity that invalidates the
schematic bareness of their initial relationships. Critics have taken too little
account of these subtle and intricate vagaries of character.

III. THE HERO AND HIS "NORMATIVE" MENTORS

Acacis and Orazia seem at first to be simple models of virtue whose chief task
is to educate and civilise the undisciplined hero, and most critics have seen
nothing but the first appearances. Certainly, Acacis and Orazia do provide
the hero with moral lessons. Acacis, for example, astonishes his self-centred

friend with his altruistic pity for the victims of his mother's usurpation, moving Montezuma to exclaim in wonder,

> How great a proof of vertue have you shown,
> To be concern'd for griefs, though not your own!   (II. iii. 36–7)

Though impressed by Acacis' altruism, Montezuma cannot at this stage imitate it, and the scene from which Montezuma's praise is taken consistently contrasts the friends' capacities for disregard of self. At the beginning of the scene Montezuma *is* concerned for griefs not his own, wishing to lessen Acacis' sorrows by sharing in them (II. iii. 5–11). His altruism, however, cannot survive a threat to his interests: discovering that Acacis is his rival, he remarks heatedly that he spares the prince's life only because he can help to secure Orazia's safety (II. iii. 62–7). Montezuma can feel concern only for those who do not encroach on his own ambitions; Acacis is distressed at misfortunes by which he has, unwillingly, benefited. Whereas the less attractive characters are imprisoned within egoistic passions, Acacis *seems* able to transcend his own sensations and enter into those of others. Although he is untouched by the prevailing passion for freedom, and although he submits willingly to bondage, he apparently has a freedom that others lack in that he is not a prisoner of himself.

In the final act Acacis pleads against the sacrifice of his friends:

> Hold, hold, such sacrifices cannot be
> Devotion's, but a solemn cruelty:
> How can the Gods delight in humane blood?
> Think 'um not cruel; if you think 'um good.
> In vain we ask that mercy which they want,
> And hope that pitty which they hate to grant.   (v. i. 92–7)

Enslaved by savage passions, Zempoalla had portrayed the gods in her own image, reserving all her worship for the "Great God of Vengeance" (I. ii. 50, 81). By contrast, Acacis' concern for the rights of others, his desire to step outside the circle of his own sensations, leads him to glimpse the designs of just and merciful gods. Acacis' concern for his fellows reflects God's will and nature in human terms, whereas Zempoalla's cult of savage and vengeful gods deifies the worst aspects of human nature, creating an incongruity even greater than that of seeking divinity in the physical (and animal) passions.

Orazia too has qualities which are genuinely admirable and which influence Montezuma's moral growth. In particular, like Acacis, she opens the hero's egoistic mind to the possibility of altruism, echoing Acacis' concern for griefs not his own:

> Think half your sorrows on *Orazia* fall,
> And be not so unkinde to suffer all.   (III. i. 54–5)

She shows a similar spirit when she forgives Montezuma and fears for his life (IV. i. 19–22); as in Acacis' protest against human sacrifice, the outward-going concern for others is here portrayed as a reflection of divine goodness. In Dryden's world, however, divine qualities are attained only briefly, and Orazia soon forfeits her nobility by desiring Montezuma's death. Nevertheless, she regains her altruism, and reaches the zenith of her ennobling influence, when she refuses to escape from Zempoalla without her father (IV. ii. 69–84). Voluntarily returning to prison, she draws both Montezuma and Acacis in her wake: this willing assumption of fetters, very different from the hero's original quest for unlimited freedom, symbolises the recognition of human bonds that is the essence of this episode. But here, too, the heroine's altruistic splendour is soon to be tarnished.

In discussing Acacis and Orazia critics have chosen to concentrate on their exemplary qualities, such as those outlined above. The qualities are certainly there, but they do not present the whole picture—especially of Acacis. Orazia's flaws are the less complex, and appear principally in the scene of fatal jealousy, which has already been discussed, and during the preparations for sacrifice, where her fatal jealousy reappears. Such is her possessiveness in the sacrifice scene that she even forbids Montezuma to beg the Ynca's life of Zempoalla, preferring that her father should die rather than live through her lover's intercession with her rival (v. i. 43–52); selfish passion triumphs over filial duty, and Orazia falters in the altruism that had inspired the return to her imprisoned father.

Acacis' flaws, however, are more extensive and interesting. For all his merits, he is a man not of immutable virtues but of noble aspirations, briefly, intermittently, and precariously realised. The gap between aspiration and ability is most clearly revealed in his last speech to Montezuma:

Dear *Montezuma*.
I may be still your Friend, though I must dye
Your Rival in her love; Eternity
Has room enough for both, there's no desire,
Where to enjoy is only to admire:
There we'l meet friends, when this short storm is past.   (v. i. 162–7)[16]

Whereas Zempoalla seeks unbounded fulfilment of passion, Acacis hopes for the absence of desire; his ambitions, however, are no less impracticable than his mother's, for in life he is necessarily imperfect, his ideals thwarted by passion, his friendship marred by rivalry. Acacis is not a friend of the Cavalier variety, enjoying a telepathic communion of souls with his partner and capable of an unshrinking sacrifice of love to friendship; on the contrary, his passions isolate him from his friend and make magnanimous resignation impossible. In revealing himself as the prisoner of passion, moreover, Acacis shows that his love, like Montezuma's, is not different in *kind* from that of the villains (here Dryden departs markedly from Platonic and *précieuse* tradition): echoing the incantation scene, Acacis describes his passion as part of the "storm" of the temporal world, and as a bondage from which eternity will free him; he thus differs from his mother neither in the nature of his passions nor in his ability to control them, but simply in his attitude towards them. In portraying his seeming exemplar of virtue as the tragic slave of passion, Dryden creates a further departure from the facile oversimplifications of much earlier love-and-honour literature, in which noble but unfortunate rivals were capable of an immediate, painless subjugation of passion; such characters belong to an unfallen world where the passions are perfectly subordinated to the reason, whereas Dryden's reveal their creator's Christian awareness of human frailty.

Like Orazia, Acacis seems for the first three acts to be a largely exemplary figure, but, like Orazia, he loses his solely exemplary status in Act IV, revealing marked and surprising flaws. The first sign of his imperfection appears after he has engineered the lovers' escape from prison. In doing so, he at first seems to be fulfilling a conventionally ideal role, ensuring his rival's safety and happiness. But in the event he does nothing of the kind, for, instead of resigning Orazia to Montezuma as an ideal character would have done, he actually challenges his friend to a duel (IV. ii. 11−44); in romance and Platonic drama, such lapses from magnanimity characterise only the base and the comically imperfect.[17] The earlier contrast between the altruistic Acacis and the savagely jealous Montezuma, willing to destroy his friend for his love (II. iii. 1−71), turns into likeness as Acacis acquires the very imperfections that had at first stood in antithesis to his virtues. Indeed, so great is his lapse from excellence that he even begins to imitate his mother's flaws:

> Your greater merits bribe her to your side;
> My weaker Title must by Arms be try'd.   (IV. ii. 35−6)

Acacis is attempting a usurpation in love that parallels Zempoalla's usurpation in the kingdom. And, like the more obviously imperfect characters, he is allowing personal impulse to triumph over social restraint: disregarding the rights of friend and lover, he pursues a passion that, because of his mother's hatred of Orazia, must render him a stateless person, exiled from the kingdom to which he is sole known heir. Montezuma is now the one who sees that passionate egocentricity is the enemy of civilisation, recognising that an unpopulated wilderness is the only fit or possible place for Acacis to follow his desires:

> Suppose thou conquerst, wou'dst thou wander o're
> The South-Sea Sands, or the rough Northern Shore,
> That parts thy spacious Kingdom from *Peru*;
> And leaving Empire, hopeless Love pursue?   (IV. ii. 25−8)

The contrasts of Acts I and II have been reversed.

In the first three acts Orazia and Acacis instruct Montezuma in virtue. In Act IV the twin embodiments of virtue reveal very human flaws. And in Act V Montezuma outstrips both his original mentors. As Zempoalla prepares to sacrifice her prisoners, Montezuma pleads for the lives that his actions have endangered:

> 'Tis I that wrought these mischiefs ought to fall;
> A just and willing sacrifice for all.
> Now *Zempoalla*, be both just and kinde,
> And in my fate let me thy mercy finde:
> Be grateful then, and grant me that esteem,
> That as alive, so dead I may redeem.   (v. i. 37–42)

Montezuma here outgrows his original egocentricity, and in doing so eclipses Acacis, his original instructor in altruism. Acacis' selflessness had, of course, vanished in the duel episode. Most specifically, however, Montezuma's speech of self-sacrifice contrasts with Acacis' concluding speech in the previous act, in which he too had offered his life to Zempoalla:

> I'le quench your thirst with Blood, and will destroy
> My self, and with my self, your cruel joy.
> Now *Montezuma* since *Orazia* dyes,
> I'le fall before thee, the first Sacrifice;
> My title in her death shall exceed thine,
> As much as in her life thy hopes did mine:
> And when with our mixt blood the Altar's dy'd,
> Then our new Title let the Gods decide.   (IV. ii. 110–17)

Acacis still retains the spirit of the duel scene, and has not yet been illuminated by intimations of an eternity free from passion; on the contrary, he regards his death as a means of purchasing a claim to Orazia in the next world.[18] Montezuma offers his life to buy for others a benefit that, by the very nature of his offer, he cannot himself enjoy; Acacis simply offers his life in order to buy something for himself.

Montezuma's desire to "redeem" the Ynca and Orazia by sacrificing himself recalls Christ's sacrifice. The similarity, of course, is far from perfect: Montezuma does not wish to suffer for the sins of others but to ensure that his own do not cause others undeserved harm. Nevertheless, there is a degree of resemblance, and the Christ image is consistent with other images of virtue in the play, since in their moments of greatest nobility both Acacis and Orazia rise briefly to imitation of the divine. Montezuma had sought divinity in the passionate exaltation of the self; he finds it only when he lays all thought of self aside, spontaneously imitating a god of whom he has never heard. In this speech he achieves his one, momentary, escape from the prison of his selfish passions.

In desiring to save all his associates, Montezuma transcends the egocentric
jealousy which in Act IV had led him to desire Orazia's death; *ipso facto*, he
also surpasses Orazia's conduct in that act, so that he now excels both his
original mentors. Orazia does, in fact, provoke Montezuma's heroic
outburst by wishing to die in order to save her father (v. i. 35–6).
Nevertheless, she still submits to the spirit of Act IV, unwilling that
Montezuma should ask anything—even the Ynca's life—of Zempoalla (v. i.
43–4), and still possessively insistent on her lover's death: she can, she says,
bear neither that her father should die nor that Montezuma should live (v. i.
50). Indeed, she succeeds in reconverting Montezuma from his Christ-like
altruism to the "cruel jealousie" (v. i. 75) of the previous act, so that he too
attains divinity only to plunge into renewed humanity. His return to fatal
jealousy is accompanied by flame images that echo those associated with
Zempoalla, similarly equating the flames of love with the flames of the
coming sacrifice. Before achieving his moment of altruism, he had identified
the flames of love and sacrifice, regarding shared death as a form of
copulation and thus providing the first of Dryden's many sex–death images:

> Forgive me one thing yet; to say I love, . . .
> Since dying in one flame, my ashes must
> Embrace and mingle with *Orazia*'s dust.   (v. i. 29, 31–2)

"Embrace and mingle" provides an image of coition, punning, perhaps, on
the two meanings of the Latin *misceo*: to mingle and to copulate. The flame
images return with the decline of Montezuma's Christ-like altruism,
revealing that the lovers are, to the end, akin to the villainess in the
destructive voracity of their passions:

> *Mont.* As in one flame we liv'd, in one we'l dye.   (v. i. 56)

> *Oraz.* That flame not like immortal love appears
> Where death can cool its warmth, or kill its fears.   (v. i. 77–8)

Montezuma has lost his moment of insight, and the moral ascendancy
soon reverts to Acacis, whose final moral vision discredits that to which
Orazia has won Montezuma. Orazia sees in eternity only a continuation of
temporal passion, and designates Montezuma as a human sacrifice to the
"immortal love" beyond the grave; Acacis, by contrast, glimpses merciful
gods who abhor human sacrifice and offer man an eternity free from passion.
Dryden's characters may not, at this stage of his career, be psychologically
complex, but they are nevertheless complex dramatic creations: the balance
of virtue between the characters undergoes many shifts in the latter part of
the play, as painfully acquired illumination is easily lost through a resurgence
of human frailty. The Ynca too participates in the intricate fluctuations of
nobility: transcending his angry self-assertiveness, he rises to a moving

magnanimity by forgiving the man who has brought about his downfall (v. i. 25–8); immediately, however, godlike forbearance gives way to human anger, and the Ynca's forgiveness is severely tested by memories of Montezuma's presumptuous love (v. i. 33–4).

Even the dying Acacis fails to attain unalloyed magnanimity, since, in death as in life, he continues his harsh and implacable hostility towards his mother. One of Zempoalla's redeeming qualities is her strong and constant maternal affection (which is, however, consistently perverted to evil ends). Her maternal love, and its perverse consequences, are most extensively portrayed in the third act, where Acacis pleads with her for Orazia's life:

> *Zemp.* I love thee so, that though fear follow still,
> And horror urges all that have been ill,
> I cou'd for thee——
> Act o're my crimes agen,——and not repent,
> Even when I bore the shame and punishment.   (III. i. 81–5)

Sexual jealousy admittedly vies with maternal attachment, moving Zempoalla to refuse Acacis' request for Orazia's life, but even her cruelty is tinged with maternal concern, since she resents Orazia's rivalry for Acacis' love as well as Montezuma's:

> Had she triumph'd, what cou'd she more have done
> Then robb'd the Mother, and enslav'd the Son?   (III. i. 110–11)

These are subtle and striking touches, worthy of more development than they receive: the villainess is motivated by a deformed altruism that mimics and parodies the qualities of the more ideal characters.

Acacis is coldly unresponsive to his mother's clinging affection, and is justly charged by her with failing to see the mother in the Queen (III. i. 4). Surprisingly, moreover, his hostility towards her appears in its most overt and jarring form in his otherwise noble death scene: between his two speeches of moral enlightenment, on divine mercy and the eternal calm of the spirit, he lapses into a quite brutal aggravation of his mother's grief:

> *Zemp.* He faints, help, help, some help or he will bleed
> His life and mine away:
> Some water there——Not one stirs from his place;
> I'le use my tears to sprinkle on his face.
> *Aca.* Orazia.——
> *Zemp.* Fond childe, why do'st thou call upon her name?
> I am thy Mother.
> *Aca.*   No, you are my shame.   (v. i. 146–52)

Acacis' implacable repudiation of his mother mars what is otherwise a scene

of almost universal pardon: Acacis himself has just begged forgiveness from
Orazia (v. i. 133), and, in the very speech in which he rejects Zempoalla, he
goes on to beg the Ynca's forgiveness (v. i. 155–6). Later, Montezuma,
Orazia, Amexia, and the Ynca all forgive Zempoalla (v. i. 260–71). In this
pattern of general reconciliation the son's rejection of the mother stands out
as a discordant exception, and as an unpleasing blemish on the final splendour
of his enlightened virtue. Retrospectively, moreover, this final discord alerts
us to earlier ones. Whereas Montezuma and his like cultivate the private man
at the expense of the public, Acacis seems at first to cultivate the public man
to a fault, aware only of his distaste for the Queen, not of his natural ties with
the mother. He repeatedly rejects offers of freedom at the beginning of the
play, preferring to observe the dictates of honour in remaining with the
Peruvians rather than those of kin in returning to his mother. In Acacis'
situation, any other heroic character would experience an agonising conflict
between honour and duty, but for Acacis there is no conflict—only a
complacent awareness of his obligations to comparative strangers. His closest
exemplar is Oroondates, who is led by love of Statira to support Darius
in a battle against his own father (*Cassandra*, 1. ii. 39). Oroondates does,
however, feel a greater conflict than Acacis, and he later comes to feel that
his action was a sin for which the gods are punishing him
(I. v. 116). Acacis, by contrast, remains untroubled by any sense of filial
attachment. His love for Orazia does bring a partial triumph of the private
over the public man and a consequent awakening of similarities with his
mother: he attempts to usurp possession of Orazia, is imaged as an outcast
from civilisation (IV. ii. 25–8), and finally anticipates Zempoalla's passionate
self-immolation. Nevertheless, he continues to reject her to the end, refusing
to acknowledge what the latter events of the play demonstrate: that her
blood and character are part of his inheritance as surely as, in *Sir Gawain and
the Green Knight*, Morgan la Fée's are of Sir Gawain's.

At first, *The Indian Queen* seems, superficially, to be an unenterprising
continuation of romance and Cavalier traditions. Acacis illustrates the
conventional supremacy of reason over passion; Montezuma is the
passionate lover whose character must be refined by his mistress's tuition and
example; and Orazia on the whole seems to be well qualified for her
educative role. For the first three acts the play jogs along in a mostly
undistinguished manner, superior to works such as Carlell's to the degree
that mechanical competence is superior to total ineptitude: the plotting is
clear and coherent, the characters' motivation is intelligible, and the syntax
on the whole makes sense. The incantation scene is thematically important,
but the themes have to be dug out with some effort: the scene shows the
immature or mediocre writer's inability to give appropriately emphatic
expression to his ideas, and it in no way matches the sustained and complex
allegory of the parallel scene in *Tyrannick Love*. The last two acts, however,
are far more interesting. The bloodless stereotypes acquire an unexpected
complexity and fallibility, and the play acquires a unity and even grandeur of

symbolism. Zempoalla's inexorable, irreversible slide towards self-destruction becomes a general symbol of the self-annihilation to which the life of passion tends—a symbol which each character, to some degree, recreates. Each imitation of Zempoalla destroys deliberately fostered expectations of ideal magnanimity. Montezuma and Orazia, who had promised to be the perfect lover and mistress, fall victim to her spirit, jealously desiring each other's deaths. Acacis, the apparent embodiment of Reason, also falls victim to his mother's spirit, anticipating her by following the path of passion to death. Zempoalla's suicide follows hard on her son's, completing not only the fatal triumph of passion but also the defeat of trite idealism. Comforting the bereaved Queen, Montezuma offers her the consolation that had so successfully assuaged tragic passions in *Arviragus and Philicia*—namely, that one friend comprehensively embodies the identity of the other: "O that you wou'd believe / Acacis lives in me, and cease to grieve", he pleads (v. i. 284–5). Since Zempoalla's feelings for Montezuma are wholly unmaternal, the suggestion seems decidedly inept, and the Queen's suicide reveals the emptiness of the comfort. Here, briefly, Dryden provides a decoy Platonic ending for the play, but quickly allows turbulent passions to conquer. This incident typifies and brings to a climax the play's realistic examination of chimerical ideals: each of the characters has experienced the fatality of passion and the impotence of conventional idealism. In making his villainess the psychological centre of the play, an embodiment of the destructive passions that at times rule even the hero and heroine, Dryden lays the groundwork for some of his greatest dramatic achievements: in *The Conquest of Granada*, for example, Lyndaraxa increasingly controls the minds and destinies of Almanzor and Almahide, until at the end they are puppets in a scenario that she contrives and controls.

The Indian Queen is obviously not a great play. Some of its central images, such as those of mutability, are realised in a rudimentary and inadequate fashion; one of Dryden's greatest advances in *The Indian Emperour* was the discovery of a dramatic imagery commensurate with the scale of his intellectual ambitions. Furthermore, although his characters are more intricate than critics have admitted, the intricacy is arbitrarily imposed at the whim of the dramatist: Acacis *is* multifaceted and subtly shaded, but he is not an individual; he has no inner, informing identity, and his vacillations are merely expressions of an abstract theory concerning human fallibility—a theory which is almost identically realised in all three heroic characters. Nevertheless, the play is far more intelligent than its commentators have allowed, and it has the value possessed by all works in which an original artist begins to discover his *métier*.

3 The Indian Emperour

In *The Indian Emperour* (1665) Dryden realises much of the promise shown in the latter part of *The Indian Queen*. In particular, he refines and develops the intricacy of characterisation that had emerged in Acts IV and V of the earlier play. Capricious appetites now flaw the would-be paragons from the outset, and the repeated discomfiture of idealism is traced with a fertility of invention unmatched anywhere in the play's predecessor. The advance, however, is primarily one of dramatic inventiveness rather than psychological subtlety: the vacillations and self-contradictions are still arbitrarily imposed, never convincing as expressions of a whole and individualised personality. Dryden does, on the other hand, achieve unqualified improvement in his dramatic imagery. Once again generation and corruption, love and death, dominate humanity in inextricable union, but now Dryden finds images worthy of the great and tragic paradox that informs the action. The brilliantly developed symbolism of Montezuma's birthday rite, for example, would not be out of place in *All for Love* (which, indeed, also opens with fatally inapposite birthday celebrations).

The Indian Emperour also marks a change in the scale of Dryden's dramatic conception. *The Indian Queen* is alone among the heroic plays in developing a single, tightly knit line of action, and in *The Indian Emperour* Dryden experiments with the more expansive design that was to characterise all the subsequent heroic plays. Whereas Orazia and Montezuma were at the centre of all the conflicts in *The Indian Queen*, *The Indian Emperour* interweaves three lines of action, each dominated by one of the play's three women—Alibech, Almeria, and Cydaria. The three strands are connected by shared motifs and images: in each, for example, characters become prisoners of the past, and in each they experience the affinity of love and death. The thematic relationships, however, are not accompanied by sustained relationships of structure. The strands of action show little correspondence of pattern and development, and give no hint of the contrapuntal mastery that was to distinguish *The Conquest of Granada*. Exuberance of invention is not yet combined with perfection of design.

Criticism of *The Indian Emperour* is on the whole disappointing, for the play's most important concerns have gone unnoticed and the complexity of its two heroes has consistently been underrated. King simply catalogues allegedly funny speeches (*Dryden's Major Plays*, pp. 28–36). Miss Barbeau falsely regiments fickle and unstable characters into ranks of "norms" and "extremes". Kirsch and Loftis also underestimate the complexity and fallibility of Dryden's characters, Kirsch asserting that Cortez "comes as close as a mortal can to heroic perfection" (*Dryden's Heroic Drama*, p. 90), Loftis that the play demonstrates "the strength of the characters' devotion to their ideals".[1] Neither claim seems to me consistent with the evidence of the text. Alssid's analysis (I. 139—61), however, is intelligent and stimulating, containing much that is of value. But it also leaves much unsaid, and again takes an excessively laudatory view of Cortez, arguing that the play traces "The rise and triumph of Cortez' *virtù*" (I. 154). Dryden still had much to learn when he wrote *The Indian Emperour*, but the play is considerably more complex than has hitherto been allowed, and considerably less optimistic about man's capacity for "heroic perfection".

I. GENERATION AND CORRUPTION

In *The Indian Emperour*, as in *The Indian Queen*, dreams of Eden are destroyed by the anarchy of human appetite and the turmoil of sublunary change. The New World at first tempts the Spaniards to expectations of boundless and imperishable fertility: the earth is here in its natal state, untouched by post-lapsarian decay and reminiscent of Lucretius' newly created world;[2] the cyclic change of seasons is absent; and, while the cycles of day and night admittedly exist, the nights are as brief as the sun can possibly make them:

> *Cortez.* On what new happy Climate are we thrown,
> So long kept secret, and so lately known;
> As if our old world modestly withdrew,
> And here, in private, had brought forth a new!   (I. i. 1—4)

> *Pizarro.* In *Spain* our Springs, like Old Mens Children, be
> Decay'd and wither'd from their Infancy:
> No kindly showers fall on our barren earth,
> To hatch the seasons in a timely birth.
> Our Summer such a Russet Livery wears,
> As in a Garment often dy'd appears.
> *Cort.* Here nature spreads her fruitful sweetness round,
> Breaths on the Air and broods upon the ground.
> Here days and nights the only seasons be,
> The Sun no Climat does so gladly see:
> When forc'd from hence, to view our parts, he mourns:
> Takes little journies, and makes quick returns.   (I. i. 15—26)

Gradually, however, the visions of Paradise are discredited, as are all Elysian dreams in Dryden's plays: fertility is still inseparable from its universal concomitant of decay, and the sense of renewal is dissipated as the characters become increasingly enmeshed in the past.

In fact, the conquistadors' effusions are never very credible, for these hard-headed adventurers are, as we might expect, neither sensitive nor felicitous as nature poets. On the contrary, they are as blinkered in their perception of nature as the Indians later are in their perception of art. When Guyomar reports the arrival of the Spanish ships (I. ii. 93 – 122), he naïvely translates the perplexing products of civilisation into the familiar terms of his natural surroundings. Similarly, the urban Spaniards are awkward and inept in their response to the novelties of nature. Their notions of natural process are very limited, being confined to ideas of parturition and excretion (I. i. 3 – 4, 7 – 8, 15 – 18, 29 – 30), and they have to plug the gaps in their terminology with images drawn inappositely from the familiar realms of custom and artifice— the proprieties demanded during confinement (ll. 3 – 4), the hazards of repeated dyeing (ll. 19 – 20). The resulting imagery is ungainly and hybrid: the savage continent was brought forth amidst all the primness of a Spanish accouchement, and the European summers are newly hatched chicks in often dyed garments. The most startling hybrid, however, is provided by Vasquez. Not only do the mountains defecate; with some inferior version of the Midas touch, they defecate silver:

> Each downfal of a flood the Mountains pour,
> From their rich bowels rolls a silver shower.   (I. i. 29 – 30)

The Spaniards' imagery, insensitively superimposing art on nature, exactly reflects their insensitive attitude towards the New World: they are less interested in its living abundance than in its mineral wealth, its potential for yielding artefacts. The imagery, therefore, is perfectly appropriate to the characters who use it. Cortez' image of the Old World's labour is the first image of many to perplex readers of the heroic plays with its comic incongruity. Yet, startling as it is, the image is just as apt to its speaker as Guyomar's bewildered mixed metaphor of the "tall straight trees which on the waters flew" (I. ii. 108); and it warns us from the outset not to expect exemplary wisdom from the hero.

As the expectations of Eden are discredited, the Spaniards' expectations of protracted day give way to the Indians' fears of unbroken night. The transition begins immediately before the first battle, when Cydaria depicts Cortez as the agent of the night that is to engulf Mexico:

> Those closing Skies might still continue bright.
> But who can help it if you'l make it night?   (II. ii. 14 – 15)

After Cortez' misconceived celebration of nocturnal harmony (III. ii. 1 – 10), immediately and ironically belied by Orbellan's treachery, night reigns with unambiguous menace: "Amidst the Terrors of a Dreadful night" (IV. iv. 134); "I never durst in Darkness be alone" (IV. iv. 136); "Night and Despair my Fatal Foot-steps guide" (IV. iv. 174); "This is a night of Horror, not of

Love" (v. i. 134); "Poor humane kind must wander in the dark" (v. ii. 58); "Stay Life, and keep me in the chearful Light;/Death is too Black, and dwells in too much Night" (v. ii. 310–12).

The vernal Paradise in fact acquires an unexpected menace as early as the play's second scene, where the solemnities of Montezuma's birthday ominously qualify the Spaniards' images of fruition. Superficially, the sense of renewal continues. Ritual commemoration of the Emperor's birth is compounded with a love rite, imbued in turn with images of natural growth and generation: the loved one is crowned, with flowers, as "Queen of all the year" (I. ii. 18), a tutelary of the year's fecundity. But the rites of fruition are linked with those of death, for Montezuma's birthday has also been marked by the sacrifice of five hundred prisoners of war (I. ii. 4–6)—an atrocity that dispels our expectations of Paradise. Ironically, moreover, the ceremony of renewal frames the description of the approaching fleet (I. ii, 93–122), the recital of the prophecies of doom (I. ii. 123–5), and, of course, the Spaniards' arrival. The dark undertones are sustained by the ominous (and later fatal) dissensions that mar the rites. Nominally an occasion of renewal, the festival in fact contains all the causes of Mexico's disintegration, and thus initiates a fusion of illusory renewal and actual decay that is to recur throughout the play and find its most explicit formulation in the expedients of the starving, who destroy themselves in the very process of ensuring their brief survival:

> Even deadly Plants, and Herbs of pois'nous juice
> Wild hunger seeks; and to prolong our breath,
> We greedily devour our certain death.   (IV. ii. 34–6)

In its conjoined images of fruition and decay, the birthday rite discredits the opening dream of unfallen changelessness (a dream that, in various guises, haunts all Dryden's heroes) by declaring the inevitable presence of corruption within generation, of death within life: *prorepunt iuncto uita morsque pede.*[3] As we have seen, the same conjunction of opposites lies at the heart of *The Indian Queen*, and it is to dominate the later tragedies, reaching its most elaborate expression in the imagery of *All for Love.*[4] And, as we might expect, it is to be ever-present in *The Indian Emperour*, creating an inexorable movement towards the incident that counterbalances and recapitulates the birthday rite—the torture scene of the fifth act, where Cortez unwittingly dignifies another religious atrocity with incongruous imagery of erotic worship and fulfilment: " 'Tis sacred here to Beauty and to Love" (v. ii. 111).

As the play develops, the birthday rite gains further, retrospective, irony: neither of the relationships initiated with the floral garland (Montezuma–Almeria, Odmar–Alibech) comes to fulfilment, and together they share responsibility for the downfall of the Mexican empire; of the courtships initiated within the love rite, only that of Guyomar and Alibech finds fulfilment, but this courtship is pointedly *not* initiated with the symbol of vernal growth and is completed only in conditions of forbidding sterility:

> *Guy.* Northward, beyond the Mountains we will go,
> Where Rocks lye cover'd with Eternal Snow;
> Thin Herbage in the Plains, and Fruitless Fields. . . .
> We to our selves will all our wishes grant.   (v. ii. 368–70, 374)

"We to our selves will all our wishes grant" expresses the longing for self-sufficiency that animates so many of Dryden's characters, whether villains or heroes. At the beginning of the play, individualistic heroism had seemed a quest for man's lost home of Eden; now it is represented as exile in a barren desert, unclaimed and unmarked by man. In tracing the movement from fruition to unfruition, Dryden recalls that other movement with which the cycles of change were initiated: from Paradise to the wilderness. As the play proceeds, then, the original expectations of renewal are increasingly thwarted by the triumph of death and sterility. Ironically, the most successful courtship is that of Cortez and Cydaria—which results from the disruption of the love ceremony.

The disrupted courtship ceremony, with its attendant ironies, is paralleled by the two disrupted marriages (of Orbellan and Guyomar) that form the later turning points of the action. In all three, obviously, the disruption takes the form of a Spanish attack, and in all three the train of events leading to the marred ceremony is preceded by a deluded celebration of natural harmony: the opening scene, Cortez' night speech (III. ii. 1–10), and the theriophilic song (IV. iii. 1–16). In the second and third sequences the praise of Nature is immediately followed by a surprise attack (by Orbellan and Guyomar), and in each case the attacked turns the tables and prevents his attacker's (and rival's) wedding. Throughout the play, then, the celebrations of natural harmony and sexual union are quickly negated by the triumph of death. "Doubly Blest, with Conquest, and with Love" (v. ii. 379), Cortez does not, as Alssid asserts, find the "ideal reward" for his heroism (I. 161). The double blessing links the marriage of the daughter with the death of the father, bringing to its culmination the grim conjunction of opposites first adumbrated in the birthday rite. From the beginning to the end, as we shall see, death frustrates the promise of renewal.

II. LOVE AND DEATH; RENEWAL AND BONDAGE TO THE PAST

The characters' lives persistently belie the opening images of vernal renewal, for, as death overshadows fruition in the birthday rite, so it does in the lives that the rite influences. Bound to death, the characters are bound also to the dead, to a dark and fatal past whose influence tragically frustrates all dreams of life and rebirth. Appropriately, the power of the dead is first manifested in the spurious rites of renewal, where Montezuma realises that love for Almeria compels him to relive the events of *The Indian Queen*, finding defeat where he had once found victory: captive to the daughter of his former gaolers, he has thrown away all his youthful triumphs:

> Once more I have *Traxalla's* chains put on,
> And by his Children am in triumph led,
> Too well the living have reveng'd the dead! (I. ii. 176—8)

Montezuma's bondage to the dead becomes yet clearer when he attempts another ritual of love. Seeking to advance his love by magic arts (II. i. 1—109), he finds not a living mistress but a dead—Almeria's mother, Zempoalla, whose passion he had once scorned:

> *Ghost.* Know *Montezuma*, thou art only mine;
> For those who here on Earth their passion show,
> By death for Love, receive their right below.
> Why doest thou then delay my longing Arms? (II. ii. 89—92)

The daughter is the channel and surrogate whereby the passions of the mother are satisfied; imagining that he courts the living, Montezuma moves inexorably to his union with the dead, with the shade that stands behind the body of the loved one. His love makes him a puppet manipulated from beyond the grave.

Cortez' career, too, repeats the ironies of the birthday rite, for here fruition is again overshadowed and frustrated by death, and the triumph of death is again a triumph of the dead and of a dark, fatal past. Indeed, the symbolism of the rite is transferred to Cortez as soon as he intrudes into Montezuma's world. In its opposed associations, the birthday rite celebrates the opposed deities of war and love—the savage god who claims the captives taken in battle and the "peaceful power" worshipped in the courtship ceremony (I. ii. 9).[5] And, when Cortez interrupts the festival, the Indians at once identify him with the malevolent war god: the Taxallans grovel before the "roaring gods" of his artillery (I. ii. 225) and, impressed by their superstitious awe, Montezuma himself hails Cortez as the "god of Wars" (I. ii. 232). Then, however, he becomes less certain of Cortez' identity: is he, as first thoughts had suggested, the "cruel god" (I. ii. 236) who has just exacted the bloody mass sacrifice, or is he the god worshipped in the love rite, the "peaceful power" who presides over human well-being and requires incense rather than blood (I. ii. 3)? For Montezuma, Cortez now embodies the ambiguity of the rites of death and love, and the possibility that he may be merely a fellow mortal occurs only as an afterthought:

> Thy actions show thee born of Heavenly Race.
> If then thou art that cruel god, whose eyes
> Delight in Blood, and Humane Sacrifice,
> Thy dreadful Altars I with Slaves will store,

> And feed thy nostrils with hot reeking gore;
> Or if that mild and gentle god thou be,
> Who dost mankind below with pity see,
> With breath of incense I will glad thy heart;
> But if like us, of mortal seed thou art,
> Presents of rarest Fowls, and Fruits I'le bring,
> And in my Realms thou shalt be more then King.　　(I. ii. 235—45)

In his reply Cortez naturally declines apotheosis, but he also confirms the symbolism that has been transferred to him; for, as soon as Montezuma has hailed him as the god either of war or of peace, he reproduces the Emperor's antithesis by proclaiming himself either "Ambassadour of *Peace*" "Or Herauld of a *War*" (I. ii. 250, 251; italics added). And, in the event, he vindicates Montezuma's first thoughts, proving to be the Herauld of War. Throughout the play Cortez recreates the associations of the birthday rite, and indeed the imagery of the play increasingly identifies him with the "cruel god", so that the spokesman of the new faith re-enacts the darkest features of the pagan past.

The dark side of Cortez' role is soon emphasised in his first conversation with Cydaria. When he tells her of the distance between the Old World and the New, he receives a strange and evocative reply:

> Your other world, I fear, is then the same
> That souls must go to when the body dies　　(I. ii. 367—8)

To Cydaria, as to Montezuma, Cortez appears as a terrible supernatural force, an emissary of death: love and death merge strangely but (as it turns out) appropriately, for Cortez is to "Court the Daughter in the Father's Blood" (II. ii. 47) and, finally, to be "doubly Blest, with Conquest, and with Love" (V. ii. 379). In seeing Cortez as a visitant from the spirit world, Cydaria recalls and reinforces her father's menacing deification of her lover during the birthday rite, and in addition anticipates the second fatally frustrated rite of love (the incantation episode), where Montezuma is in literal truth faced with a spectral lover. Moreover, Montezuma's second love rite is in turn to be echoed and recapitulated by Cortez, for shortly after the incantation scene Cortez reveals that he too has fallen under the spell of his own past, tactlessly telling Cydaria that in her he loves the image of an earlier and dead love (II. iii. 91—6). Cydaria's response echoes and amplifies her earlier image of the lover as ambassador from the dead, for she senses that both Cortez and she are manipulated by the dead mistress from beyond the grave:

> Ah happy Beauty whosoe're thou art!
> Though dead thou keep'st possession of his Heart; . . .
> Thou Liv'st and Triumph'st ore *Cydaria* too.　　(II. iii. 97—8, 102)

As Montezuma's first reactions had foretold, Cortez is deeply implicated in the characteristics of a world untransformed by Christianity: a world in which the processes of generation are subordinate to those of death, and in which the present is controlled and determined by a fatal past; in short, a world governed by the Fall. As the ambassador of Christianity, Cortez nominally comes to release the world of natural man from its confinement to the cyclic patterns of mortality;[6] instead, as we shall see, he becomes ever more closely identified with the continuing tyranny of death.

Almeria, parallel to Cortez in her conquest of Montezuma, is parallel also in sharing her victim's bondage, similarly succumbing to a love dominated by the past and by death. Her sudden infatuation with the man she proposes to kill re-enacts Zempoalla's similar infatuation with Montezuma:

In spight of me I Love, and see too late
My Mothers Pride must find my Mothers Fate.   (IV. i. 27—8)

She too is imaged as a deity from the land of the dead—her *"Cupid* looks as dreadfully as Death" (IV. iv. 12)—and she most clearly experiences the affinity of love and death, asking Cortez to kill her (IV. iv. 147—8) and attempting to consummate her passion by sprinkling him with her blood (V. ii. 309). Four of the major characters, then, are caught up in cyclic repetitions of the past which are analogous to the cycles of mutable nature and which, like them, declare the ineradicable presence of death within fruition. In the second love rite, in fact, the two species of cycle are identified, as the periodicity of individual life is projected on to the larger span of history:

High Priest. That the sad powers of the Infernal race
May read above what's hid from Humane Eyes,
And in your walks, see Empires fall and rise.
And ye Immortal Souls, who once were Men,
And now resolv'd to Elements agen,
Who wait for Mortal frames in depths below,
And did before what we are doom'd to do; . . .
Ascend, ascend, ascend at my command.
(II. i. 14—20, 22; italics added)

The helpless re-enactment of the past is here absorbed into a larger eschatological cycle of reincarnation and repetition, linked in its turn to a wider cycle of repetitive mutability that governs whole empires.

In *Paradise Lost* Adam was to be given two successive prophecies revealing the course of human history: the first, extending as far as the Flood, is of history shaped by the character of natural man, following a cyclic movement of growth and decay; the second, of history instinct with the purposes of God, moves in a linear succession of ever greater types towards man's fulfilment in Christ.[7] Dryden exploited a similar contrast in some of his later works: in *Absalom and Achitophel*, for example, the conspirators are heirs to the Fall and slaves to the cycles of change, living out recurrent patterns of error:

> For, govern'd by the *Moon*, the giddy *Jews*
> Tread the same track when she the Prime renews:
> And once in twenty Years, their Scribes Record,
> By natural Instinct they change their Lord.[8]

At the end of the poem, by contrast, David's reassertion of the ordering Logos brings "a *Series* of new time", of "mighty Years in long *Procession*" (1028, 1029; italics added). In *The Hind and the Panther*, similarly the repetitive "rise, . . . progress, and decay" (II. 611) of error is contrasted with the "lineal course" of revealed tradition (II. 615), which is elsewhere compared to a "*Jacob*'s ladder" (II. 220) linking man with God and declaring God's unbroken line of influence in human affairs.[9] In *The Indian Emperour*, as in these later works, the history of natural man expresses the cycles of mutable nature. But Cortez brings no "Series of new time"; on the contrary, he is the chief agent of the old processes.

III. THE RULE OF PASSION: CORTEZ

As the sport of mutability, man is vitiated by change and passion, his reason and resolution vacillating according to the unstable whims of bodily impulse: "*There is no constant existence, neither of our being, nor of the objects*," wrote Montaigne, deriving the mutability of the mind from that of the world: "And we, and our judgement, and all mortall things else do uncessantly rowle, turne, and passe away."[10] Passion and caprice are ubiquitous. Dryden does at first present his characters as exponents of "a single idea" (Chase, *The English Heroic Play*, p. 103), as stereotypes arranged in elaborate patterns of exact contrast—though Montezuma's early vacillations between feeble love and aggressive rationalism hint at complications to come. Despite its enticing plausibility, however, the geometrical order proves to be a Procrustean oversimplification, irrelevant to the changeful intricacies of human reality. Consider, for example, the trio of Montezuma, Almeria, and Alibech. From the outset, Montezuma exemplifies *par excellence* the subordination of public interests to private passion, allowing his love for Almeria to master and destroy his political judgement. Almeria inherits her mother's craving for boundless freedom, scorning all responsibilities that oppose her desires. And Alibech provides a clear and simple contrast to her sister and her Emperor, subordinating personal affection to the good of the nation by offering herself to the brother who serves his country best (I. ii. 159–61, III. i. 25–56). Yet Alibech, still more than Montezuma or Almeria, is the engineer of Mexico's downfall: she urges

Odmar to betray the city, and Odmar, acting on her advice after its justification has passed, destroys his father's kingdom. The two sisters, though morally opposed, are ultimately alike in their historical role. And so, ultimately, are the two opposed brothers, the honourable Guyomar and the base Odmar. Certainly, Guyomar defeats the Spaniards, whereas Odmar turns Spanish defeat into Spanish victory; but it is Guyomar, in his egocentric secretiveness about his victory plan (IV. ii. 98 — 105), who induces Alibech to believe that all hope is lost and to corrupt Odmar into readiness for future villainy; moreover, when the city has fallen, the lustful Odmar and the romantic Guyomar are alike in demanding Alibech's death (v. i. 60 — 80), so that honour and villainy are equal in their sexual as in their political destructiveness. Indeed, many of Guyomar's conventionally honourable acts, from his preservation of Cortez (III. i. 105 — 14) to his retreat into the wilderness (v. ii. 368 — 75), work against his country's interests.

A further false antithesis marks the rivalry of Cortez and Orbellan. Without fail, Cortez receives all the acclaim proper to the ideal and magnanimous lover, whereas Orbellan seems simply to be type-cast as the unworthy suitor, neither receiving nor deserving love. His unworthiness grows into outright villainy with his attempt to assassinate Cortez, but the assassination attempt does not mark the end of his development. Having returned from the Spanish camp, he resolves to renounce his former baseness:

> From Virtues rules I do too meanly swerve:
> I by my Courage will your Love deserve.   (III. iv. 54 — 5)

Within seconds, however, Cortez has contemptuously killed him as a "degenerate Coward" (III. iv. 58); death, ironically, cramps Orbellan within the stereotype that he has outgrown, and even Alibech, his sister, can only disparage his memory (IV. ii. 126 — 9). Conversely, Cortez continues to receive loud praises despite his increasing destructiveness and dishonour. In the episode of Orbellan's death, indeed, villainous and heroic rival exchange roles. Orbellan is striving for reform and redemption, whereas Cortez' harsh treatment of his rival contravenes both a specific oath (III. ii. 24) and, as I shall show, expected heroic practice. Cortez is not a model of heroic perfection but a man of complex and serious flaws, which are worthy of extended analysis.

The enthusiastic encomia which Kirsch, Barbeau, and others have bestowed on Cortez pay little regard to the realities of the text. No one has even heeded the obvious fact that, in the play's first scene, Cortez is every bit as mercenary and cynical as his companions. He, for instance, is the first to gild the forcible acquisition of wealth with divine sanction:

> Heaven from all ages wisely did provide
> This wealth, and for the bravest Nation hide,

> Who with four hundred foot and forty horse,
> Dare boldly go a New found World to force.   (I. i. 31—4)

This marriage of human greed and divine decree will later bear fruit in the
rack scene. Indeed, Cortez' claim is suspect even in the utterance. He claims
that Spanish bravery will be divinely rewarded with Mexican gold, but
Pizarro's reply immediately reveals that the Spanish enterprise is less
impressive than Cortez pretends, since the four hundred and forty would be
powerless were not the Indians destroying themselves:

> Our men, though Valiant, we should find too few,
> But *Indians* joyn the *Indians* to subdue,
> *Taxallan*, shook by *Montezumas* powers,
> Has, to resist his forces, call'd in ours.   (I. i. 35—8)

Cortez' first heroic speech is undercut as soon as it is made, and the pattern of
the play has been set from the start.

Pizarro's comments on the shortage of Spanish troops inspire Vasquez to a
convenient blend of justice and self-interest:

> Rashly to arm against so great a King
> I hold not safe, nor is it just to bring
> A War, without a fair defiance made.   (I. i. 39—41)

Pizarro's rejoinder is blunt and cynical: "Declare we first out quarrel: then
Invade", he proposes (I. i. 42). As a result of these two suggestions, Cortez
modifies his no-nonsense assertion that he has come "to force" (to rape?) the
new-found world:

> By noble ways we Conquest will prepare,
> First offer peace, and that refus'd make war.   (I. i. 51—2)

"And that refus'd": Cortez regards the refusal of peace terms as inevitable,
and his proposal merely rephrases Pizarro's, for both men wish to give a
specious respectability to the invasion by preceding it with an empty show of
negotiation; Cortez' "noble ways" are tawdry indeed. The dramatic context
forbids us to wrest "that refus'd" into a conditional sense: Cortez had been
unequivocally committed to the use of force, only changing his mind as a
result of Vasquez' far from disinterested and Pizarro's bluntly cynical
suggestions; and he is later to admit to the meretricious deception that he is
clearly planning here.

The cynicism of the first scene discredits the heroics of the second: we
cannot share Montezuma's enraptured admiration of Cortez's magna-
nimity, and we must detect a hollow ring in Cortez's high-sounding
protestations:

Having no convincing answers to give his accusers, Cortez starts to make concessions to them, firstly offering to take "The edge of War . . . from the Battel" (II. ii. 48)—an offer which he wholly fails to honour—and then proposing to delay the battle for a day (II. ii. 54—5). As Alibech is quick to see, this second concession invalidates all his previous arguments:

> This grant destroys all you have urg'd before,
> Honour could not give this, or can give more.   (II. ii. 56—7)

Observing that he will be fighting women, including Cydaria (II. ii. 58—60), she adds a final thrust: "Kill her, and see what Honour will be won" (II. ii. 61). Women are to be slaughtered in battle by Spanish artillery; Dryden once again foreshadows the triumph of death over the generative principle, echoing the birthday rite and confirming Cortez' kinship with the malevolent god.

Pressure from Alibech and Cydaria produces a complete reversal in Cortez' position. Honour had been an inner quality of soul, dearer than life itself. Now, within thirty lines, it becomes a mere external, beneath consideration: "Honour be gone, what art thou but a breath?" (II. ii. 67), he exclaims, resolving to abandon the campaign. He is too late, however, for battle has already been joined, and he accordingly changes his mind once again, discovering renewed esteem for honour:

> Retire, fair Excellence, I go to meet
> New Honour, but to lay it at your feet.   (II. ii. 78—9)

The honour which Cortez here dedicates to Cydaria is to be earned amid the slaughter of her father's subjects. Crassly insensitive to Cydaria's painfully divided allegiances, he embarks on the course predicted by Alibech, courting the daughter in blood, not yet of the father, but of the subjects who serve and protect him.

When the first battle is joined, Cortez does not, as he had promised, take "the edge of War" from the fighting. Instead, the Indians are massacred by artillery, and he is loud in his demands that the fleeing enemy be slaughtered (not demands characteristic of the ideal hero):[14]

> Command our Horse to charge them in the rear.
> You to our old *Castillian* Foot retire,
> Who yet stand firm, and at their backs give Fire.   (II. iii. 14—16)

Appropriately, this scene of carnage is the immediate prelude to the scene in which Cortez' love becomes most heavily imbued with the taint of death: his altercation with Cydaria after the fighting is the place where the truth about his former mistress slips out, and where Cydaria begins to feel that her love is dominated from beyond the grave. Only one act of magnanimity lightens the intimations of doom, and even here the magnanimity is more apparent than real. Cortez sets free the brother of the woman he loves—in the hope that to do so will further his suit:

> Haste, lose no time, your Sister sets you Free,
> And tell the King, my Generous Enemy,
> I offer still those terms he had before,
> Only ask leave his Daughter to adore.   (II. iii. 169–72)

Liberation of valiant foes is *de rigueur* in the romances,[15] but Cortez scarcely equals the disinterested magnanimity of his romance counterparts; Dryden borrows the ideal gesture from romance, but gives it a motive less altruistic than is usual.

Cortez' behaviour in the next act, however, is far more spectacularly non-ideal. Orbellan, his rival for the hand of Cydaria, steals into the Spanish camp by night in order to assassinate him, but Guyomar overhears the assassination plot and sends a message of warning. Vasquez and Pizarro receive the message and raise the alarm. And, seeing Orbellan in flight, but not yet realising his identity or his intentions, Cortez gives him an unequivocal promise of protection and safety: "Upon my Life I'le set thee safe and free," he swears (III. ii. 24). But then he learns the truth.

The path of perfection is clear: Cortez has tied himself with an unwary promise and must observe it to the letter, whatever the disadvantage to himself.[16] But the path of perfection is not for Cortez, and, instead of discharging his promise with unyielding principle, he wriggles unconvincingly:

> *Orb.* Yet you must spare me for your Honours sake;
> That was engag'd to set me safe and free.
> *Cort.* 'Twas to a Stranger, not an Enemy:
> Nor is it prudence to prolong thy breath,
> When all my hopes depend upon thy death——
> ——Yet none shall tax me with base perjury,
> Something I'le do, both for my self and thee.   (III. ii. 56–62)

Cortez' first three lines are devoted to a quibble motivated by frank personal interest: the "Stranger" and "Enemy" are one and the same person, and the substance of Cortez' argument is that he should not now keep his word because to do so would be inexpedient; mercenary reflections intrude on the poses of honour. Cortez then implicitly admits what his quibble had sought to deny, realising that to kill Orbellan on the spot would expose him to the charge of perjury. He therefore devises a course that will preserve his name (though it will not, in the event, honour the terms of his promise). Leading his rival from the camp, he forces him to fight a duel, claiming that he has now discharged his promise: "I sav'd your Life, now keep it if you can" (III. iii. 8). This is, however, mere word play, for Cortez promised to set

Orbellan "safe and free" and has not done so; his promise to Orbellan meets the same fate as his undertaking to mitigate the horrors of war.

When a wound prevents Orbellan from continuing the duel, Cortez honourably spares him, though the ill grace with which he does so dims the lustre of his magnanimity. Honour is here not a fit of virtue in the soul but an external code to be resentfully respected, and, as so often in Dryden, we sense a discrepancy between the ideal code and its frail representative:

> Unlucky Honour that controul'st my will!
> Why have I vanquish'd, since I must not Kill?   (III. iii. 30—1)

If Cortez' magnanimity is dimmed here, it is extinguished by his subsequent course of action, which is to pursue Orbellan hotfoot towards the town and kill him there: Orbellan enters "in hast and out of breath" (III. iv. 16), and within twenty lines the Spaniards arrive. Although Cortez halts the duel because of Orbellan's wound, he immediately leads an attack aimed specifically at his rival, and kills him while the same wound still leaves him defenceless: Cortez' concern is merely with external respectability, with a "nobility" of the kind displayed in the peace terms.

The ignobility of Cortez' behaviour becomes yet more apparent when this episode is compared with its source. Cortez' rivalry with Orbellan for the hand of Cydaria is extensively derived from one of the histories in *Cassandra*, in which Arsaces/Artaxerxes competes with Arsacomes for the hand of Berenice (see Appendix, pp. 160—2). Yet throughout the history Arsaces treats Arsacomes with the punctilious generosity that Cortez so conspicuously lacks. When Arsaces incapacitates Arsacomes in a duel, he spares him without any of Cortez' reluctance and resentment: "I had time enough to have slain Arsacomes," he says, "if I had had a minde to it; but how great Interest soever I had in his death, I was not able to give it him, being he was no longer in a condition to defend himself" (IV. iv. 23). He procures medical aid for his rival (p. 24) and, though he is under no promise to do so, sets him free (p. 26). Whereas Cortez pursues Orbellan to the town with all possible speed, Arsaces deliberately *retards* the advance of the army (p. 26). His attack on the town takes place considerably later (IV. v. 33—5), and during the attack he again deliberately spares Arsacomes' life: "Arsacomes may live also," he declares, "since I cannot give him his death without advantage" (p. 35). Arsaces also differs from Cortez in emerging victorious from his attack on the town. Whereas Arsaces consistently acts both with honour and military prudence, Cortez discredits his honour and needlessly endangers his military enterprise. Yet Kirsch claims that "every decision which Cortez makes demonstrates his worthiness" (p. 90).

Imprisoned in Mexico, Cortez is visited by Almería, who plans to avenge Orbellan's death. Quickly, however, she falls in love with the man she proposes to kill. Here, once more, Dryden is using a standard romance situation: in *Cleopatra*, for example, Artaxus falls in love with the heroine as he is preparing to kill her (v. ii. 511). More generally, romance heroes and heroines are frequently troubled with a violent or evil lover: Oroondates has Roxana, Statira Perdiccas, Berenice Arsacomes, Thalestris Neobarzanes (all in *Cassandra*); Elisa has Tigranes, Olympia Adallas, and Cleopatra Tiberius as well as Artaxus (*Cleopatra*); Cyrus has Thomiris, Mandana the King of Assyria and many others (*Cyrus*). The conventional response, predictably, is for the ideal character to remain immovably faithful to the ideal partner, greeting the new lover with anything from firm rejection to vituperative repugnance. At first, Cortez seems to be conforming to the standard pattern, meeting Almeria's advances with tactful but firm rejection (IV. i. 55−96). After she has left, however, he delivers a very curious soliloquy. In general terms, its sentiments are conventional enough, but, if it is read in the light of its dramatic context (and Dryden's speeches too seldom are), it must indicate a degree of perplexed responsiveness to Almeria, for her declaration of love moves Cortez to troubled reflections on the tormenting inconstancy of desire:

> In what a strange Condition am I left,
> More then I wish I have, of all I wish bereft!
> In wishing nothing we enjoy still most;
> For even our wish is in possession lost:
> Restless we wander to a new desire,
> And burn our selves by blowing up the Fire:
> We toss and turn about our Feaverish will,
> When all our ease must come by lying still:
> For all the happiness Mankind can gain
> Is not in pleasure, but in rest from pain.   (IV. i. 105−14)

The confused and shifting sentiments of this speech imply that Cortez' reactions to Almeria are less simple than first appearances had suggested, and his next encounter with her confirms the implications of his perplexed soliloquy. He does continue to reject her, but he now seems decidedly susceptible to her charms, and certainly does not give her the unequivocal rebuff that Oroondates and his like invariably give to Roxana and hers:[17]

> You tempt my Faith so generous a way,
> *As without guilt might constancy betray:*
> But I'm so far from meriting esteem,
> That if I Judge, I must my self Condemn;
> Yet having given my worthless heart before,
> What I must ne're possess I will adore;
> Take my devotion then this humbler way;
> Devotion is the Love which Heaven we pay.   [*Kisses her hand.*
>   (IV. iv. 23−30; italics added)

The last three lines emphasise the warmth of Cortez' reaction with a startling echo of words earlier addressed to Almeria by the love-sick Montezuma:

> Madam, this posture is for Heaven design'd,   [*Kneeling.*
> And what moves Heaven I hope may make you kind.   (I. ii. 37−8)

Indeed, Almeria is thwarted not by Cortez' triumphant fidelity (for he is becoming increasingly responsive) but by Cydaria's timely arrival and outraged protest.

Cortez' altercations with Cydaria have in some measure prepared us for his reactions to Almeria. Within seconds of their first meeting, he had confidently promised Cydaria eternal devotion, boasting that his was a love "which must perpetual be" (I. ii. 371). Later, he reaffirms the perfection of his love, declaring that the Spaniard's "greatest Honour is in loving well" (II. iii. 66)—though, with inconsistency typical of Cortez, love had earlier been "the noblest frailty" for which honour could be abandoned (II. ii. 71). But then complications set in, for Cortez' protestation provokes an exchange in which Cydaria's penetrating questions make him increasingly apologetic about Spanish forms of courtship, until he lamely dissociates himself from the practices he had initially extolled:

> I have no reason, Madam, to excuse
> Those ways of Gallantry I did not use.   (II. iii. 89−90)

The proud equation of Spanish love and Spanish honour, itself inconsistent with earlier pronouncements, is here in turn quickly and red-facedly abandoned (at our peril, therefore, do we see in such pronouncements firm principles shared by hero and author).[18] And the dispute with Cydaria gives a further sign of Cortez' instability of principle: desperately improvising answers to her charges, he lets slip the truth about his former mistress and, becoming more desperate than ever in his improvisations, propounds an axiom strikingly at variance with his vow of unchanging love:

> The object of desire once tane away.
> 'Tis then not Love, but pitty which we pay.   (II. iii. 121−2)

Such a proposition does not augur inflexible constancy: memories of a mistress in the grave here elicit from Cortez a principle that compromises his vow of constancy to Cydaria; and, in the second encounter with Almeria, a woman strangely parallel to the dead mistress (her "*Cupid* looks as dreadfully as Death" [IV. iv. 12]) threatens to push the principle to its logical conclusion.

Like the image of the dead mistress, that of the deadly Cupid provides a further conjunction of death and love, investing Almeria with the equivocal properties of the birthday rite: she is a love deity associated, by a sinister paradox, with the realms of death, confirming her ambiguous role by brandishing a dagger at the man she wishes to seduce. And Cortez pays overtly religious homage to the grim Cupid, giving it the "Devotion" which is the due of "Heaven" (IV. iv. 30). In doing so, he associates himself once more with the darker aspects of pagan worship, briefly exchanging the role of deity for that of votary; Almeria, the imagery suggests, would be a fit partner for him. Consequently, the hastily resurrected idealism with which he calms the outraged Cydaria seems false and oversimplified, misrepresenting the tortuous intricacies of the encounter:

> With what injustice is my Faith accus'd?
> Life, Freedom, Empire, I at once refus'd;
> And would again ten thousand times for you. . . .
> Could you have heard my words!   (IV. iv. 43 – 5, 61)

"Could you have heard my words!" is quite flagrantly inappropriate, for we can hardly suppose that Cydaria would have listened equably to Cortez' expressions of adoration and "Devotion".

Cortez' decisions do not consistently demonstrate his worthiness. On the contrary, every decision he makes demonstrates his inability to control dishonourable passions—an inability that reveals the impotence of romance ideals in a world of real humanity. His greatest failure, and his most overt contravention of romance practice, lie in his encounter with Orbellan, where his ignobility can be demonstrated by contrast with the nobility of his prototype: the career of the selfish Cortez forms a precise antithesis to that of the magnanimous Arsaces; and, whereas Arsaces' just and prudent attack on his rival's town brings victory, Cortez' rash and dishonourable attack brings defeat and imprisonment. Like the young Montezuma's imprisonment, Cortez' is a fitting consequence and image of his subservience to discreditable passions, an outward token of an inward impotence. The impotence continues in victory: as the Spaniards loot, torture, and kill, Cortez wanders ineffectually from place to place, entrusting Cydaria to a treacherous protector, turning up too late to save Montezuma from the rack, leaving Cydaria once again, and playing no useful role when her life is threatened. The earlier acts had demonstrated Cortez' failure to control the selfish and bellicose passions of his own nature; in Act V the failure is horrifyingly magnified into total powerlessness over the destructive forces that he has unleashed. The fifth act confirms the lessons of the previous four, exposing the impotence of fake nobility in a world of chaos and cruelty.

To be sure, Cortez' intentions (or rather his afterthoughts) are of the best:

> On pain of death kill none but those who fight;
> I much repent me of this bloody night:
> Slaughter grows murder when it goes too far,
> And makes a Massacre what was a War.   (V. ii. 106 – 9)

Cortez' scruples, however, assail him only when the massacre is a *fait accompli*, and he alone is responsible for deciding to force a town that he could have taken without bloodshed. When Cortez was in prison, Montezuma offered to surrender on the terms originally stipulated by the Spaniards:

> *Mont.* He fiercely answer'd I had now no way
> But to submit, and without terms obey:
> I told him, he in Chains demanded more
> Then he impos'd in Victory before:
> He sullenly reply'd, he could not make
> These offers now; Honour must give, not take.   (iv. ii. 13 – 18)

The demands of Cortez' honour have altered yet again, for he can only be magnanimous where magnanimity will inflate his reputation, and his self-regarding obduracy at this point renders inevitable the slaughter which he later so loudly deplores; yet, after all the killing, he offers the Indians the very terms that he had refused to countenance while he was in prison (v. ii. 356– 7). Cortez wants war to be as it is in the romances, where the mass carnage seems unimportant and imperceptible in comparison with the splendour of heroic enterprise. But war in *The Indian Emperour* is real war, divested of meretricious glamour.

In the fifth act, appropriately, the Spaniards' affinities with the "cruel god" appear in their most flagrant form. The rack scene demonstrates beyond doubt that the Spanish religion is identical with the cult of Huitzilopochtli and provides the grimmest image of the triumph of death over the forces of renewal. As Cortez enters the torture chamber, he bestows on it a startlingly unwarranted consecration: " 'Tis sacred here to Beauty and to Love" (v. ii. 111). The incongruity of Cortez' consecration repeats the incongruity of the birthday rite and amplifies it, for the rites of love are now only a tenuous and mocking memory amidst the victory of bloodlust. The opening rites are, however, most completely and strikingly repeated in Almeria's death scene: when Montezuma mistook Cortez for the malevolent god, he offered to gratify him with the blood of human sacrifice, feeding his "nostrils with hot reeking gore" (i. ii. 239); now, in her last moments, Almeria honours the Emperor's offer, dedicating to Cortez the blood that streams from her wound: "Stand fair, and let my Heart-blood on thee flow," she commands (v. ii. 309). The roles of the second prison scene have been reversed, Almeria now being the votary and Cortez (once more) the deity; as death claims her, Almeria sees the man she loves in the guise of the savage god, at last giving him the tribute which has increasingly seemed to be his due. Throughout the play the nature of the birthday ritual has been reflected in the nature of passion, both ritual and passion exemplifying the primacy of death in the union of generation and corruption. Now Almeria unites ritual with the passion that it expresses and symbolises, providing at once a

sacrificial rite and a sexual consummation. Her blood-letting recalls and
vindicates the many images that have associated Cortez with the destructive
war god—images that forbid us to share Alssid's enthusiasm for the rewards
which Cortez celebrates in the play's final couplet:

> While I loud thanks pay to the powers above,
> Thus doubly Blest, with Conquest, and with Love.   (v. ii. 378—9)

The double blessing provides the last of many conjunctions of death and
love, with death, as usual, predominating: many have been killed but few are
to be married. Indeed, in thanking the divine powers for Conquest and Love
Cortez exactly reproduces the worship of the opening ceremony, which had
celebrated the god of war and "The peaceful power that governs love" (I. ii.
9). Nothing has changed. Here, more clearly than ever, we see that Cortez is
not a force of renewal but the re-embodiment of a bloody past. The
inexorable, cyclic repetition of the past had at first been manifested in the
limited realms of the personal life; now, as the incantation scene had
predicted, it is fully visible in the processes of history.

   The Indian Emperour is the most pessimistic of the heroic plays, and one of
the most pessimistic of any of the tragedies, equalling *Cleomenes* and outdone
only by *Oedipus*. All the heroic plays are dominated by the cycles of renewal
and decay, but in *The Indian Emperour* renewal is no more than a tenuous
illusion amidst all-pervasive ruin. All Dryden's heroes embody a potentially
tragic paradox, striving for divinity and allying themselves to death, but
none realises the paradox in a more terrible form than Cortez, whose
divinity consists of symbolic identity with the Aztec god of slaughter. Of all
Dryden's heroes, Cortez most closely recalls Achilles, who attains a similarly
savage godhood, at once attaining divinity and renouncing humanity. *The
Indian Emperour*, however, is even bleaker than the *Iliad*. Though the
fighting around Troy is relentless, there are memories of times when the
campaign had been fought more nobly; and, in the final book, Achilles'
return to humanity is accompanied by his unexampled compassion in
sharing the grief that he has inflicted on Priam. In *The Indian Emperour*,
however, there is no nobler past and no final transcendence of hatred; there is
only a monotonous transition from the old savagery to the new.

4 *Tyrannick Love*

Perhaps because of the haste with which it was composed,[1] *Tyrannick Love* (1669) is the most uneven of the heroic plays. It shares *The Indian Emperour*'s failure to combine multiplicity of plot with unity of structure, for the several strands of narrative have no constant source of coherence, entering instead into temporary, shifting, and incidental relationships, with the result that there is no consistently maintained counterpoint. An actual decline in craftsmanship, however, is evident in the frequent and tedious debates. Never expressing or furthering an inexorable accumulation of conflicts, the debates are for the most part dragged in as a result of arbitrary complications, and serve principally to reduce the strain on Dryden's invention: his characters are not revealed and shaped in action, as they are tested and changed by the circumstances which they endeavour to master; rather, they label themselves in a series of facile, self-contained set-pieces. Recent criticism has, admittedly, oversimplified the debates, interpreting fluid battles between fallible mortals as inflexible contrapositions of Truth and Error. Nevertheless, the debates betray a lamentable artistic laziness.

Once again, Dryden presents an ironic view of man's claims to grandeur and perfection. Here, however, the ironies are often crude and undramatically conceived, and Dryden repeatedly relies on his heroines to expound issues that he has failed to incorporate in the substance of the drama. In doing so, he creates a contradiction which he never satisfactorily resolves. His heroines are at times the reliable analysts of Maximin's flaws, clumsily compensating for Dryden's failure to contrive circumstances that extort unwitting self-revelation from his villain. At other times, however, the heroines are themselves portrayed with an irony that thoroughly destroys their authority as moralists. They thus fulfil two distinct functions that are never wholly reconciled. Clumsy, too, is Dryden's handling of Catharine in Acts II and III, where his dramatic inventiveness totally deserts him: in these acts Catharine serves almost entirely as a homilist, untouched by the events that she interprets, awkwardly extraneous to the mainstream of the drama. Only in the last two acts does Dryden, if not integrate, at least activate all the elements of his drama.

I. THE RED HERRING OF SIR ROBERT FILMER

As in the earlier plays, the characters of *Tyrannick Love* seem at first to be immutable stereotypes arranged in trite geometrical patterns. As usual, the patterning and stereotyping break up and vanish as human fallibility asserts itself, claiming even the seeming models of piety and duty. Here, however, the false geometry is excessively extensive and emphatic, and is complicated belatedly and often crudely. As a result, the deceptive schematism seems to dominate the play at the expense of the asymmetries and ironies that invalidate it. Nevertheless, the ironies are there, and they have gone largely unnoticed.[2] The prevailing fashion has been to treat Catharine and Berenice as unfailing embodiments of wisdom and virtue and to construct from their pronouncements an alleged account of Dryden's own politics and theology.[3] Their exhortations to passive trust in Providence have been taken as Dryden's own, and have even been used to foist on Dryden the political philosophy of Sir Robert Filmer. The result has been a gross misrepresentation of Dryden's political and artistic intelligence. Weak play though it is, *Tyrannick Love* is not merely an enacted dialogue on political duty; it is not Dryden's *Crito* and it contains no Socrates, no perfect and unchanging source of wisdom. None of the characters is Dryden in disguise and none consistently possesses an infallible clue to the play's enigmas; all at times apply inadequate oversimplifications to intractably complex events.

Throughout the play, Catharine and Berenice do counsel passive trust in Providence, opposing the schemes of the self-styled agents of Heaven's will; and, since recent interpretations of *Tyrannick Love* have all assumed that Dryden shares his heroines' creed of inaction, they have concluded that the play preaches the virtues of quiescence in the face of usurping tyranny. In the most thorough-going exposition of this view, Miss Barbeau treats *Tyrannick Love* as part of an *œuvre* much influenced by the doctrines of Sir Robert Filmer—including the principle that rebellion against a usurper is impermissible *even for the purpose of restoring the rightful monarch* (*Intellectual Design of Dryden's Heroic Plays*, pp. 41–3, 48–9).[4] We can only determine the heroines' moral authority by examining their words and actions in their dramatic context. As a preliminary, however, I would like to consider the more general and obvious flaws in the conventional view (and in particular of Miss Barbeau's reading), so that close analysis of the play will not proceed under the shadow and constraint of mistaken preconception.

Patriarcha was not published until 1680. Filmer's other political works were first published between 1648 and 1652; none were reissued until 1679; and they exercised no notable influence before the time of their republication, when they became the canonical statement of Tory principles in the Exclusion crisis and its aftermath.[5] *Tyrannick Love*, then, antedates Filmer's heyday by a decade, and there is no *a priori* reason for us to expect the play to reveal his influence. The chief objection to the Filmer case, however, rests not on external factors but on the clear evidence of the text. Miss Barbeau persistently claims that Porphyrius is brought, with Dryden's blessing, to recognise the evils of rebellion against even a bloody and illegitimate ruler (*Intellectual Design of Dryden's Heroic Plays*, pp. 17, 77, 100), but in building her case she ignores one vital and obvious piece of contrary evidence, for the play is only brought to a happy ending because Porphyrius disregards Berenice's teachings and takes upon himself the responsibility of insurrection: Berenice certainly thwarts Porphyrius' attempt to assassinate Maximin (v. 435–6), but the hero soon leads a second, successful rebellion:

> *Centurion.* Arm, arm, the Camp is in a mutiny:
> For *Rome* and Liberty the Souldiers cry.
> *Porphyrius* mov'd their pity as he went,
> To rescue *Berenice* from punishment,
> And now he heads their new-attempted crime.   (v. 606–10)

Maximin's assassination is certainly the work of the initially ignoble Placidius, but Porphyrius' simultaneous, independent rebellion is the immediate, indispensable cause of Berenice's survival, for by itself Maximin's death would have been too late to halt the execution. The dénouement of the play thus fails to endorse the submissive attendance on Providence advocated by Berenice and Catharine, and the beneficent designs of Heaven are accomplished only when passive trust cedes to active human assistance. As Dryden was later to write, "The Pilot's Prayer to *Neptune* was not amiss, in the middle of the Storm: *Thou may'st do with me,* O *Neptune, what thou pleasest, but I will be sure to hold fast the Rudder.* We are to trust firmly in the Deity, but so as not to forget, that he commonly works by second Causes, and admits of our Endeavours with his concurrence."[6]

The amazingly obvious evidence of Porphyrius' final rebellion thoroughly discredits the view that Dryden espoused a doctrine of extreme nonresistance. (Needless to say, he would not have countenanced rebellion against a *legitimate* monarch, no matter how tyrannical.) Nevertheless, the ending of the play is by no means heretical. Roper (*Dryden's Poetic Kingdoms,* p. 61) and Barbeau notwithstanding, Filmer neither expressed nor created a Royalist orthodoxy when he condemned armed opposition to reigning usurpers, even on behalf of a rightful claimant; on the matter of resisting usurpers Filmer was atypically (though not uniquely) pacific. Bodin, the fountain-head of much Royalist thought, approved the forcible deposition of usurping tyrants,[7] and many Royalist writers followed him, enthusiastically asserting the subject's duty to oust or slaughter a usurper when a rightful claimant was available; the killing of Athaliah (II Kings 11:1–16) was frequently cited. Among Filmer's contemporaries, Sir Dudley Digges, John Bramhall, Griffith Williams, and Michael Hudson all permitted rebellion against usurpers, as, after the Restoration, did Roger Coke, Clarendon, and Sir Philip Warwick.[8] Dryden, therefore, does not set himself apart from Royalist orthodoxy merely by approving (as he clearly does) of Porphyrius' final rebellion against Maximin. Moreover, within the alien constitutional premises of the Roman narrative, he provides rightful claimants to Maximin's throne in the two Emperors elected by the Senators:

"whom they chuse no *Roman* should oppose" (v. 662), says Porphyrius, vindicating a claim that stood well before the death of Maximin and interpreting Roman law in conformity with the pronouncements of Bodin, who discussed Maximin's deposition and concluded that the Senate had acted constitutionally.[9] *Tyrannick Love* is simply not an exhortation to passive toleration of usurpers. On the contrary, its ending repudiates the doctrine of passivity which its two heroines have consistently upheld, and suggests that the critic who takes the two heroines as "norms" is drastically oversimplifying Dryden's dramatic intentions.

Even in the works which Dryden produced in Filmer's heyday, the case for Filmerism is by no means as clear-cut as recent scholarship has maintained. King, for example, sees in *The Spanish Fryar* (1680) the principles that Miss Barbeau sees in *Tyrannick Love*:

> Filmer warned that "if government be hindered, mankind perisheth", and he concluded:
>
> > The first usurper hath the best title, being, as was said, in possession by the permission of God; and where a usurper hath continued so long, that the knowledge of the right heir be lost by all the subjects, in such a case a usurper in possession is to be taken and reputed by such subjects for the true heir, and is to be obeyed by them as their Father.
>
> This is what Torrismond means when he says:
>
> > Kings Titles commonly begin by Force,
> > Which Time wears off and mellows into Right:
> > So Power, which in one Age is Tyranny,
> > Is ripn'd in the next to true Succession:
> > She's in Possession.[10]

This speech is certainly a close paraphrase of Filmer, but we cannot take it as evidence that Dryden himself endorsed Sir Robert's views: Torrismond is here decidedly not Dryden's mouth-piece, since his defence of the Queen is clearly prompted not by political wisdom but irrational passion:

> I see no Crime in her whom I adore,
> Or if I do, her Beauty makes it none:
> Look on me as a man abandon'd o'er
> To an eternal Lethargy of Love.   (IV. pp. 181–2)

Indeed, he is so blinded by love for the usurper that, when he learns that the true heir still lives, he immediately decides to kill him:

> I dare him to the Field with all the ods
> Of Justice on his side, against my Tyrant:
> Produce your lawfull Prince, and you shall see
> How brave a Rebell Love has made your Son.   (IV. p. 182)

This is the man whom King would see as a political oracle. The Filmerian sentiments in *The Spanish Fryar* are an expression not of Dryden's settled reasoning but of Torrismond's confused desperation. Furthermore, the dramatic point of Torrismond's Filmerian speech, as of his threat to kill the true heir, lies in its ironic inappositeness. Filmer's contention that a usurper "hath the best title" when "the knowledge of the right heir be lost by all the subjects" is inapplicable to *The Spanish Fryar*, in which the true heir is from the outset known by one subject—and turns out to be Torrismond himself, the would-be regicide. With *The Spanish Fryar*, as with *Tyrannick Love*, the case for Filmerism rests on a misunderstanding of the textual evidence.

Let us now return to Dryden, untroubled by the ghost of Filmer.

II. VILLAIN AND SAINT

In Maximin Dryden magnified and elaborated the figure of the passionate aspirant to divinity, engaged in an implacable rebellion against the restrictions of mortality and moral responsibility, and in Maximin he moved nearer to the combination of traits that was to characterise both heroes and villains throughout the mature tragedies. For the first time the struggle against the mutable world becomes, in a crude and rudimentary way, a battle against time itself: bereaved of Charinus and rejected by Porphyrius, Maximin fatuously decides that he will be his own heir (IV. 667–72); and, repenting Catharine's execution, he actually imagines that he can countermand it after the event (V. 383–5). For the first time, moreover, Dryden portrays the life of divine illusion as one of histrionic fantasy, of drama within drama; for, as Alssid has shown (II. 279–81), all Maximin's schemes are those of a dramatist seeking to abolish the real world and enthrone that of his imagination. When the palace sorcerer shadows forth the events of the coming day (and of Dryden's play), a "Curtain" is drawn to reveal the "Scene" of what is to come (I. 100, 98). When Maximin wishes to seduce Catharine, he attempts to draw her into an erotic masque enacted by aerial spirits (IV. 43–148). And, thwarted, he consigns her with scarcely more success to a dramatic spectacular of death, revealing the scenic masterpiece of the wheel with the further drawing of a curtain (V. 242), but finding it reduced by angelic intervention to the banality of a mere "Puppet-show" (V. 311). The world for Maximin is the product of his dramaturgy, and he can concede to his subjects only "The will of Puppets danc'd upon a wyre" (IV. 301); but, in the end, the vociferous puppeteer has become an inanimate mummer in the enigmatic "dumb-show of death" (V. 645) that greets the victorious Porphyrius.

In his downfall, Maximin creates a by now familiar irony, enslaving himself to the change and decay that he deludedly combats. The vanity of his histrionic battle with change is most extensively illustrated in the masque of aerial spirits, whose actors are themselves slaves of the transient: as genii of the air, they are trapped in the eternal war of elements intrinsic to mutable matter (IV. 56—78) and are powerless before Amariel's freedom "from Elements" (IV. 173). Although intended to assert Maximin's control over nature, the masque in fact symbolises his bondage to change, and even the charm designed to further his love dwells on the impotence of senile passion:

> *Love and Time with reverence use,*
> *Treat 'em like a parting friend,*   (IV. 137—8)

sing the spirits; for,

> *If a flow in Age appear,*
> *'Tis but rain, and runs not clear.*   (IV. 147—8)

The passions that promise transcendence of sublunary things merely ensnare Maximin in the decay that he fears—as Catharine recognises:

> Yet man, by pleasures seeks that Fate which he would shun;
> And, suck'd in by the stream, does to the Whirl-pool run.
>
> (IV. 417—18)

Here Catharine identifies the great, fundamental contradiction of Maximin's life: the passions that intoxicate him with sensations of divinity covertly corrode his being and carry forward the work of mortality.

During the first half of her career Catharine seems to stand in simple antithesis to Maximin,[11] embodying all the virtues that are contrary to his vices; as so often, however, the heroic and the evil move into surprising likeness, and Catharine's own combat with the mutable sphere becomes increasingly theatrical and increasingly destructive. When we first see her, converting Apollonius with her marriage of reason and faith and her call to eternal rewards, she on the whole provides unexceptionable standards whereby to judge Maximin's irrational and suicidal obsession with earthly ephemera. But already we have a slight foretaste of the cold retreat into self that is increasingly to characterise her pursuit of celestial glory. In embracing Catharine's cause Apollonius of necessity embraces immediate martyrdom, becoming a truly heroic figure and, for the moment, the prime object of our admiration. And, at first, Catharine does justice to his heroism, urging him to "Lose not that Courage which Heav'n does inspire" (II. 237); but quickly her interest shifts from her neophyte to herself, and the speech of comfort concludes in a remarkable and peremptory burst of patrician haughtiness:

Go, and prepare my Seat: and hovering be
Near that bright space which is reserv'd for me.   (II. 241—2)

For Catharine, Apollonius' redemptive suffering is now merely a subsidiary
element in the saga of her own martyrdom: she is not fortifying one who is a
heroic witness of Christ in his own right; rather, she is instructing a servant
who is to be sent ahead on her behalf to arrange the celestial furniture; and we
note that, of the two martyrs, only Catharine is to have the privilege of
seated bliss, for Apollonius' lot is to be an eternity of respectful "hovering".

For the next one and a half acts Catharine continues to provide
wholesome doctrine: whereas Maximin covets the power of the gods, she
acquiesces humbly in divine dispensation; whereas he is enslaved to the
material, she teaches the freedom conferred by indifference to external
fortunes (III. 36—41); and, whereas he juggles varying notions of de-
terminism in order to justify his pursuit of passion (IV. 297—308, 370—9),
she asserts the freedom of the will and declares that it is properly employed in
the regulation of desire:

But you may make your self a God below:
For Kings who rule their own desires are so. . . .
Your mind should first the remedy begin;
You seek without, the Cure that is within.   (IV. 382—3, 396—7)

Only once do we have a hint of the insensitive self-absorption with which
Catharine had dispatched Apollonius to martyrdom—when, refusing
Placidius' offer to restore her crown, she paraphrases Lucretius' famous
commendation of the lot of the detached spectator:

No happiness can be where is no rest:
Th' unknown, untalk'd of man is only blest.
He, as in some safe Cliff, his Cell does keep,
From thence he views the labours of the Deep:
The Gold-fraught Vessel which mad tempests beat,
He sees now vainly make to his retreat:
And, when from far, the tenth wave does appear,
Shrinks up in silent joy, that he's not there.   (III. 46—53)[12]

At first, Lucretius is on the whole acceptably baptised. In a subsequent scene
(IV. 352—447), for example, Catharine again echoes him in order to urge
disengagement from the wild "Ocean" (IV. 368) and "Whirl-pool" (IV. 418)
of earthly passion, praising the heavenly calm whence

    you may see
Poor humane kind all daz'd in open day,
Erre after bliss, and blindly miss their way.   (IV. 404—6)[13]

But, despite the wide currency of its sentiments,[14] the first Lucretian paraphrase invites slight disquiet from the start. Disengagement from worldly turmoil is commendable enough, but we do not expect an exemplary Christian to associate herself, even in metaphor, with the self-congratulatory contemplation of human suffering. Dryden was later to find "*something of a malignant joy*" in Catharine's Lucretian source,[15] and we may detect something similar in her version of it, for the pauper's "silent joy, that he's not there" is conspicuously untinged with compassion for those who are in the sinking vessel. Moreover, the imagery of this speech is to gain in significance and complexity as the play progresses, and as the storms that Catharine coldly contemplates become less intangibly abstract than those of earthly passion in general; for, in each of the subsequent tests of her ideals, when Berenice and Felicia in turn beg to be saved from death, Dryden echoes and reworks the theme of peril by water; and in each case Catharine imitates the action of the pauper, following Lucretius' image with increasing literalness. However simple and desirable it may be in theory, withdrawal from human concerns can be cruel and devastating to those left behind.

Not until the end of Act IV are Catharine's ideals and ambitions subjected to extensive scrutiny. Hitherto, her moral choices have been easy and clearly defined: Placidius has offered her the crown of empire, and she has rejected it for that of martyrdom; she has rebuffed an aged lecher; and, with angelic help, she has emerged unscathed from a rather timid erotic dream. Now, however, she is presented with an ingenious inversion of Placidius' temptation: there, moral priorities coincided comfortably with personal ambition, and Catharine declined an unwanted human glory for the sake of a celestial glory that she much desired; now she is asked to sacrifice her ambitions for the sake of another, to defer celestial exaltation and accept human obscurity, for Porphyrius proposes that she save Berenice's life by escaping from Maximin and, consequently, from martyrdom. While Catharine's refusal to save Berenice does not discredit her beyond doubt, it does for the first time raise substantial questions about her conduct and place her in a decidedly equivocal position. And we should remember that there is no moral reason why Catharine should not comply with Porphyrius' plan, for St Augustine declared that Christians were permitted to flee from persecution, provided only that priests did not desert their congregations in times of trial.[16]

When Berenice falters at the prospect of death, she is at once portrayed as a traveller endangered by raging water, fearing to be engulfed in her "Voyage" (IV. 489) over the "Torrent" (l. 479) of death; and, at once, she and Porphyrius beg Catharine to rescue her from the torrent. Critics always assume on *a priori* grounds that Catharine is in the right in the ensuing discussion. But, in fact, Dryden portrays the debate as an inconclusive draw, and at first weights the arguments against the saint. Porphyrius and Berenice cogently urge that God's own example commends the course of mercy (IV. 513 – 14) and that Catharine's vocation may entitle her to sacrifice her own life but not another's (IV. 531−2). And, in reply, Catharine can only repeat her determination for her own instant salvation, for her "Crown of Martyrdom" (IV.512) and an immediate entry to "future life" (IV. 528) − a determination that throws doubt on her claim to be separating "The will of Heav'n" from her "private interest" (IV. 515, 516). Then, however, the debate turns in Catharine's favour, and she rises to a sublime sense of election and duty:

> But I am plac'd, as on a Theater,
> Where all my Acts to all Mankind appear,
> To imitate my constancy or fear.   (IV. 537−9)

Here Catharine's sense of mission and commitment appears at its most noble and convincing. Her theatrical view of herself is nevertheless curious, briefly disrupting the dramatic illusion and creating an as yet enigmatic linkage between her and Maximin; for, like her antagonist, she is possessed by a dramaturgic vision that must override the very existence of her fellows.[17] Catharine's argument is strong, but we must be surprised that, when her authority seems to be at its height, Dryden chooses to identify his saint as both protagonist and controller of a dramatic spectacle.

Nevertheless, Catharine gains control of the debate, and Porphyrius is reduced to the lame argument that escape is morally justified because it is physically possible (IV. 542−3). But, if Porphyrius declines into sophistry, Catharine simply withdraws from the realm of rational argument into a dogmatic assertion of her own destiny:

> Thus, with short Plummets Heav'ns deep will we sound,
> That vast Abyss where humane Wit is drown'd!
> In our small Skiff we must not launce too far;
> We here but Coasters, not Discov'rers are.
> Faith's necessary Rules are plain and few;
> We, many, and those needless Rules pursue:
> Faith from our hearts into our heads we drive;
> And make Religion all Contemplative.
> You, on Heav'ns will may witty glosses feign;
> But that which I must practise here, is plain:
> If the All-great decree her life to spare,
> He will the means, without my crime, prepare.   (IV. 544−55)

Catharine's arguments are appropriate to opposing the insufficiency of human reason to the clarity of revealed Biblical truth; Tillotson, for example, uses the doctrine of the few plain rules to argue that, although many Biblical passages are obscure and controversial, the few precepts necessary for salvation are all contained in clear texts of commonly agreed meaning.[18] But Catharine opposes Porphyrius' dim reasonings not to uncontested Biblical authority but simply to her own, heavily contested, sense of right (which Tillotson himself might have questioned);[19] and, in doing so, she plumbs the "vast Abyss" just as deeply and confidently as the opponent whose presumption she reproves. What to make of her un-reasoned sense of mission we do not yet know (and perhaps never do). But she has not conclusively won the dispute, and the image of the coast-hugging skiff which opens and shapes her speech arouses our disquiet, for Catharine here instinctively reworks and reapplies the ocean image of her Lucretian speech: jealously guarding her ambitions from the claims of others, she mimics the pauper's secure quiescence, untroubled in her fancied inability to venture from the coast in order to save Berenice.[20] Moreover, the Providential *laissez-faire* with which she concludes matters is eventually questioned when armed action brings Berenice the safety that pious passivity had failed to secure. At the very least, the life of beneficent action emerges as more acceptable to human sensibilities than that of ruthless contemplation.

As soon as Catharine has disposed of the dilemma presented by Berenice, she is faced with a still more exacting one, posed this time by her mother, Felicia. Once again, Dryden introduces the dilemma by echoing (now more closely) Catharine's Lucretian image of the tempest-beaten vessel: Felicia has newly disembarked, having survived a fierce storm at sea (v. 158−74), but at once finds that she has escaped drowning only to fall into another, equal danger, from which Catharine refuses to save her. Catharine's own imagery suggests the parallel, portraying fear of death as fear of a terrifying and alien flood:

> Here we stand shiv'ring on the Bank, and cry,
> When we should plunge into Eternity.   (v. 233−4)

Now having Felicia in his power, Maximin offers Catharine the choice of satisfying his lust or retaining her virginity at the cost of her mother's life; and Felicia, lacking her daughter's inflexible contempt of the world, bombards her with terrified pleas for life. Once again, an earlier, originally easy moral choice—martyrdom or adultery—recurs in a perplexingly altered form: Might there not be a charity in sin?[21]

Catharine's choice of chastity rather than kin is dramatically conventional and morally plausible (though not, perhaps, morally inevitable),[22] but Dryden handles the choice in a thoroughly disconcerting manner, going out of his way to arouse our discomfort. For, like the debate with Porphyrius and Berenice, the debate with Felicia is conceived dramatically rather than ideologically; Dryden does not present an unchanging contrast between a consistently authoritative hierophant and a consistently erring novice, but instead keeps shifting and perplexing the balance of authority and persuasiveness, toying with the audience's sympathies and forcing them to a continual revision of judgement. Felicia's first appeal to Catharine is moving in its bewildered transition from confidence to incredulous doubt, from

"My life is safe, when it depends on her" to "Speak quickly, speak and ease me of my fear" (v. 189, 192). Catharine's first response, by contrast, is frigidly unattractive, showing what is by now an expected and characteristic self-absorption:

> Alas, I doubt it is not you I hear.
> Some wicked Fiend assumes your voice and face,
> To make frail Nature triumph over Grace.
> It cannot be——
> That she who taught my Childhood Piety,
> Should bid my riper age my Faith deny:
> That she who bid my hopes this Crown pursue,
> Should snatch it from me when 'tis just in view.   (v. 193–200)

Catharine does not see her mother as an independent being with a private, human agony: instead, she immediately classes her as a demonic play-actor in a script important only in reference to herself, and sees in her pleas nothing more than an attempt to "snatch" her own glory; the jarringly strident accusation shows that desire for the martyr's crown is unmixed with any comprehension of Felicia's suffering. As in her farewell to Apollonius, Catharine fails to see an autonomous, intrinsic importance in the experiences of others, regarding her fellows merely as subsidiary figures in her own drama of salvation, significant only as foils to her own starring role. She is one of Dryden's many heroic solipsists.

Soon, however, the debate swings in Catharine's favour. Felicia becomes evasive, claiming (unconvincingly) that she had merely wanted her daughter to temporise in order to delay the execution (v. 216–19), and Catharine replies with dignified and moving counsel against the fear of death:

> Here we stand shiv'ring on the Bank, and cry,
> When we should plunge into Eternity.
> One moment ends our pain;
> And yet the shock of death we dare not stand,
> By thought scarce measur'd, and too swift for sand.   (v. 233–7)

Death, however, is not necessarily as easy as Catharine maintains, and the unveiling of the wheel moves Felicia to a further, more pressing appeal. Seizing on Catharine's image of the swimmer shivering on the bank, she recalls the occasion on which she had plunged into the Nile in order to save her daughter from drowning:

> I, from far, all pale and out of breath,
> Ran and rusht in——
> And from the waves my floating pledge did bear,
> So much my Love was stronger than my fear.
> But you——   (v. 269–73)

"But you——": Felicia's contrast remains unspoken, but our memory supplies all the contrast that is needed, for here is the final, clearest echo of Catharine's image of the sinking, tempest-beaten vessel: Felicia's readiness to risk death in the flood stands against Catharine's sympathy with the landsman's complacent security, hinting once more at the cold self-absorption that marks the heroine's quest for celestial glory. And, indeed, so wrapped is she in self that she gives no sign even of having heard Felicia's appeal, her mother's speech provoking no acknowledgement of any kind, no hint of shared recollection. Catharine's imaginative isolation becomes still more apparent and disconcerting when Felicia repeats her terror at the "horrid pains" (v. 300) which threaten her. The heroine responds, characteristically, by counselling acquiescence in the evident designs of Heaven, urging her mother to accept her agony as a merciful dispensation of Providence:

> Heav'n is all mercy, who that death ordains.
> And that which Heav'n thinks best is surely so.   (v. 301–2)

But, although the prospect of her mother's torture cannot disturb Catharine's acquiescence in "that which Heav'n thinks best", there is another prospect that quickly shakes her submissive composure: that of dying "bare and naked" (v. 303); sternly inflexible when exhorting others to meet extreme agony, her sermons upon Providence falter with surprising ease at a threat to her own decorum.[23] Her imagination, impervious to her mother's suffering, is exclusively dedicated to contriving the fit dramatic spectacle of her own death. And, when Amariel preserves her modesty by destroying the wheel, his chief function is to assert dramatic decorum: in Act IV he had intervened to censor Nigrinus' tamely erotic masque, and now too he is as much the agent of theatrical propriety as of divine compassion, intruding not to thwart Maximin's cruelty but to halt the tasteless dramaturgy which is its vehicle, vindicating Catharine's sense of theatre at the expense of her antagonist's; indeed, the first reaction to his intervention is that of disappointed spectator vulgarity, in Maximin's critical damning of the feeble "Puppet-show of death" (v. 311).

Thwarted by Amariel, Maximin determines to assert his omnipotence with more foolproof means of execution. And, in her reply, Catharine reaches the zenith of her sense of election, disdaining her self-deifying captor as a helpless robot who exists only to serve the ends of her own salvation:

> No, Heav'n has shown its pow'r, and now thinks fit
> Thee to thy former fury to remit.
> Had Providence my longer life decreed,
> Thou from thy passion hadst not yet been freed.
> But Heav'n, which suffer'd that, my Faith to prove,
> Now to its self does vindicate my Love.

A pow'r controls thee which thou dost not see;
And that's a Miracle it works in thee.   (v. 328−35)

Formerly the champion of free will, Catharine now turns about-face into a
strikingly deterministic position and asserts that an invisible power "con-
trols" Maximin, fitting him for murder by extinguishing the love that had
restrained his original bloodlust (ll. 334, 330−1);[24] in the ecstasy of
imminent martyrdom, she disconcertingly mimics her opponent, in effect
conceding him only "The will of Puppets danc'd upon a wyre" (IV. 301).
And, in doing so, she grossly distorts the real nature of Maximin's
experiences. For one thing, Maximin's love—the motive of all his
contradictory responses to Catharine—has not been extinguished, and
indeed the saint is his "Love" in the very line that precedes her speech
(v. 327). Humiliation at his bondage impels him to seek freedom by destroy-
ing his captor (v. 192). But, after Catharine has pronounced him divinely
transformed from lover to murderer, continuing love comes close to
inspiring penitence. In the doubts and conflicts that assail Maximin after
Catharine's speech, we see beyond doubt that he is not a mere automaton
divinely programmed to the exaltation of Catharine's soul and the loss of his
own: on the contrary, he wilfully stifles the promptings of reform:

Were penitence no shame, I could repent.
Yet 'tis of bad example she should live;
For I might get th' ill habit to forgive.
Thou soft Seducer of my heart, away.   (v. 352−5)

From her farewell to Apollonius to her final denunciation of Maximin,
Catharine shows that she can see others only as celestially ordained
subordinates in her quest for heavenly glory. Her spiritual detachment from
the world is also an imaginative detachment from the lives and sufferings of
those around her; like later characters (Nourmahal and Aureng-Zebe, for
example), she cannot see others as autonomous beings, each with a purpose
of his own, each a private and complete sphere of sensations. This is why her
career of sanctity becomes at crucial points (again anticipating the careers of
Nourmahal and Aureng-Zebe) a career of theatrical illusion: the world
which her imagination forms is not the world in which she lives but one in
which her fellows are divested of autonomy and identity, becoming hollow
shells of humanity, insubstantial extensions of her own unique existence.
They are all subordinates in a drama that she dominates: Apollonius is to be a
mere celestial stage-hand, arranging the spectacle of her entrance to glory;
Berenice's fate must subserve her exemplary performance "on a Theater";
Felicia is a demonic tempter acting the part of her mother; and Maximin is a
puppet whose motions are guided by the needs of her soul. Even her
guardian angel functions solely as a dramatic censor. Significantly, Dryden's
sources provide no precedent for Catharine's egomania. Neither

Metaphrastes nor *Le Martyre de Sainte Catherine* have a counterpart to
Felicia, and, although both attribute to the Empress a brief lapse of
courage,[25] neither relate that she beseeched the Saint to relinquish her
martyrdom. In *Le Martyre*, indeed, Sainte Catherine *is* prepared to forgo
martyrdom on condition that Maximin adopt the Christian faith and cease
the persecution (v. ii. p. 75); she thus lacks Catharine's obsessive spiritual
ambition and is prepared to relinquish her martyr's crown for the sake of a
greater good.

Unlike the compassionate Dorothea of the Dekker-Massinger *Virgin
Martyr*, and unlike even Corneille's Polyeucte, who hopes by his death to
unite his wife with her first love, Catharine does not grace her life with a
single good work, and she dies in the state of frigid self-concern in which she
has lived. As the mother and daughter leave for martyrdom, Felicia berates
Maximin with an ugly reversal of the sentiments of the dying Christ:

> That mercy, Tyrant, thou deny'st to me,
> At thy last breath may Heav'n refuse to thee.   (v. 339−40)

As we might expect, Felicia's vengefulness moves Catharine to re-
monstrance, but her remonstrance does not, as we might also expect, replace
disfigurement of Christ with imitation. Rather, she simply continues her
self-directed concern with the dramatic decorum appropriate to the
spectacle of martyrdom:

> No more, dear Mother; ill in death it shows
> Your peace of mind by rage to discompose:
> No streak of blood (the reliques of the Earth)
> Shall stain my Soul in her immortal birth;
> But she shall mount all pure, a white, and Virgin mind;
> And full of all that peace, which there she goes to find.   (v. 345−50)

In thus attempting to safeguard her decorum, however, Catharine produces
one of the most grotesque and indecorous images in any of the heroic plays,
for the metaphor of childbirth is quite startling in the particularity of its
reference. In refusing to contaminate her "immortal birth" with any "streak
of blood", Catharine is contrasting the glories of her spiritual nativity with
the messy actualities of human birth, when the baby may emerge from the
womb "with a few streaks of blood on its head, face and body".[26] Vainly
asserting her maternal claims on Catharine, Felicia had recalled not only her
plunge into the Nile but the pains that she had endured in labour (v. 256);
now, in an appropriately jarring image, Catharine moves from reproof of
her mother to repudiation of her mother's womb—to her final, most
inhumane, gesture of disengagement from earthly claims. And, on this note,
she departs for martyrdom.

Catharine has her triumphant salvation, but it is a triumph attended by troublesome and perplexing questions. For her career of single-minded self-exaltation has been ruthless, destructive, and devoid of all that is normally considered charitable and Christ-like; after all, when his disciples were endangered by a storm at sea, Christ did not imitate the Lucretian spectator. Catharine's triumph appears the more troublesome when set against the misery of the pagan Valeria, who consistently displays the altruistic self-sacrifice that Catharine so conspicuously lacks, yet dies a lonely and unrewarded death. If Catharine does represent the ultimate spiritual attainment possible to mankind, she also illustrates how much common humanity must be sacrificed in the course of such extraordinary attainment.

After the moral untidiness of the ending—of the enigmatic "dumb-show of death" (v. 645)—Nell Gwyn's reassertion of familiar, everyday realities brings a positive and necessary relief, but a relief that may introduce fresh doubts about the alien world that is so abruptly snatched from our view. In the twinkling of an eye Valeria rises, changed, in the spiritual body of Nell Gwyn, vociferously disrupting the "dumb-show", parodying the resurrection of St Catharine, and exposing Dryden's noblest and most selfless character as an absurd mirage, a spurious idealisation of a base reality. Art has been not an imitation of reality but a puzzling sleight of hand, and we are left with a sense not of completed destiny but of interrupted illusion, and of the moral disparity between the illusion and the reality. Perhaps Dryden is merely offering a wry apology for dramatic earnestness. But perhaps Nell's raucous assault on dramatic illusion undermines the histrionic martyrdom enacted by her sister "Slater'n"; for, in the Epilogue's final, grating and indecorous, rhyme, the saint is dragged violently into the world of rampant vulgarity which succeeds to that of staid hagiography:

> Here *Nelly* lies, who, though she liv'd a Slater'n,
> Yet dy'd a Princess, acting in S. *Cathar'n.*   (ll. 29–30)

III. BERENICE

Berenice, Catharine's peer as a champion of Providence, is also too fallible to be taken as a mere auctorial mouth-piece. Once again, Dryden reveals his heroine's failings gradually, changing and at times perplexing our estimate of her conduct. We have no cause for misgiving in the first act, where Berenice opposes Maximin's capricious tyranny with dignity and compassion for the oppressed (I. 269–302), but in Act II her dignity is displayed only to be disconcertingly abandoned. Remonstrating with the impetuous and lovesick Porphyrius, Berenice at first presents an appearance of unalloyed virtue and self-restraint, since she discourages her former suitor by claiming that her love is now, as duty bids, given wholly to Maximin (II. 16–37), and she opposes his designs on Maximin's life by urging a passive reliance on Providence (II. 45–69). Towards the end of the encounter,

however, a brief hint of a more perplexed and uncertain personality
emerges: Berenice's Providentialism remains, at this stage, unchallenged, but
we do learn that inclination and duty are less in harmony than she has
persuaded herself:

> Love blinds my Vertue: if I longer stay,
> It will grow dark, and I shall lose my way.   (II. 74 – 5)

> I must withdraw; but must not let him know
> How hard the precepts of my Vertue grow!   (II. 91 – 2)

The dramatic skill is minimal, for Berenice merely informs the audience in
two asides that her pretensions are in excess of the facts; Dryden was not yet
equipped to portray the subtle and unconscious vacillations that mark
Almahide's misinterpretation of her own motives. Nevertheless, the point
has been made, however perfunctorily: Berenice's fidelity to Maximin is not,
as she has claimed (and is to claim again), a perfect assimilation of will to duty
but a painful struggle with a rival affection. In this respect, at least, life is
more complex and cruel than her ingenuous idealism has suggested. Slight in
itself, this first glimpse of uncertainty brings about a startling change of
atmosphere, for Berenice's dignity at once evaporates as her imperfectly
suppressed love forces her into the ridiculous role of a pay-mistress rationing
out a subsistence supply of kisses:

> *Ber.* Love blinds my Vertue: if I longer stay,
> It will grow dark, and I shall lose my way.
>   *Por.* One kiss from this fair hand can be no sin; . . .
> Give me but one.
>   *Ber.*———Then let it be your last.
>   *Por.* 'Tis gone! . . .
> ———Let but one more be added to the sum,
> And pay at once for all my pains to come.
>   *Ber.* Unthrifts will starve if we before-hand give:
>   [*Pulling back her hand.*

I'le see you shall have just enough to live.   (II. 74 – 6, 79 – 80, 83 – 6)

The combination of high principle and bathos reappears in the next act,
when Berenice discusses with Porphyrius the consequences of his refusal to
marry Valeria. Learning that rejection of Valeria is certain to cost Porphyrius
his life, she declares that his death is preferable to his infidelity, discovers that
she can avert the danger by seeking a divorce from Maximin, but prefers to
die herself rather than to do so—though she would welcome a divorce
initiated by Maximin himself (III. 265 – 310); and, having resolved on death
rather than divorce, she delivers a speech of banal sentimentality, anticipat-

ing her ghost's attendance on the living Porphyrius:

> My earthy part——
> Which is my Tyrant's right, death will remove,
> I'le come all Soul and Spirit to your Love.
> With silent steps I'le follow you all day;
> Or else before you, in the Sun-beams, play.
> I'le lead you thence to melancholy Groves,
> And there repeat the Scenes of our past Loves.
> At night, I will within your Curtains peep;
> With empty arms embrace you while you sleep. . . .
> All dangers from your bed I will remove;
> But guard it most from any future Love.
> And when at last, in pity, you will dye,
> I'le watch your Birth of Immortality.   (III. 312–20, 323–6)

Here Berenice returns to a Platonic interpretation of her relations with Maximin and Porphyrius, forgetting the perplexity of Act II. More startlingly, she also forgets present realities, for she has just learned that Porphyrius must marry Valeria or die, and has just urged him to choose the course of death; in envisaging for her lover a long life free "from any future Love" she is shying away from the consequences of her own demanding idealism and flying in the face of all available evidence. In her Platonic ecstasy she thus suppresses unwelcome realities—both psychological and external—and creates an idyll of faithful longevity that disguises the immediate and pressing dangers to her lover, fitly combining sentimental banality with sentimental self-deception. In her self-indulgent fantasy, she moves into kinship with Catharine and Maximin, for she too retreats from the perplexity of life into a private world of theatre, conjuring up a histrionic immortality in which she will "repeat the Scenes" (l. 318) of former happiness. But her world of theatre, too, is ultimately to disintegrate in the Epilogue, where Dryden burlesques her sentiments, transforming her promises of incorporeal love into Nell Gwyn's crude sexual propositions:

> Gallants, look to't, you say there are no Sprights;
> But I'le come dance about your Beds at nights.
> And faith you'l be in a sweet kind of taking
> When I surprise you between sleep and waking.
>   (ll. 11–14; italics reversed)

As art gives way to life, Berenice's Platonic, sentimental fictions are transformed into the known realities of Nell's sensualism.

The conjunction of idealism and absurdity reappears in Berenice's scene on the scaffold, which is consistently marked by an extraordinary aesthetic incongruity; for, when imminent death seems to demand heroic sublimity,

Berenice remains a figure not of high seriousness but bathetic comedy. Her first speech from the scaffold, for instance, is exemplary and selfless, imploring that Heaven may protect Maximin and that he, after her death, may forgive her (v. 423–8). We might expect this morally outstanding speech to be given commensurate dramatic weight and finality. Not so, however, for Berenice is immediately upstaged by Maximin:

> How much she is to piety inclin'd!
> Behead her while she's in so good a mind.   (v. 429–30)

Nevertheless, Berenice proceeds to give still greater proofs of selflessness: refusing to preserve her own life at the cost of her husband's, she alerts Maximin to two disguised assailants, one of whom turns out to her dismay to be Porphyrius (v. 436–49). At first, we are given no clue as to how to judge Berenice's action: does it display perfect goodness or an overzealous sense of principle? With her next speech, however, Berenice begins to provide us with clues, reviving the doubts we had felt about her in Act III. Here, once more, she describes and differentiates her ties with Maximin and Porphyrius, with the husband she has saved and the lover she has condemned: for Porphyrius she has reserved

> A Love which never knew a hot desire,
> But flam'd as harmless as a lambent fire:
> A Love which pure from Soul to Soul might pass,
> As light transmitted through a Crystal glass:
> Which gave *Porphyrius* all without a sin;
> Yet kept entire the Right of *Maximin*.   (v. 457–62)

Berenice here resurrects and elaborates the Platonic fictions of her Act III fantasy, again refusing to acknowledge the emotional perplexity which had briefly surfaced in Act II—and which is inevitable in any dual attachment. And, if the painful self-revelations of Act II are by now dim in our memories, subsequent speeches are to confirm the shallowness of the present one.

Berenice now realises that her protection of Maximin was not the unambiguous act of beneficence that she had imagined it to be, and that the moral complexity of life does not answer to the moral simplicity of her code. In realising this, she also realises that, however perfect her fancied distribution of emotional claims, she has not managed to sustain such ideal proportion in her recent actions, since by paying her debt to Maximin she has necessarily defaulted on her debt to Porphyrius; once again, the patterns of life fail to reflect those envisaged in her ideals:

> *Porphyrius* I must dye!
> That common debt to Nature paid must be;
> But I have left a debt unpaid to thee.

To *Maximin*——
I have perform'd the duty of a Wife;
But, saving his, I cast away thy life.
Ah, what ill Stars upon our Loves did shine,
That I am more thy Murd'rer than he mine.   (v. 469—76)

Her sense of fatal enigma does not, however, last. Death is soon prettified, and the tragic, unintelligible problem of Berenice's complicity in her lover's execution is supplanted by the romantic, easily surmounted problems of a sugary eternity:

    Ber. If I dye first, I will——
Stop short of Heav'n, and wait you in a Cloud;
For fear we lose each other in the crowd. . . .
'Tis want of knowledge, not of Love, I fear,
Lest we mistake when bodies are not there;
O as a mark that I could wear a Scroul,
With this Inscription, *Berenice's Soul.* . . .
This sigh of mine shall meet it [Porphyrius' last sigh] half the way,
As pledges giv'n that each for other stay.
                              (v. 485—7, 490—3, 500—1)

Once again, Berenice plunges into disconcerting absurdity, and once again the dramatic context assures us that the absurdity is deliberate, for Berenice's insistence on material identification—if not a body, at least a label—decisively and pointedly debunks the claims of her recent Platonic speech: her love is clearly *not* one

        which pure from Soul to Soul might pass,
    As light transmitted through a Crystal glass;

Porphyrius' body is less transparent, more the object of her eyes, than she has formerly allowed; for all her imagined subordination of body to soul, her view of the spiritual is dominated and limited by corporeal experience.[27] The erstwhile champion of Providence now forfeits her credibility by falling into the most trivial doubts about God's competence, imagining that he may have neglected to make incorporeal souls recognisable. Years later, with obvious blindness, Don Sebastian was to echo Berenice by fearing that Almeyda's soul would prove unrecognisable in Paradise.[28]

Here, as her life of idealism reaches its climax and approaching martyrdom calls for tragic dignity, Berenice arrives at her nadir of bathos and foolishness. In her protest against the "ill Stars" (v. 475) she had briefly glimpsed a Providence less simple, less benign in the face of human inaction, than the one in which she had trusted throughout her life. Immediately, however, she suppresses the vision and takes refuge in an escapist reverie of anodyne fatuity—though her mistrust of Heaven persists in her fears about Porphyrius' recognisability. Her code has not even brought her the benefit of moral authority, and it is soon swept aside when Porphyrius' rebellion brings the safety that pious resignation had failed to secure. Thus, in the play's closing pages, Dryden brings his lovers' opposing ways of life to opposing conclusions: Berenice's pursuit of the ideal culminates in a ludicrous escapist fantasy; Porphyrius' life of pragmatism in decisive action. There should be no doubt as to which course we are to approve.

Berenice, then, is not an infallible moralist but an ingenuous idealist. Her politics, in fact, are the politics not of Dryden, nor even of Filmer, but of Madeleine de Scudéry,[29] and her relations with Maximin and Porphyrius provide not a paradigm of political duty but an extended allusion to La Calprenède's version of the Herod and Mariamne story (see Appendix, pp. 162–3). Dryden portrays Berenice as a romance heroine in a bewilderingly unromantic world, trusting in facile formulae that are irrelevant to the problems she faces and inhabiting a realm of impossible fiction that is appropriately exploded by Nell Gwyn's final reassertion of reality.

Comparison with *Le Martyre de Sainte Catherine* emphasises Dryden's willingness to consign his tyrant to human vengeance, to allow that rebellion may contribute to the sum of human happiness, and to transform the straitly ideal into the perplexedly human. Maxime, the closest counterpart to Dryden's Porphyrius, is wholly unsuccessful in his love for the Empress ("Va, sors de ma présence, ennemy de ma gloire" [III. iii., p. 43]; contrast with Berenice's tortured and equivocal reactions). He is similarly unsuccessful in his rebellion and is eventually executed (v. v. pp. 78–80). As in Metaphrastes, the Empress suppresses an inconsequential hesitation (IV. iv. pp. 61–2) and desires, courts, and undergoes martyrdom. Porphire, despite his hatred of Maximin's cruelty, indignantly refuses to join Maxime's conspiracy, *claiming that Heaven alone has the right to punish tyrants* (II. iv. pp. 32–5); as in Metaphrastes (col. 300), he too is martyred. Maximin, however, survives, faced only with the impersonal threat of an outraged and insurgent Empire. Dryden thus modifies the French play's idealism of statecraft and character, and uses his characters' imperfection and pragmatism as the bases for an unhistorical happy ending.

5 The Conquest of Granada

To pass from the early heroic plays to *The Conquest of Granada* (1670–1) is to pass from tentative and uneven experiments to a work revealing a sustained assurance and sense of purpose. Nevertheless, the increase in mastery brought no radical change of preoccupation, Almanzor's flaws and aspirations being those of Montezuma and Zempoalla, and Almahide's those of Acacis and Berenice. In the earlier plays, however, Dryden's artistry often lags behind his ambitions, for, although he attempts to banish romantic stereotype and assert the intricate frailty of real humanity, his strokes of realism are often as mechanical and contrived as are the oversimplifications that he questions. The old Montezuma's alternations between the roles of incisive rationalist and abject lover are arbitrary and externally imposed, never credible as the conflicting expressions of a single, entangled personality. Similarly, Berenice can only inform the audience in asides that her Platonic façade conceals a perplexed and anguished mind; Dryden could not at this stage portray a character unceasingly haunted by a bewildering ambiguity of motive. Furthermore, although he subverts heroic ideals by revealing the aspirants to divinity as the slaves of mortality, the bondage to mortality is often dramatised in a rudimentary and ineffectual manner. Sporadically, a rich and multifaceted image (such as that of Montezuma's birthday rite) reflects the interdependence of florescence and decay, love and death. Never, however, does Dryden create a convincing psychological union between heroic passion and the deathward impulse. Almeria's attempt to consummate her love by sprinkling Cortez with her blood is an outward gesture, thematically significant but not proceeding from an intelligible psychological impulse. Nor does Dryden convey the grandeur and tantalising plausibility of the illusions that ensnare and often destroy his characters. Zempoalla voices her immortal longings with a perfunctory baldness unequal to the transcendent scale of her ambitions. Maximin certainly declares his ambitions with greater verbosity, but the dreams that he seeks to communicate remain indistinct and flimsy. His illusions of timelessness, for example, move him merely to bathos and eccentricity, to an irritable cancellation of a past execution and to a ludicrous scheme of succeeding himself on the throne.

In *The Conquest of Granada* Dryden's invention is for the first time largely commensurate with his ambitions: in portraying Almahide he mastered the skills that had eluded him in his portrayal of Montezuma and Berenice; the commingling of passion and death is for the first time derived from a profound and overmastering psychological compulsion; and the battle with time and mortality is sustained by illusions of seductive grandeur and hallucinatory credibility. Furthermore, Dryden here achieves a structural mastery that he was never later to surpass: the many strands of his plot move in a perfectly balanced imitative counterpoint, travelling inexorably towards an eventual integration, when all the characters' careers are enmeshed in Lyndaraxa's final web of illusion; and the movement of the contrapuntal design complements the process of psychological exploration and revelation, for the careers of the hero and heroine develop in increasing mimicry of those of the villains and their dupes, who enact and elucidate the confused and irrational motives behind the masks of heroic and Platonic idealism.

Nevertheless, recent studies of the play have done little justice to the breadth of its conception and the integrity of its execution. Alssid does attempt to analyse the play's linear and contrapuntal structure, but he distorts the design by oversimplifying its components, too often viewing perplexed and erring mortals as adamantine moral stereotypes. In particular, he misrepresents Almanzor's career by misinterpreting the role of his instructress, seeing the frail and deluded Almahide as an oracular moralist and her empty, perilous code of Platonism as an agent of spiritual transfiguration. King and Barbeau, however, treat *The Conquest of Granada* less as a drama than as a repository of philosophical and political ideas, King seeing it as a satire on contemporary intellectual fashions, Barbeau as a dramatised political discourse. Both identify themes of genuine importance: Dryden certainly, for example, deals with a bastard Hobbism that sanctions the appetitive pursuit of boundless fancy; certainly, too, he depicts the political dangers of uncontrolled individualism. These concerns, however, are very subordinate parts of the larger and more profound concern with man's Faustian inability to accept the constraints of sublunary life, his rebellion not only against society but against the very premises and axioms of mortal existence. King and Barbeau isolate peripheral parts of a rich and intricately unified design and treat them as self-sufficient *raisons d'être* of the drama. Moreover, they are compelled by their own distortions to deny Dryden's coherence of design: King asserts that the play's satire is indiscriminate and disunified (*Dryden's Major Plays*, pp. 79–80), Barbeau (evidently without censure) that the "surface" of heroic drama "is often a disguise rather than an indication of what the play is really about" (*Intellectual Design of Dryden's Heroic Plays*, p. 21). This chapter will seek to avoid the well-worn paths of Hobbes-hunting and political exegesis and attempt to show that *The Conquest of Granada* has the artistic coherence which King denies to it and which Barbeau appears to consider unimportant—that the play is, indeed, a richly inventive and minutely integrated work.

I. HEROES AND VILLAINS IN PART I

Since the political themes of *The Conquest of Granada* have been extensively analysed, there is no need to spend long in repeating the causes of Granada's downfall. The kingdom disintegrates because its members, intent on the unbounded fulfilment of passion, refuse to contain desire within the order imposed by society, preferring instead the perilous freedoms of the state of nature. Lyndaraxa, haunted by the ambition "to live without controul",[1] foments rebellion and finally betrays her city; Abdalla, frankly subordinating reason to passion, rebels to further his love; and Zulema and his fellow Zegrys all pursue private desire at the expense of public good. Although Abdelmelech's passion does not undermine his loyalty, it does undermine his patriotic achievements by inducing fatal leniency to Lyndaraxa and her kin. And even Boabdelin shares in the common guilt, repeatedly sacrificing the needs of his kingdom to the demands of his jealousy. The triumph of passion over the bonds of civilisation is reflected in the repeated violation of oaths,[2] which implies a descent into the Hobbesian condition of nature.[3]

This is all familiar enough, and no one would deny that the unruly passion of Lyndaraxa, Zulema, and Abdalla is a source of anarchy. This uncontroversial evaluation of the villains and dupe, however, leads inevitably to the still vexed question of how we are to evaluate Almanzor, himself often unruly and passionate, but variously interpreted as a figure of "primitivistic purity",[4] a flawed but ultimately reformed character,[5] or a butt of unrelieved ridicule.[6] This question can only be settled by a closer attention to textual evidence, and to the scope and structure of the drama, than has hitherto been displayed.

In the first two acts Almanzor is a designedly enigmatic figure. Dryden baffles his spectators into shifting and equivocal responses to the hero, suspending them between admiration, censure, and laughter, and providing no criteria whereby to form a settled judgement: magnanimous courage seems to be disconcertingly alloyed with egocentric caprice, but the hard evidence of the text does not, so far, permit us to be confident in our misgivings. Almanzor's ambiguities are well illustrated by his very first action in the play—his unquestioning assistance of the Abencerrages against the numerically superior Zegrys. His automatic, attractive support for the underdog draws him, luckily, to the better side and invites our approval. If his action is conventionally noble, however, it is only fortuitously just, since he does not know the circumstances of the dispute (see Appendix, p. 164). Indeed, far from slurring over the arbitrariness of Almanzor's aid, Dryden chooses to accentuate it, making the hero opt explicitly against an informed appraisal of the situation:

> I cannot stay to ask which cause is best;
> But this is so to me because opprest. (I. I. p. 32)

Circumstances, of course, left no leisure for enquiry, and we cannot safely condemn or deride Almanzor on the strength of this incident alone. Nevertheless, our doubts have been raised from the outset. Almanzor's generosity seems to be erratic and unthinking, beneficent only by coincidence; magnanimity and unreasoning impulsiveness commingle in proportions that are as yet unquantifiable. As Almanzor's career progresses, however, we realise that magnanimity is only the fitful, superficial, and at times deceptive adornment of a nature inveterately impulsive and unreasoning. Furthermore, as Almanzor reveals his true character, so he moves into increasing harmony with the villains of the Zegry circle—the very group that he had opposed in his first, ambiguous act of heroism. The increasingly emphatic parallels between hero and villains provide clear textual evidence, hitherto neglected, of Dryden's sustained censure of Almanzor's conduct.

With the benefit of hindsight, we can see that the pattern of parallels begins to emerge in Act II of the first part—an act that, on second reading, we see to be shaped and dominated by the forces of unreason. The act consists of three episodes arranged in A−B−A form, the first episode being paralleled and counterbalanced by the third. In the first, Abdelmelech declares his love of Lyndaraxa to Zulema (I. II. pp. 38−9), and is thus introduced declaring unreason to the future agent of unreason, the passion that is to destroy him to the man who is to set his destruction under way. In the third, Abdalla confesses that he too loves Lyndaraxa, learns that he can only win her by seizing his brother's throne, and allows Zulema to destroy the last vestiges of his loyalty. Zulema now emerges as the clear enemy of reason, formulating the first of many assaults on its authority and bolstering his attack by recourse to transparent sophistry: "Reason's a staff for age," he urges, "But Youth is strong enough to walk alone"; moreover, since Boabdelin was born before their father began to reign, Abdalla is in truth "a Monarch's eldest Son"; and, viewing "reason . . . through Loves false Optiques", Abdalla allows himself to be persuaded (I. II. p. 44). Act II thus begins and ends with the introduction of an irrational, tragic obsession with Lyndaraxa. And, flanked by these parallel episodes, forming the centre of the A−B−A structure, is a single, brief event—Almanzor's impulsive decision to free Arcos:

> But since thou threatn'st us, I'le set thee free,
> That I again may fight and conquer thee.   (I. II. p. 40)

Like his instinctive defence of the outnumbered in Act I, Almanzor's promise to free his enemy is a conventionally magnanimous gesture (see Appendix, p. 164), and, like its earlier counterpart, it is equivocally portrayed, combining nobility of action with irrationality of motive; for Almanzor acts not out of a generosity that transcends partisanship[7] but out of an egocentric and wilful desire to repeat the pleasure of conquest. There is still no solid evidence against him, since his acts are still beneficent, no matter how impetuous his motives. But his impetuosity is not intrinsically beneficent,

and by setting capricious impulsiveness in a framework of blind irrationality
Dryden hints at the dangers of Almanzor's rashness and prepares for more
substantial correspondences between the hero and the villains. None of this,
of course, is immediately apparent (for, after all, the irrationality of
Abdelmelech's love is not exposed until the following act); rather, Act II is
like a slow introduction in which, after repeated hearings, we begin to hear
the concealed outlines of the main subject.

The inchoate correspondences of Act II, in fact, quickly acquire clarity and
substance, since at the beginning of Act III Almanzor's obstinate de-
termination to liberate Arcos actually drives him to join the rebellion
conceived by Lyndaraxa, Zulema, and Abdalla in the last portion of the
previous act; the two lines of plot, suggestively juxtaposed in Act II, are now
overtly integrated. Furthermore, in joining the rebellion Almanzor as-
sociates himself with the rejection of reason that had characterised the final
stages of Act II. "Loves false Optiques" had induced Abdalla to accept
Zulema's sophistries; Almanzor, looking through Friendship's Optiques,
does not even require the comfort of fallacy:

> *Abdal.* And when I shew my Title, you shall see
> I have a better right to Reign, than he.
>   *Almanz.* It is sufficient that you make the claim:
> You wrong our Friendship when your Right you name.
> When for my self I fight, I weigh the cause;
> But Friendship will admit of no such Laws:
> That weighs by th' lump, and, when the cause is light,
> Puts kindness in to set the Ballance right.
> True, I would wish my friend the juster side;
> But in th' unjust my kindness more is try'd.   (I. III. p. 46)[8]

Heroic idealism is now explicitly and exultantly irrational, and no longer
beneficent: Almanzor here joins the Zegrys as blindly and impulsively as he
had opposed them in his first act of heroism.

The irrationality of Almanzor's ideals, however, assumes a far darker
colour in the middle of the same act. During the first engagement of the
rebellion Lyndaraxa, irked by the lull in battle, rants in vehement bloodlust:

> Methinks it is a noble, sprightly Sound.
> The Trumpets clangor, and the clash of Arms!
> This noyse may chill your Blood, but mine it warms. . . .
> Curse of this going back, these ebbing cryes!
> Ye Winds waft hither sounds more strong, and quick:
> Beat faster, Drums, and mingle Deaths more thick.
> I'le to the Turrets of the Palace goe,
> And add new fire to those that fight below.   (I. III. p. 52)

This speech is in itself crucially significant, since it establishes Lyndaraxa as the cardinal embodiment of the twin and conjoined principles of sensuality and death. Her sexual power is ultimately to destroy both her lovers, and the chaos that she inflicts on Granada is but a larger consequence and projection of her fatal eroticism (she will "add new fire to those that fight below"). In her own mind, furthermore, she mirrors the conjunction of sensuality and carnage that she inspires, gaining a voluptuous *schadenfreude* from the sound and spectacle of death. In her psychology, as in her influence, she typifies the union of Eros and Thanatos. Her effusive craving for slaughter, however, is given still further significance by the speech that follows it. *As soon as she has vented her frustration at the lull in battle* she leaves, making way for Almanzor, *who immediately vents his own keen frustration at the same lull*:

> We have not fought enough; they fly too soon:
> And I am griev'd the noble sport is done.   (I. III. p. 52)

Perverse bloodlust and heroic ardour meet and coalesce.

In this first moment of palpable affinity with Lyndaraxa, Almanzor is united with her by a passionate joy in battle—that is, by the very impetuous bellicosity that had led him to promise freedom to Arcos. Retrospectively, Dryden strengthens the links between Almanzor's impulsive gesture and the flanking scenes of surrender to Lyndaraxa, the incarnate principle of unreason. Act II is a piece: in its three episodes Abdelmelech, Almanzor, and Abdalla successively prepare for submission to a single mistress. Indeed, Dryden immediately amplifies his reappraisal of Act II by echoing and then reverting to the Arcos incident. In his celebration of battle Almanzor illustrates the glories of war by producing Ozmyn as his captive, as he had produced Arcos in the previous act. And his headstrong delight in battle leads him to praise his second captive exactly as he had praised his first, expressing gratitude to an opponent who dares to put up stimulating opposition:

> We have not fought enough; they fly too soon:
> And I am griev'd the noble sport is done.
> This onely man of all whom chance did bring
>
> > [*Pointing to* Ozmyn.
> To meet my Arms, was worth the Conquering.
> His brave resistance did my Fortune grace;
> So slow, so threatning forward he gave place.
> His Chains be easie and his Usage fair.   (I. III. p. 52)

Immediately afterwards he orders the release of Arcos, thus confirming the parallel between the two conquests. In the capture of Ozmyn, however, the darker side of Almanzor's heroic idealism once more becomes apparent. Magnanimously demanding fair and easy usage for his prisoner, he delivers Ozmyn into the custody of Selin, his mortal enemy. Only through a magnanimity different in kind from Almanzor's is Ozmyn saved from the consequences of his captor's crass action.

Lyndaraxa's celebration of bloodlust leads into an amplification of her ambition "to live without controul", in which she claims an arbitrary, divine mastery over the events of the battle:

> I'le to the Turrets of the Palace goe,
> And add new fire to those that fight below.
> Thence, *Hero*-like, with Torches by my side,
> (Farr be the *Omen*, though,) my Love I'le guide.
> No; like his better Fortune I'le appear:
> With open Arms, loose Vayl, and flowing Hair,
> Just flying forward from my rowling Sphere.
> My Smiles shall make *Abdalla* more than Man;
> Let him look up and perish if he can.   (I. III. p. 52)

The self-apotheosis, however, is plainly mere self-dramatisation, a mannered assumption of mythological roles and iconographic conventions: she toys with the role of Hero but decides that, on balance, she prefers that of Fortune. Pursuing a god-like freedom which life cannot grant, she flies from reality to a fictitious and ultimately insubstantial realm of art. The brief remainder of her life is co-extensive with the brief triumph of her artistry: as her meteoric career of illusion proceeds, she draws all the flawed and passionate characters into the all-encompassing theatrical masquerade with which she obliterates reality.

Indeed, Almanzor's ensuing speech simultaneously provides both his first moment of contact with Lyndaraxa and the first hint of his dissociation from the real world. His image of "the noble sport" suggests a failure to distinguish the first act's festal games of combat (the scene, appropriately, of his début) from the genuine slaughter which they precipitated, and he confirms his want of discrimination by entrusting Ozmyn to the "Usage fair" of a man intent on his death: concerned only to act the part of the romance hero,[9] Almanzor fails to see the consequences of romantic gestures in a complex and treacherous world; blind to the true implications of his actions, he lives in a specious game-world of make-believe nobility, a counterfeit reality that is to be increasingly absorbed into Lyndaraxa's more powerful vein of illusion. Even at this point, in fact, Dryden accentuates the affinity of hero and villainess by creating clear parallels between their realms of pretence, for Almanzor's "sport" image recalls the imagery that thas recently characterised Lyndaraxa's irresponsible cruelty:

> *Abdel.* Just heav'n, must my poor heart your May-game prove
> To bandy, and make Childrens play in Love.   (I. III. p. 49)

Furthermore, Dryden cannot have been blind to the pun entailed in Lyndaraxa's first essay at self-dramatisation—in the role of "*Hero*".

Lyndaraxa and Almanzor move into conjunction at the mid-point of Act III (and consequently of the play). This central point of contact is flanked by two parallel episodes whose correspondence further emphasises the hero's incipient subservience to the evil illusionist. The preceding part of the act, dominated by the dissensions of Lyndaraxa's *ménage à trois*, once more anatomises the defeat of Abdalla's reason, the triumph of passion becoming both cause and image of the rebellion that follows: "like a Captive King", Abdalla's reason is "born away: / And forc'd to count'nance its own Rebels sway" (I. III. p. 47). Abdalla then uses a succession of images to characterise the delusion that proceeds from the sacrifice of reason: of lethargy, of a nightmare of terrifying paralysis, and of magical, dehumanising transformation. Here, for the first time, Lyndaraxa is revealed as the mistress of illusion:

> Love like a Lethargy has seiz'd my Will.
> I'm, not my self, since from her sight I went;
> I lean my Trunck that way; and there stand bent.
> As one, who in some frightful Dream, would shun
> His pressing Foe, labours in vain to run. . . .
>   This enchanted place,
> Like *Cyrce's* Isle, is peopled with a Race
> Of dogs and swine, yet, though their fate I know,
> I look with pleasure and am turning too.   (I. III. p. 47)

Interestingly (I will return to this point later), Abdalla's analysis of malignant sexual obsession, with his imagery of dream-like illusion, is immediately followed by Almahide's first entrance (I. III. p. 50), marked by the Zambra (pp. 50–1) which she herself has arranged (I. I. p. 38)—and which is entirely concerned with the illusions of an erotic dream. The correspondence is at first totally enigmatic, but it does help to highlight the clear parallel, soon to emerge, between Almanzor's infatuation with Almahide and Abdalla's with Lyndaraxa. In the great moment of contact between the hero and the villainess, when his thirst for battle merges with her thirst for blood, Almanzor shows himself subject to the forces embodied in Lyndaraxa, subservient to her as a symbol if not as a person. After this crucial conjunction, counterpoising the dupes' helpless contemplation of their enslavement, comes Almanzor's capitulation to Almahide, where he quickly appropriates the language of Abdalla's devotion, worshipping Almahide with Lyndaraxa's litany: within a few lines he repeats the imagery of paralysis (he is "numm'd, and fix'd"), of lethargy, and of usurpation within the mind:

> I'm numm'd, and fix'd, and scarce my eyeballs move;
> I fear it is the Lethargy of Love!
> 'Tis he; I feel him now in every part:

Like a new Lord he vaunts about my Heart,
Surveys in state each corner of my Brest,
While poor fierce I, that was, am dispossest.   (I. III. p. 54)

These echoes do not reveal all their implications at once, instead tantalising
us with elusive similarities; Dryden clarifies the enigmatic patterns of Act II
only to create further inchoate and teasing symmetries.

At the beginning of Act III Almanzor joins Abdalla's conspiracy; at the end
he leaves it. At first, military dissociation seems to coincide with moral
dissociation, for, when Zulema declares himself as a rival for Almahide's
hand, hero and villain are opposed as Platonic idealist and cynical sensualist:
when Almanzor selflessly insists on Almahide's unconditional release,
Zulema replies with earthbound opportunism:

If you will free your part of her you may;
But, Sir, I love not your Romantique way.
Dream on; enjoy her Soul; and set that free;
I'me pleas'd her person should be left for me.   (I. III. p. 58)

This schematic contrast is, however, to be challenged repeatedly, and is
ultimately revoked in the scene of attempted seduction. Indeed, the contrast
is promptly blurred when Almanzor, denied custody of Almahide, brushes
aside Abdalla's excuses and delivers the first of his fully-blown rants,
asserting his invincible mastery of the Prince's fate; for the boasts of
Almanzor's quintessentially heroic speech are identical to those with which
Zulema had prompted Abdalla to villainy:

Zul. Man makes his fate according to his mind.
The weak low Spirit Fortune makes her slave;
But she's a drudge, when Hector'd by the brave.   (I. II. p. 44)

Almanz. There's not a starr of thine dare stay with thee:
I'le whistle thy tame fortune after me:
And whirl fate with me wheresoe're I fly.   (I. III. p. 59)

The speech in which Almanzor perfects his characteristic style thus hints
once again that the boundless dreams of heroism and villainy are suspiciously
akin. And the affinities between the hero and the villains continue to
proliferate despite his return to Boabdelin's camp. Faced with understand-
able doubt as to his good intentions, Almanzor urges the king to lose no time
in securing—and rewarding—his loyalty:

I am your fortune; but am swift like her,
And turn my hairy front if you defer. . . .
Great Souls by kindness onely can be ti'd;
Injur'd again, again I'le leave your side.   (I. IV. p. 60)

Almanzor's loyalties are still, like Lyndaraxa's, frankly subject to the fluctuations of self-interest, and in posturing as the "hairy" personification of Fortune he echoes and parodies the self-dramatisation that had accompanied Lyndaraxa's speech of bloodlust:

> No; _like his better Fortune_ I'le appear:
> With open Arms, loose Vayl, _and flowing Hair._
>
> (I. III. p. 52; italics added)

The parallel is complemented by one closer at hand: immediately after Almanzor's reunion with Boabdelin, Lyndaraxa enters and echoes both her own earlier self-dramatisation and the hero's recent mimicry of it: "I will be constant yet, if fortune can," she declares (I. IV. p. 61). Such reciprocation of assumed, histrionic roles is to become increasingly evident as the heroes are drawn into an imitative world of baseless fictions, fabricated by the unnatural artistry of the evil illusionists. More immediately, the double parallel invites us to view the ensuing display of temporising, in which Lyndaraxa evasively refuses both flight with Abdelmelech and commitment to Abdalla, as a further commentary on Almanzor's still unstable and self-serving loyalties.

As Almanzor's career conforms ever more to that of Lyndaraxa, Dryden initiates a career of better fortitude, measuring the progress of false heroism against one of ever-increasing dissociation from the counterfeit reality conjured up by the villainess's perverse mimesis. In the tower that Lyndaraxa commands, immediately after Lyndaraxa has toyed with her two lovers, Selin brings Benzayda to delight in the spectacle of Ozmyn's death. Selin, of course, has been given his chance of vengeance both by Lyndaraxa's treachery (Ozmyn was captured during the insurrection) and by Almanzor's crassness, and his scheme is animated by the spirit that united its two tutelaries in their chief moment of contact, for he shares Lyndaraxa's sensual delight in death and Almanzor's failure to distinguish the reality of slaughter from the ritualised and imitative games of the bullfight. Moreover, he expects Benzayda to share them too: she is to witness "A Scene of Vengeance, and a Pomp of death" and "To judge the lingring Souls convulsive strife" (I. IV. p. 67). We recall that Ozmyn's father, presiding over the game that led to the present vendetta, sat "Judge-like, . . . to praise, or to arraign" the skill of the combatants in the "pomp and Sports" of Boabdelin's betrothal celebrations (I. I. p. 29). Benzayda, however, cannot take an aesthetic view of death; she would not share Lyndaraxa's visual delight in "purple, which the blood of Princes, dies" (II. II. p. 112). Abjuring the deluded, theatrical life of falsely idealised carnage, she also abjures the primitive and antisocial egocentricity of Lyndaraxa and Almanzor, engaging in a painful and self-sacrificing attempt to satisfy conflicting obligations, and reversing the amoral manipulation of loyalties with which the authors of her predicament had preceded her entrance.

Benzayda's release of Ozmyn is followed and paralleled by Almanzor's release of Ozmyn's sister, Almahide. But the episodes are very different in character, for Benzayda's selflessness—"Think not of me, but fly your self away" (I. IV. p. 69)—is abruptly followed by Almanzor's noisy demands for recompense (and recompense for undoing mischief he has himself caused): "You wonnot hear! you must but Hear and grant," he insists, "For, Madam, there's an impudence in want" (I. IV. p. 71). Furthermore, he takes a small but significant step in the direction of the villains' sensuality: weakening in the Platonic idealism that he had shown to Zulema, he implicitly rejects the Platonic notion that true love can subsist without carnal nourishment, as the chameleon feeds on air:[10]

> My Love is languishing, and sterv'd to death;
> And would you give me charity, in breath?   (I. IV. p. 71)

Almanzor's desires are not yet wholly reprehensible, since Almahide is not yet wholly out of reach. Nevertheless, he is no longer content to dream on and enjoy his mistress's soul; the initial, tentative, parallels between heroic and villainous love are gradually being strengthened.

The strengthening continues in Act V, where Abdalla, Ozmyn, and Almanzor successively meet with obstacles in love and go into exile. Firstly, Lyndaraxa rebuffs Abdalla, who begs shelter after his defeat in battle. Next, Abenamar refuses his blessing to Ozmyn's love. And then Almanzor reappears, demands Almahide's hand, and is sentenced to death, but is saved when Almahide makes his survival the price of her marriage to Boabdelin. Now committed to Boabdelin, Almahide seeks unsuccessfully to discourage and quell Almanzor's passion, engaging in an altercation whose imagery provides further echoes of Abdalla's dream-like illusion, further hints of the hero's entrapment in the counterfeit, make-believe world over which Lyndaraxa presides; significantly, the imagery of fantasy is combined with that of a theatrical "scene":

> *Almah.* 'Twas but a dream, where truth had not a place:
> A scene of fancy, mov'd so swift a pace
> And shifted, that you can but think it was.   (I. V. p. 84)

Furthermore, Almanzor again compromises his original idealism by rejecting Almahide's Platonic counsel and longing for carnal sustenance, though he now knows that she is irrevocably bound to another: sisterly love, he protests, is

> like thin food to men in feavours spent;
> Just keeps alive; but gives no nourishment.   (I. V. p. 84)[11]

Shortly afterwards he goes into exile; immediately after Almanzor's exit

Abdalla's flight is announced (I. v. p. 85); and then we learn that Ozmyn and
Benzayda too have fled (I. v. p. 86).

At the end of Part I, therefore, passion has brought Almanzor and Abdalla
to parallel states of physical and psychological isolation, exile and illusion
cutting them off from society and from reality itself. In Almanzor's case,
particularly, the two solitudes are inseparable, since his expulsion from
society is a correlative of his solipsistic inability to comprehend any order
that is not shaped by his own will:

> Where'ere I goe there can no exile be;
> But from *Almanzor's* sight I banish thee: . . .
> Stay thou with all thy Subjects here: but know,
> We leave thy City empty when we go.   (I. v. p. 80)

At this point, curiously, Almanzor's condition is less distinct than usual from
that of Ozmyn and Benzayda. They too, thwarted by society, try to ignore it
and to comprehend all space within the sphere of their passions: recognising
that they are between Scylla and Charybdis, hostile parents and hostile
Spaniards, Ozmyn cannot think where to go; but Benzayda has the answer:

> I'le fly to you; and you shall fly to me:
> Our flight but to each others armes shall be.
> To providence and chance commit the rest;
> Let us but love enough and we are blest.   (I. v. p. 77)

The two exiles are, of course, opposite in character: Almanzor is cast off by
society because his anarchic and amoral passion refuses conformity to any
discipline, whereas Ozmyn and Benzayda flee because they see a moral order
and harmony which their corrupt and fragmented society cannot accom-
modate. Nevertheless, their ambition to find the world in each other's arms
and to leave all else to Providence is a piece of idealistic illusion, reminiscent
of the fantasies of Berenice; they must perforce return to society and seek to
reconcile it to their moral vision. In this they are only partially successful,
since, although they redeem individuals, they are powerless to transform the
degenerate state: at the trial by combat Ozmyn, the sole conscious agent of
justice, is overcome, and victory goes to egocentric force. Only in
Christianity do Ozmyn and Benzayda find an order answering to their
aspirations.

Part I provides a sustained and unified portrayal of the dissociation from
civilisation and reality that plagues the adherents of love and passion. By the
end, cohesion is destroyed, perception baffled or distorted: Ozmyn and
Benzayda flee from civilisation, abandoning hope of a reality answering to
their idealistic vision; Abdalla defects, blinded by passion into denying an
order whose legitimacy he had well understood; Almanzor, unable to
envisage any obstacle to his boundless aspirations, is cast off by an order that

he cannot comprehend; Lyndaraxa holds out in the Albayzin, cherishing futile dreams of absolute autarky; Abdelmelech, placing deluded love above political wisdom, secures a fatal clemency for Lyndaraxa and Zulema; and even Boabdelin is absorbed in the cares of love to the neglect of those of state.

II. HEROES AND VILLAINS IN PART II

The design of the first part is complemented in the second, which interweaves a number of spurious (or at best ineffective) reversals of the descent into illusion and social fragmentation: Ozmyn and Benzayda secure a narrow, domestic concord but bring no peace to their warring clans; Zulema and Lyndaraxa obtain a deceitful reconciliation with the king they had betrayed; Abdalla, the quintessential self-deceiver, is killed; and Abdelmelech falsely persuades himself that his deluded love is quenched. The most prominent component of this pattern, however, is the career of Almanzor, whom Almahide seeks, with only specious success, to purify and civilise through the transfiguring power of love. With the frailty character- istic of Dryden's heroes, Almanzor hoists himself into conformity with Almahide's instructions only to plummet into renewed imperfection. Furthermore, the elaborate series of trials through which Almahide guides Almanzor is (*pace* Alssid and others)[12] merely a series of masquerades, imitative of but detached from permanent realities, for the virtues that she inculcates are eidola—shadows, to use Esperanza's metaphor (II. v. p. 149)— of the substantial values that emerge with the triumph of Christianity: the loyalty that she teaches is misdirected, and her Platonic sexual code is less a set of moral values than of literary conventions, derived from an imitative, less- than-real world and alien to the realities both of Almanzor's nature and her own. By Act v the idealistic transformations and reconciliations have proved nugatory or impotent, and the pretended reform of Zulema and Lyndaraxa has secured the triumph of evil and illusion: coherence of a sort is restored, but it is the coherence of universal participation in Lyndaraxa's final deception. The pagan civilisation of Granada is itself founded upon falsehood, embodying no principles of coherence and enshrining no truths that will lead its citizens from their diverse and incommunicable illusions to a communal enlightenment. Only when Christianity supplants the false and ephemeral order are regeneration and unity possible.

Act I of the second part begins the abortive movement towards order and enlightenment, portraying a series of accommodations between passion and society: Ozmyn and Benzayda fall into Spanish hands and move Ferdinand to clemency with their display of noble love; Zulema, pardoned because of Abdelmelech's love for his sister, reflects cynically on the clemency he has received; and Boabdelin is forced to ask his wife to reconcile him with her lover, Almanzor. Ozmyn and Benzayda's relationship with the Christian power is at this stage fragile and superficial, justified merely by the

adventitious demands of honour (II. II. p. 103); at the end of the play the
relationship is renewed, now grounded upon the immutable principles of
faith (II. V. p. 162). Zulema's reconciliation with Boabdelin is, however,
wholly fraudulent: "Feign'd Honesty shall work me into Trust," he reveals
in a soliloquy, "And seeming Penitence conceal my Lust" (II. I. p. 97).
Zulema's renewed alliance, a façade to conceal and a contrivance to further
his lust, is a vastly distorted accentuation of the renewed alliance that
Almanzor is soon to undertake. The extent of the distortion should not be
minimised: Zulema is a sinister and misshapen shadow of Almanzor.
Nevertheless, his self-serving and lust-motivated alliance remains in the
background to qualify and comment on Almanzor's—and, as the play
develops, shadow and prototype gain in resemblance.

Act II provides a series of transformations brought about by the power of
love. Inspired by love of Benzayda, Ozmyn self-sacrificingly defends Selin's
life and consequently brings about the old Zegry's reform. This wholly
beneficent transformation is inverted in the following episode, in which
Lyndaraxa relentlessly undermines Abdelmelech's pretended hostility and
leads him to an avowal of renewed love. She follows up this victory by
confirming Abdalla in his deluded trust:

> *Abdal.* My love makes all your Acts unquestion'd go:
> And sets a Soveraign stamp on all you doe.
> Your Love I will believe with hoodwink'd eyes;
> In faith, much merit in much blindness lies.   (II. II. p. 111)

This episode is in turn—seemingly—inverted in the following encounter,
where Almahide tries to lead Almanzor from Abdalla's species of love to a
love without passion, transcending thoughts of possession. In the earlier part
of the encounter, Almanzor reaches a new stage in his mimicry of Abdalla
and his association with the realms of fantasy which Lyndaraxa pre-
eminently controls: images of theatre, dream, enchantment, illusion linked
with immobility ("while you think / To walk . . ."), and sexual fantasy
echo comprehensively the analysis of Abdalla's sexual obsession, glance at
the Zambra, and recall the Prince's recent celebration of erotic illusion:

> *Almanz.* My quick imagination will present
> The Scenes and Images of your Content:
> When to my envy'd Rival you dispence
> Joyes too unruly, and too fierce for sence.
> *Almah.* These are the day-dreams which wild fancy yields,
> Empty as shadows are, that fly o're fields.
> O, whether would this boundless fancy move!
> 'Tis but the raging Calenture of Love.
> Like a distracted Passenger you stand,
> And see, in Seas, imaginary Land,

Cool Groves, and Flow'ry Meads, and while you think
To walk, plunge in, and wonder that you sink.
    Almanz. Love's Calenture too well I understand;
But sure your Beauty is no Fairy Land!   (II. II. p. 114)

This is the most extensive parallel so far between the hero and the dupe.
Soon, however, Almahide inspires Almanzor with more austere and resolute
thoughts: with a facility that bodes ill for the permanence of the change he
deserts one area of theatre for another, leaping into the apparel of Orrery's
Clorimun[13] and seeming content to deserve what Boabdelin merely
possesses:

    Almah. Your Vertue to the hardest proof I bring:
Unbrib'd, preserve a Mistress and a King.
    Almanz. I'le stop at nothing that appears so brave;
I'le do't; and now I no Reward will have.
You've given my Honour such an ample Field,
That I may dye, but that shall never yield.   (II. II. p. 114)

For his renunciation of reward he is promptly rewarded with Almahide's
scarf.

At his first opportunity to justify his boasts, however, Almanzor fails
miserably. Incensed when Boabdelin forces the return of the scarf, he refuses
to intervene during a Spanish attack and allows the King to be captured (II. III.
p. 119). Almahide has to start all over again:

    Almah. Almanzor vow'd he would for honour fight;
And lets my husband perish in my sight.
    Almanz. O, I have err'd; but fury made me blind:
And, in her just reproach, my fault I find!   (II. III. p. 119)

Penitent, Almanzor arranges to exchange the captured Abdalla for the
captured Boabdelin and seems at last to have dissociated himself from his
alter ego:

    Abdal. Your benefits revenge my crimes to you:
For I my shame in that bright Mirrour, view.
    Almanz. No more; you give me thanks you do not ow,
I have been faulty; and repent me now.   (II. III. p. 120)

But, although the exchange scheme seems to set the seal on Almanzor's
reform, it creates its own complications, since the truce brings him into
contact with two tempters from the opposing side—Arcos and Lyndaraxa
(now in the Spanish camp), father and spiritual mistress. Almanzor easily
resists Arcos' inducements to a further change of allegiance and in doing so

regains and intensifies the Orreryan mood of the previous act, falling into
renewed imitation of Clorimun and his successors:

> Then be it so: let me have no return
> From him but Hatred, and from her, but Scorn.
> There is this comfort in a noble Fate,
> That I deserve to be more fortunate.   (II. III. p. 125)

This is the scene in which Almanzor most fully manifests the public and
sexual virtues in which Almahide instructs him; yet this is also the scene that
Dryden chooses to recall and invert when Almanzor, submitting to Arcos, is
initiated into the true values of Christianity. The hero is truly redeemed only
when he relives and reverses this encounter.

The exchange with Lyndaraxa, however, is by no means so smoothly
managed. Indeed, Dryden's stagecraft suggests from the outset that this is to
be the crisis of Almanzor's career, for the two characters have not until now
appeared on-stage together. For the first time, the hero faces in the flesh the
woman who for so long has invisibly mastered his spirit: hitherto,
Lyndaraxa has been an elusive lamia, vanishing before his gaze; hero and
villainess have been as Castor and Pollux, each able only to fill the place
vacated by the other. Appropriately, the scene is commensurate in its
psychological importance. Appropriately, too, Lyndaraxa approaches as
Almanzor reaches the apogee of his forced Platonic idealism (and of his
career as Almahide's pupil), so that she overshadows the make-believe while
it plays itself out: as Almanzor exclaims "let me have no return", the stage
direction reads, "*Here* Lyndaraxa *comes neer and hears them.*" She then
proceeds irrevocably to strip away the veneer of unassimilable ideals that
Almahide has imposed on him. At first, Almanzor does repeat his Platonic
claims, asserting once more that he serves without desire of reward;
Lyndaraxa, however, sees that his love is still carnal and quickly forces him to
abandon his idealistic posturing:

> *Lynd. Almanzor* cannot be deluded, twice.
> *Almanz.* No; not deluded; for none count their gains,
> Who, like *Almanzor*, franckly give their pains.
> *Lynd. Almanzor*, do not cheat your self, nor me;
> Your Love is not refin'd to that degree.
> For, since you have desires; and those not blest,
> Your Love's uneasie, and at little rest.
> *Almanz.* 'Tis true; my own unhappiness I see:
> But who, alas, can my Physician be?   (II. III. p. 127)

Stripped of the artificial role in which Almahide had cast him, Almanzor
plunges into renewed impersonation of Abdalla, once again using images of
the abdication of reason, of enchantment, and of illusion entailing bondage,

and now clearly preferring illusion to unclouded perception:

> Love is that madness which all Lovers have;
> But yet 'tis sweet and pleasing so to Rave.
> 'Tis an Enchantment where the reason's bound:
> But Paradice is in th' enchanted ground.
> A Palace void of Envy, Cares and Strife,
> Where gentle hours delude so much of Life.
> To take those Charms away; and set me free
> Is but to send me into misery.
> And Prudence, of whose Cure so much you boast,
> Restores those Pains, which that sweet Folly lost.   (II. III. p. 128)

In his first encounter with Almahide, Almanzor had spoken in Abdalla's voice, addressing the heroine in images appropriated from the cult of the villainess. Now he goes one better, rehearsing his love in Lyndaraxa's formulae to Lyndaraxa herself. Although he rejects his temptress's advances, the visible stage action does provide a striking image of the identity of heroic and villainous love: Lyndaraxa now supplants Almahide as the corporeal audience of protestations that all along have revealed her spiritual ascendancy over Almanzor.

In this critical encounter Lyndaraxa appears quite overtly as the mistress of theatre, enticing Almanzor from his brief participation in Almahide's Orreryan scenario and investing him with a role in her own rival drama. When she commences her temptation, for example, she does so with imagery of a triumphal masque enacted by personifications of Granada's towers:

> The Genius of the place its Lord will meet:
> And bend its tow'ry forehead to your feet.
> That little Cittadel, which now you see,
> Shall then, the head of Conquer'd Nations be:
> And every Turret, from your coming rise
> The Mother of some great Metropolis.   (II. III. pp. 126—7)

Lyndaraxa is not merely dealing in vacant hyperbole. Rather, she thinks in terms of a staged allegory such as Dryden himself was later to contrive in *Albion and Albanius*—where the personification of London enacts an exact reversal of Lyndaraxa's triumphant conception:

> Behold! . . .
> My Turrets on the ground
> That once my Temples crown'd![14]

Almanzor responds by dissociating himself from Lyndaraxa's dramaturgy,

arguing that he is not fitted for the role in which she casts him: "I am not that
Almanzor whom you praise," he protests (II. III. p. 127). Nor, we soon learn,
is he the Almanzor whom Almahide, or anyone else, praises: seemingly
resisting Lyndaraxa's casting, he here unwittingly anticipates the renewed
transformation of Almanzor into Abdalla. Soon afterwards, he himself takes
up the masque image, casting Lyndaraxa as a personification in an enacted
psychomachia:

> I in the shape of Love Despair did see:
> You, in his shape, would show Inconstancy.   (II. III. p. 128)

Lyndaraxa in her turn sustains and makes blatant the histrionic motif,
offering to act the part of Almahide in Almanzor's sexual fantasies: "Court
me in jest," she proposes, "and call me *Almahide*" (II. III. p. 128). This turn in
Lyndaraxa's drama, of course, has little organic connection with her pageant
of triumphant towers: her art is chaotic, unnatural, and ephemeral.
Nevertheless, this final, explicit attempt at play-acting does give us the clue
with which to interpret the dramaturgic manoeuvres of the whole scene. By
forcing us to see the encounter as a piece of theatre within theatre, Dryden
calls attention to the confusion and exchange of identities that dominates the
scene. Lyndaraxa consciously acts the role of Almahide, while Almanzor
unconsciously slips into that of Abdalla. Simultaneously, with a single script,
the pair enact three dialogues: between Lyndaraxa and Almanzor, between
Almahide and Almanzor, and between Lyndaraxa and Abdalla. The two
parallel infatuations—of hero for heroine and of dupe for villainess—
coalesce: posing as Almahide's surrogate, Lyndaraxa elicits from Almanzor
the suppressed, unideal reality of his passion for the woman whom she
personates; and, in the act of revealing this reality, Almanzor mimics the
lover of the siren who for the nonce assumes Almahide's role. Thus,
although he resists Lyndaraxa's direct advances, he reveals that he is still
controlled by the spirit that she embodies, subservient to her as a symbol if
not as a person. When he bribes his way into Almahide's apartment at night,
he does so hounded by the desires that Lyndaraxa has brought into renewed
prominence.

Almanzor's renewed subservience to Lyndaraxa's spirit, however, first
appears in war rather than love. In his great victory over the Spaniards he
once more celebrates the joys of battle, regaining the mood in which he had
released Arcos and captured Ozmyn:

> 'Tis War again; and I am glad 'tis so;
> Success shall now by force and courage goe.
> Treaties are but the combats of the Brain,
> Where still the stronger loose, and weaker gain.   (II. IV. p. 133)

Two noteworthy aspects of this speech align Almanzor with Lyndaraxa and her entourage. Firstly, he again commits himself to the cause of unreason, deriding the brain and exalting the body. Secondly, he belittles the contracts devised by reason and yearns instead for a covenantless condition in which the prize goes to the strongest; in short, for the Hobbesian condition of nature. Thus rededicating himself to Lyndaraxa's principles, he prepares the way for the seduction attempt, for this too is actuated by a libertine contempt for reason and for the bonds formulated by civilisation; ironically, Almanzor's greatest triumph and greatest failure as a romance hero spring from a single code of life.

Act IV had at first seemed to promise the triumph of enlightenment over illusion, for Abenamar had at last relinquished his deluded cruelty, renouncing the world of dream to which Abdalla and Almanzor still cling and comparing himself to a man "just waking" (II. IV. p. 132). Almanzor's Lyndaraxa-like paean to combat, however, at once interrupts the banishment of illusion, since, as soon as Abenamar has repudiated dream, the hero enters and celebrates the somnambulistic trance of battle:

> [The hero] shoots the Gulph; and is already o're.
> And, when th'Enthusiastique fit is spent,
> Looks back amaz'd at what he underwent.   (II. IV. p. 133)

As soon as Almanzor has left, however, the attack on illusion reappears, albeit in a more tragic and malign form: Abdalla, the arch-dreamer, is destroyed and Abdelmelech, recognising Lyndaraxa's baseness, persuades himself that his love is quenched. In doing so he echoes Abenamar's awakening, reviewing and renouncing the images of enchantment, illusion, and dream favoured by Abdalla and Almanzor; but, unlike Abenamar, he still longs for the comforts of dream:

> These Arts have oft prevail'd; but must no more:
> The spell is ended; and th' Enchantment 'ore. . . .
> O that you still could cheat, and I believe! . . .
> I'm now awake, and cannot dream again!   (II. IV. pp. 135–6)

Almanzor himself is now given the opportunity to participate in the process of enlightenment. When, driven by lust, he arrives at Almahide's chamber, he reveals conclusively that his mistress's guidance has been without effect: human instruction has failed and the time has come for supernatural intervention. Accordingly Almanzor is visited by his mother's ghost, who in a few lines comprehensively censures all that he now stands for: the misguided loyalty painstakingly inculcated by Almahide, the delight in battle for its own sake, and the pursuit of sensual love:

> Yet bred in errors thou dost mis-imploy
> That strength Heav'n gave thee, and its flock destroy. . . .

Heaven does not now thy Ignorance reprove;
But warns thee from known Crimes of lawless Love.   (II. IV. p. 140)

Almanzor, however, pays no heed, rejecting illumination and plunging into intensified sensuality.

The ensuing scene reveals the full spuriousness of Almanzor's transfiguration through love. Revoking all his protestations of unmercenary integrity, he completes his long absorption into the villains' world: the original antithesis between the sensual Zulema and the Platonic Almanzor is decisively negated as the two men arrive simultaneously at the same place with the same intentions. The hero's movements are now geared to those of Zulema, who is now Almanzor's evil genius as he was formerly Abdalla's. Indeed, Almanzor immediately confirms the abandonment of the antithesis with Zulema by rejecting Platonism and insisting on carnal recompense: repudiating the self-denying claims that he has mouthed at Almahide's instigation, he remains true to the admission extorted by Lyndaraxa:

> *Almah.* You know you are from recompence debarr'd,
> But purest love can live without reward.
> *Almanz.* Pure love had need be to it self a feast;
> For, like pure Elements, 'twill nourish least.   (II. IV. p. 141)

Similarly, he repudiates the honour that in his Platonic flights had seemed invincible: "Let [Honour] in pity, now, to rest retire; / Let these soft hours be watch'd by warm desire" (II. IV. p. 142), he begs, forgetting the proud boasts of Act II:

> I'le do't: and now I no Reward will have,
> You've given my Honour such an ample Field,
> That I may dye, but that shall never yield.   (II. II. p. 114)

Lest we should fail to notice the gap between promise and performance, Almahide explicitly contrasts the hero's mercenary ravings with the calm and superhuman renunciation that he had seemed to offer: "how August and god-like" he had seemed in his repudiation of reward; but "How little, and how mercenary now!" (II. IV. p. 143). In abandoning the Platonism that had fitfully distinguished him from Zulema, Almanzor once again falls into mimicry of his evil counterpart, echoing the villain's assault on Abdalla's tottering reason and imitating its libertine scorn for the restraints that reason and virtue impose on desire: brushing aside Abdalla's protest that "Reason was giv'n to curb our headstrong will", Zulema had derided virtue's "lean holy face" and insisted that youth was "strong enough" to dispense with reason (I. II. p. 44); now, when Almahide echoes Abdalla by praising reason as the "curb of headlong Will", Almanzor parallels Zulema by disparaging reason and virtue, urging Almahide to remove "dull

Reason . . . / And tedious formes; and give a loose to love" (II. IV. p. 142). Not only does Almanzor reach Almahide's boudoir at the same time as Zulema and with the same intentions; when he is admitted, he also speaks with the same voice.

Almanzor does ultimately control his lust when faced with the threat of Almahide's suicide, seeming to regain the selfless idealism in which she had instructed him and promising never to "disturb" her virtue again (II. IV. p. 144). But even this reasserted nobility does not survive for long. Indeed, hints of coming complications appear almost at once, for the speech of unqualified self-denial is followed by one that is far more hesitant, uncertain, and human:

Alas, I am but half converted yet:
All I resolve, I with one look, forget.
And like a Lyon whom no Arts can tame;
Shall tear, ev'n those, who would my rage reclaime. (II. IV. p. 144)

As the lion image reveals, Almanzor still instinctively resists the disciplines of civilisation; and, as the last line predicts, he is very soon to turn against the woman who has sought to impose them.

As soon as Almanzor has left, Zulema enters, takes over the assault on Almahide's chastity, and is detected by Abdelmelech. Lyndaraxa, however, assumes control of events, stands truth on its head, and creates her final, climactic deception, arraigning Almahide on a charge of adultery with Abdelmelech. All characters except Ozmyn and Abenamar are now the pawns and puppets of the villainess: Zulema acts only by her script ("second what I say, and do not fear," she tells him [II. IV. p. 145]), Boabdelin becomes the blind instrument of her will, and Abdelmelech, who has long submitted voluntarily to her fictions, becomes a helpless star marionette in her final piece of stagecraft. Almanzor, too, falls victim: whereas Almahide's reproofs barely touched an answering chord, Lyndaraxa's words command instant and instinctive assent, and he is shamefully ready to believe the worst of his mistress. The seduction attempt, his most extensive surrender to the spirit of the villains, thus proves to be an immediate (and fitting) prelude to his credulous participation in Lyndaraxa's greatest masquerade. His subservience to her is complete.

As in her temptation of Almanzor, Lyndaraxa is here undertaking a piece of deliberate dramaturgy. Indeed, she plagiarises her initial ruse from Seneca's *Hippolytus*, for, like Phaedra, she turns the tables on the innocent party by acquiring his sword and producing it as evidence of guilt (*Hippolytus* 896–7). In this great coda to her career Lyndaraxa appears openly as the puppet-mistress, standing over the action, controlling the minds and movements of her creatures, inspiring the theatrical pageant of death in the Vivarambla; significantly, the tournament occupies the scene of the bullfight, an event that prefigured and symbolised the aesthetic manipulation of death that was to distinguish Lyndaraxa's career. This universal, overt submission to her puppetry provides an extended staged metaphor, imaging and confirming the veiled psychological homage that all characters have paid to the spirit that she embodies: subservience to the symbol leads in the end to subservience to the person.

The symbolic significance of Lyndaraxa's ascendancy provides the answer to an important (but unasked) question: why should Dryden give so much prominence to the suspected adultery of Abdelmelech and Almahide? The two characters have so far followed separate courses, and their relationship has been so neutral and nebulous that the false pairing seems, at first sight, to lack any point or irony. Once more, the answer lies in the permutable quality of the hero's and dupes' attachments. Almanzor's seduction attempt is aptly followed by Lyndaraxa's dramaturgic manipulation of Abdelmelech, since both successively develop the interchange of roles enacted in her temptation of Almanzor, where the love of hero for heroine had been transubstantiated into that of dupe for villainess. In the seduction attempt Almanzor had continued the translation of identities, approaching Almahide's apartment in the spirit of Abdalla, in harmony with Zulema, and under the sway of Lyndaraxa, remaining true to the role in which his temptress had cast him. Abdelmelech, by contrast, arrives at the spot in an attempt to rectify a confusion of identities, wishing to subject the usurping queen to the rightful one, the false Almahide to the true: "That Queen you scorn'd, you shall this night, attend," he tells Lyndaraxa (II. IV. p. 136). His attempt, however, is futile. Lyndaraxa easily takes over, elaborating the permutation of identities which she had contrived in her temptation of Almanzor and which her unwitting pupil had sustained and developed in his temptation of Almahide. Her triumphant fiction entails a comprehensive reversal and exchange of roles: the heroine becomes the villainess and the villainess the heroine; to Abdelmelech is attributed the lechery of Zulema, to Zulema the loyalty of Abdelmelech. Furthermore, her fabricated translation of identities parallels and elucidates the psychologically real translation that we have just witnessed in Almanzor. Lyndaraxa has been the invisible superintendent of a scenario in which her spiritual helot, aping her brother Zulema, has tried to sleep with Almahide; she now openly contrives an identical scenario, centring instead upon her corporeal lover, who similarly becomes the dummy of Zulema, being forced to bear his guilt. Her fiction parallels and reflects the hero's abortive seduction scheme, pairing Almanzor with Abdelmelech, the lover of Almahide with the slave of Lyndaraxa. Almanzor's homage to the heroine's person is homage also to the spirit of the villainess; and, now cast as the rival of Abdelmelech, Almanzor has fully assumed the mantle of the dead Abdalla.

Almanzor does, of course, oppose Lyndaraxa's cause, fighting to vindicate Almahide's chastity. He does so, however, without faith in her innocence: paradoxically, therefore, the unwitting agent of truth is still the double of Abdalla, who had fought to exonerate a mistress he knew to be false (II. IV.

p. 134). Nor does the trial by combat of itself prove anything. In her first, tentative and shallow, flirtation with Christianity Almahide does represent the trial as a test case of divine (and poetic) justice:

> Let me thy godhead in thy succour see:
> So shall thy Justice in my safety shine,
> And all my dayes, which thou shalt add, be thine.   (II. v. p. 149)[15]

In the event, however, the trial is not a manifestation of providential justice but a final, theatrical parade of the baseless and chimerical values which have informed Granada's chaotic and divided society. Ozmyn, the sincere champion of innocence, is wounded and overcome, and victory is reserved for the disingenuous but muscular Almanzor; Lyndaraxa goes virtually unpunished, and Almahide quickly falls under renewed suspicion. Nor is Almanzor's restored trust in Almahide a direct and unmediated result of his heroism. Victory alone, we know, would not have converted him, for before the combat he had been confident both of his own triumph and Almahide's guilt: "I'le leave her, when she's freed; and let it be / Her punishment, she could be false to me" (II. v. p. 148). Almanzor is converted not by the self-sufficient efforts of his prowess but by Zulema's confession; he is freed from his psychological dependence on the villain only when the villain himself repents and releases him.

Lyndaraxa, however, survives, and in the immediate aftermath of the tournament Almanzor remains his old self. His greedy, forcible snatching of kisses (II. v. p. 156) shows that his love is as impulsively corporeal as ever. More serious, however, is his continued disregard of the Ghost's teachings: echoing Abdalla's blind, quasi-religious faith in Lyndaraxa (II. II. p. 111), he blasphemously declares the worship of Almahide to have been the sole purpose of his creation:

> Your new Commands I on my knees attend:
> I was created for no other end.
> Born to be yours, I do by Nature, serve,
> And, like the lab'ring Beast, no thanks deserve.   (II. v. p. 154)

In this spirit, unchanged and unregenerate, Almanzor leaves for his last battle in the pagan cause; when he returns, he has been transformed by supernatural interposition; and the chief on-stage event in the intervening period has been the death of Lyndaraxa.

Lyndaraxa's death speech is also the death speech of the old Almanzor. Very early in his career, Almanzor had arrogantly defied his captors with the words, "Stand off; I have not leisure yet to dye" (I. I. p. 35). Now, in the moment of death, Lyndaraxa vainly echoes his boast: "Dye for us both; I have not leysure now," she commands Abdelmelech (II. v. p. 160). She

continues to echo Almanzor throughout the ensuing speech, impotently
reviving his pose as the arbiter of destiny:

> A Crown is come, and will not fate allow. . . .
> Sure destiny mistakes; this death's not mine;
> She dotes, and meant to cut another line.
> Tell her I am a Queen.   (II. v. p. 160)

Lyndaraxa's death speech comprehends the quintessence of heroic illusion,
emptily sustained in the face of a reality that even the greatest hero cannot
transcend: here Almanzor's aspirations, no less than Lyndaraxa's, are
denuded of force, splendour, and credibility by the "ugly skeleton" (II. v. p.
160). Stage events again provide a visible, outward symbol of the meaning
of what has just passed: Lyndaraxa's corpse is carried off-stage; and, as soon as
she has been removed, the new Almanzor enters.

In his public actions, then, Almanzor does achieve an erratic and
misguided development. But this development (such as it is) is inseparably
linked to a gradual inner degeneration: the military ardour and sexual
importunity of the penultimate act both spring from a contempt for reason
and civilisation. Almahide's Platonic expectations merely assist the hero's
decline by imposing demands with which he cannot cope and, consequently,
temptations which he is unequipped to resist. Only in the final stages of the
play does his true education begin. Unflinchingly aware of the untidy
anomalies of historical progress, Dryden does not portray the Spanish
victory as an unequivocal triumph of justice: Ferdinand, after all, enthrones
Lyndaraxa. Nevertheless, the large, tangled movements of history do
provide circumstances propitious to individual enlightenment: Almanzor's
progress has only just begun, but the "unquarried gem" (I. III. p. 53) is at
length on the way to revealing its proper lustre.

So far, the most conclusive and glaring evidence for the "anti-heroic" case
can be summed up as follows: Abdalla's essential fault is that he allows his
passion to vanquish his reason; Zulema's villainy consists largely in feeding
the fires of unreason; and Almanzor persistently flouts reason in terms
indistinguishable from those of the dupe and the villain. If we are to praise
Almanzor, we must praise Abdalla just as loudly. To state the matter in this
way, however, is to trivialise the subtlety and richness of Dryden's design.
Abdalla enslaves himself to Lyndaraxa, urged on by the Mephistophelean
promptings of his evil genius Zulema. Throughout the play Almanzor
figures in a duplicate triangle, aping Abdalla, subservient to Lyndaraxa,
shadowed by Zulema. Seen on his own, Almanzor may appear to be
superficially portrayed, to exist solely within the confines of his own
rhetoric. To see him on his own, however, is to miss the point. By
surrounding the hero with projections of his instinctual self, reflexes of the
dark motives masked by the idealistic rhodomontade, Dryden achieves a
characterisation that is both profound and brilliantly stage-worthy. Were

the play to receive the modern revival that it merits, it would deserve the attentions of the most gifted producers and designers, so that its complex symmetries of character could be visibly reflected in corresponding symmetries of movement, diction, colour, and dress.

III. ALMAHIDE AND LYNDARAXA: THE FAILURE OF IDEAL LOVE

In serving Almahide, I have argued, Almanzor serves also the spirit of Lyndaraxa. Unwittingly, Almahide courts such irony, for Lyndaraxa dominates her life as much as Almanzor's: if the villainess is Almanzor's spiritual mistress, she is Almahide's spiritual shadow; nowhere does Dryden show greater psychological insight than in his exposure of the unconscious affinities that bind the heroine to the villainess.

Almahide consistently casts herself in the role of a Platonic heroine, cherishing Almanzor with an incorporeal love that is without desire and danger and poses no threats to her marriage with Boabdelin. But her pretensions exceed her capabilities, and her misguided idealism brings increasing perplexity and peril, until her tortured vacillations between husband and lover become ironically parallel to the calm double-dealing of Lyndaraxa. Dryden does not create an antithesis between idealised and corrupt sexuality. On the contrary, he suggests that the conduct of a Lyndaraxa is implicit in the codes of Platonism and preciosity to which the play's sexual idealists naïvely cling.

In portraying the dealings of Lyndaraxa, Zulema, Abdalla, and Abdelmelech, Dryden produced one of his closest adaptations of romance material, borrowing extensively from "The History of the Prince Ariantes, of Elibesis, of Adonacris, and of Noromante" (*Cyrus* IX. i. 12—74). But, although he follows Scudéry's narrative closely, Dryden radically alters its significance. Elibesis (Lyndaraxa's counterpart) is guilty not of a crime against civilisation itself but of an offence against the punctilious love code that dominates the romance: the rebellion that she foments is without lasting consequence, and she is punished only for her amorous duplicity, losing her beauty and her admirers (IX. i. 73), and suffering the mortification of seeing her first lover (Abdelmelech's counterpart) ascend to the throne (X. iii. 231). She is a cheat in the game of preciosity. Dryden, of course, alters and deepens the nature of her transgression, turning her into a malignant incarnation of all the anarchic and destructive impulses of the human mind. He also, however, shows that the forces which she typifies are latent even in those who play the game of preciosity; indeed, that her life-style is implicitly adumbrated in the *précieuse* doctrine that Almahide and Isabel naïvely mouth. Whereas Elibesis is the antithesis of the *précieuse*, Lyndaraxa represents the reality behind the *précieuse* façade; here, as always, Dryden rejects the tenets of romance even as he imitates its subject matter.

The affinity of idealist and siren is implicitly suggested even in the passages of conventional romance doctrine which glorify the mistress's authority over the lover:

> *Almah.* That absolute command your love does give
> I take; and charge you, by that pow'r, to live.   (I. v. p. 83)

> *Isabel. Granada,* is for Noble Loves renown'd;
> Her best defence is in her Lovers found.
> Love's a Heroique Passion which can find
> No room in any base degenerate mind:
> It kindles all the Soul with Honours Fire,
> To make the Lover worthy his desire.
> Against such Heroes I success should fear,
> Had we not too an Host of Lovers here.
> An Army of bright Beauties come with me;
> Each Lady shall her Servants actions see:
> The Fair and Brave on each side shall contest;
> And they shall overcome who love the best.   (II. I. pp. 96—7)

> *Almah.* No Lover should his Mistriss Pray'rs withstand:
> Yet you contemn my absolute Command.   (II. v. p. 155)

Some of these sweeping and inflexible formulae sanction a Lyndaraxa as much as an Almahide or an Isabel; none convincingly distinguishes ideal love from the villainess's corrupt eroticism. Isabel's celebration of "Heroique Passion", for example, is repeatedly disproved by events: love in general produces human degradation and does not even inspire valour efficiently, as Lyndaraxa discovers after imagining that she can invest her lover with invincibility, playing Guinevere to Abdalla's Lancelot:

> My Smiles shall make *Abdalla* more than Man;
> Let him look up and perish if he can.   (I. III. p. 52)

The only lover without a "degenerate mind" is Ozmyn, and he explodes Isabel's case by losing almost every battle that he enters. The inspiration of the *précieuse* may have some worth in the game-like world of the bullfight, but it is a romantic irrelevance in war. If Lyndaraxa is the play's dramatist, seeking to divert events into conformity with her perverse artistry, Isabel is the play's novelist: her speech is a historical romance in miniature, suppressing the unpalatable realities of treason and infiltration and inventing a causality of trite and counterfeit glamour.[16]

The truth is that the chief female influence to bring victory to Spain is that of Lyndaraxa. In the account of the final battle, descriptions of Isabel's intervention are closely shadowed by those of Lyndaraxa's more decisive aid:

> *Qu. Isab.* I will advance with such a shining train,
> That Moorish beauties shall oppose in vain. . . .
>   *Alabez.* Fair *Lyndaraxa*, and the Zegry line
> Have led their forces with your troops to join.   (II. v. p. 157)
>   *D. of Arcos.* Our troops then shrunk; and still we lost more ground:
> Till, from our Queen, we needful succour found.
> Her Guards to our assistance bravely flew,
> And, with fresh vigour, did the fight renew.
> At the same Time——
> Did *Lyndaraxa* with her troops appear,
> And while we charg'd the front, ingag'd the rear.
> Then fell the King (slain by a *Zegry's* hand.)   (II. v. p. 158)

Acknowledging the women's contribution to the war, Ferdinand himself continues the pairing of Isabel and Lyndaraxa:

> All stories, which *Granada's* Conquest tell,
> Shall celebrate the name of *Isabel.*
> Your Ladies too, who in their Countries cause,
> Led on the men, shall share in your applause.
> And for your sakes, henceforward, I ordain,
> No Ladies dow'r shall question'd be in *Spain.*
> Fair *Lyndaraxa*, for the help she lent,
> Shall, under Tribute, have this Government.   (II. v. p. 160)

Here, in the play's final paean to *frauendienst*, the worlds of the *précieuse* and the villainess are at last explicitly united. Indeed, Ferdinand's panegyric leads both in sequence and in logic to Lyndaraxa's enthronement, which she celebrates with a hideous parody of the mistress—servant relationship, planning to treat Abdelmelech as her Bajazet (II. v. p. 160). Her plagiarism of Marlowe continues her aesthetic, dramaturgic pleasure in human torment and debases the equally bookish contrivance of purifying amorous service which the ingenuous idealists seek to foist on life.

Almahide does try to use her mistress—servant relationship for public-spirited ends, but the unqualified terms in which she formulates her rights— "No Lover should his Mistriss Pray'rs withstand"—endorse Lyndaraxa's behaviour as much as her own; indeed, this most uncompromising assertion of her authority is closely juxtaposed with Lyndaraxa's planned humiliation of her lover. Significantly, Ozmyn and Benzayda take no part in the equivocal rites of *frauendienst*: Ozmyn obeys his mistress out of respect for the merit of particular exhortations rather than conformity with the inflexible roles of convention.

The ambiguity of conventional formulae is reflected throughout the play
in patterning that brings the heroine and villainess into increasingly close
conjunction. As early as Lyndaraxa's début scene, Dryden brings the two
women into a striking but as yet enigmatic association: Lyndaraxa has been
impelled into her career of evil by a desire to take over the role of Almahide:

> *Abdal.* Why wou'd you be so great?
> *Lyndar* ————————— Because I've seen,
> This day, what 'tis to hope to be a Queen.
> Heav'n, how y'all watch'd each motion of her Eye: ⎫
> None could be seen while *Almahide* was by;   ⎬
> Because she is to be her Majesty.   ⎭
> Why wou'd I be a Queen! because my Face
> Wou'd wear the Title with a better grace.   (I. II. p. 42)

In the following act, the elusive symmetries are sustained in Almahide's own
début scene, marked by the Zambra which she herself has arranged.
Almahide thus makes her first appearance in the guise of a stage manager, so
that Lyndaraxa is not the only dramatist in the cast. The heroine's
supervision of a piece of mild bawdry is itself slightly incongruous (the song
describes an erotic dream culminating in a nocturnal emission), but more
disturbing is the fact that the song's erotic dream clearly recalls the dream
imagery that has recently characterised Abdalla's blind infatuation with
Lyndaraxa; still enigmatic, the conjunction of heroine and villainess is
nevertheless gaining emphasis.

Immediately afterwards, the two women move into opposition, for
Almahide's Zambra is interrupted by Lyndaraxa's insurrection, and the
heroine's timid horror at warfare is contrasted with the villainess's gloating
sadism (I. III. p. 52). The contrast, however, is immediately blurred: in her
speech of bloodlust Lyndaraxa casts herself as the personification of Fortune,
adorned with "loose Vayl, and flowing Hair" (I. III. p. 52), and in doing so
appropriates an image from Almahide's Zambra:

> *From the bright Visions head*
> *A careless vail of Lawn was loosely spread:*
> *From her white temples fell her shaded hair.*   (I. III. p. 50)

Within seconds, however, Almahide retrieves the image: "*veyl'd*" (I. III. p.
53), she approaches Almanzor and, with histrionic deliberation, uncovers
her beauty to the hero's gaze.[17] When the infatuated Almanzor speaks to
Almahide in the tones of Lyndaraxa's lover, he addresses a woman who is
enacting an image shared with Lyndaraxa and derived from the bawdy
fantasy of the Zambra dance, itself a recollection of Abdalla's dream-like
obsession with Lyndaraxa. Even at this point, heroine and villainess engage
in an intricate reciprocation of roles.

In suggesting that Almahide should petition Almanzor, Esperanza injects a surprisingly unideal note by using the unattractive analogy of the corrupt subversion of justice:

> Heav'n never meant misfortune to that Face.
> Suppose there were no justice in your cause,
> Beauty's a Bribe that gives her Judges Laws.   (I. III. p. 53)

Succeeding events sustain the disturbingly unideal note that this analogy introduces. Naïvely blind to the pitfalls of real life, Almahide entertains the belief that she can use her sexual charms without courting sexual danger—an illusion that, in increasing defiance of the facts, she is to retain throughout the play. In the event, however, ignoble realities defeat ideal expectations: Almahide plays with fire and gets burnt, calling up forces that threaten her contract with Boabdelin and thus give new relevance to the image of subverted law. Hereafter, Lyndaraxa and Almahide are parallel in condition as well as imagery, for both vacillate uncertainly between a contracted partner and a lover, Lyndaraxa from a cynical sense of self-interest, Almahide from a tortured conflict between obligation and desire. The parallel is emphasised by a fleeting but close verbal echo when, in Act IV, the two women in turn guard their thoughts from inspection by the interloping lover:

> *Lynd.* For why should you my secret thoughts divine?   (I. IV. p. 66)

> *Almah.* Why do you thus my secret thoughts pursue?   (I. IV. p. 72)

The parallels, however, do not fall fully into place until Part II. Callously playing off two lovers against one another, Lyndaraxa persistently casts her shadow on Almahide's perplexed relationships with Boabdelin and Almanzor, pointing to the confused weakness behind the masks of wifely perfection and Platonic idealism—for the heroine's intentions are more entangled, less in harmony with duty, than she normally cares to admit. She faces up to her perplexity on only one occasion, when she ponders the consequences of her consent to recall Almanzor on Boabdelin's behalf:

> I'le cherish Honour, then, and Life despise;
> What is not Pure, is not for Sacrifice.
> Yet, for *Almanzor*, I in secret mourn!
> Can Vertue, then, admit of his return?
> Yes; for my Love I will, by Vertue, square:
> My Heart's not mine; but all my Actions are.
> I'le, like *Almanzor* act, and dare to be
> As haughty, and as wretched too as he.
> What will he think is in my Message meant!

> I scarcely understand my own intent:
> But Silk-worm-like, so long within have wrought
> That I am lost in my own Webb of thought.   (II. I. pp. 102–3)

In this unique passage of intense self-doubt, Almahide vainly casts herself in successive simple heroic roles, finding them inadequate as she becomes more and more lost in the elusive complexities of her thoughts. The one thing that is clear (both to herself and to us) is her continuing love for Almanzor—a love reaffirmed when she admits sexual responsiveness to his importunities (II. IV. p. 142) and, of course, when she overtly declares her unextinguished passion to him (II. V. p. 155).

Almahide's perplexity is in many ways scarcely surprising: her love for Almanzor is abundantly clear before her marriage,[18] and Boabdelin is left in no doubt that she far prefers his rival, that she is only proceeding with the marriage because of her promise, and that she will not even do thus unless Boabdelin frees Almanzor (I. V. pp. 81–2). What does make the soliloquy surprising is her preceding argument with Boabdelin, in which she seeks to calm his violent and capricious jealousy. The following assertion, for example, is flatly contradicted in her moments of private introspection:

> But know, that when my person I resign'd,
> I was too noble not to give my mind:
> No more the shadow of *Almanzor* fear;
> I have no room but for your Image, here.   (II. I. p. 101)

"I was too noble not to give my mind"—"My Heart's not mine; but all my Actions are"; "I have no room but for your Image, here"—"Yet, for *Almanzor* I in secret mourn": the contradictions are absolute and irreconcilable. Almahide performs a similar *volte-face* when she admits to herself the ambiguity of the motives behind her consent to Almanzor's recall, for to her husband's face she had fiercely resisted charges that her quick consent betrayed continuing love for the hero (II. I. pp. 101–2). She is clearly so confused about her emotions that she is unintentionally misrepresenting them to her husband. Self-deceivingly, she plays the part of a heroine (such as Davenant's Evandra or Orrery's Princess Katherine)[19] whose passions are subject to the facile redirection of reason (see Appendix, pp. 165–6). Once again, however, the simple roles of convention are incompatible with the intricate imperfections of real humanity, and Almahide's dual attachment drives her to a state of mental chaos reminiscent of Lyndaraxa's:

> *Almah.* I scarcely understand my own intent.   (II. I. p. 103)

> *Lynd.* For I my self scarce my own thoughts can ghess.
>
>   (I. IV. p. 61)

The dispute with Boabdelin has already uncovered the conflict between the optimistic fantasies of convention and the unwelcome complexities of reality..During this exchange Almahide attempts to invest her marriage with the imagery of lyric idealism—imagery that is wholly out of keeping both with the forced compromise of the union and with the immediate circumstance of Boabdelin's brooding and cynical jealousy:

> *Almah.* So, two kind Turtles, when a storm is nigh,
> Look up; and see it gath'ring in the Skie:
> Each calls his Mate to shelter in the Groves,
> Leaving in murmures, their unfinish'd Loves.
> Perch'd on some dropping Branch they sit alone,
> And Cooe, and hearken to each others moan.   (II. I. p. 100)

The flight to convention again aligns the heroine with the villainess, for, whereas Almahide innocently seeks a substitute for sincerity in prefabricated and inappropriate formulae, Lyndaraxa brazenly imports into her Hobbesian jungle the alien accents of Chloe or Phyllis betrayed:

> Go Faithless Man!
> Leave me alone to mourn my Misery:
> I cannot cease to love you, but I'le die.   (I. IV. p. 63)

Indeed, the ideal fantasy of cooing doves is itself tinged with the spirit of Lyndaraxa, since it proceeds from an envy of animal life that calls up fleeting echoes of her libertinism:

> All Creatures else a time of Love possess:
> Man onely clogs with cares his happiness;
> And, while he shou'd enjoy his part of Bliss,
> With Thoughts of what may be, destroys what is.   (II. I. p. 100)

Though nominally a reflection upon Boabdelin's jealousy, Almahide's protest against the burden of consciousness perhaps betrays already her fear of her "own Webb of thought".

Almahide's confusion is sustained in all her dealings with Almanzor in Part II. In their first meeting after his return (II. II. pp. 113–15) she blunderingly makes the ill-considered gesture of presenting him with her scarf (a conventional token of favour and commitment), thus causing Boabdelin predictable and understandable resentment (II. III. pp. 115–17). The scarf—intended to express wifely gratitude, inevitably seeming to denote wifely betrayal—perfectly symbolises the ambiguity and uncertainty of Almahide's emotions. As Boabdelin dwells sneeringly on the gift before wife and rival, Almahide falls into increasingly desperate play-acting, seeking to delude Almanzor with a useless show of marital harmony (pp. 116–17). At the beginning of the scene Boabdelin had compared marriage to a theatrical stage set (p. 115),[20] and at its climax he scoffs at Almahide's "well acted vertue" (p. 117). Although his suspicions do no justice to Almahide's anguished perplexity, his imagery is very much to the point: we here perceive more acutely than ever the empty theatricality of Almahide's marriage.

The next encounter—the seduction attempt—is still more damaging. As Almanzor, tormented with lust, brushes aside her Platonic precepts, Almahide herself learns their inefficacy and is forced to an avowal of desire; Platonism is a flimsy shield, and death provides the only barrier to lust:

> You've mov'd my heart, so much, I can deny
> No more; but know, *Almanzor*, I can dye,
> Thus far, my vertue yields; if I have shown
> More Love, than what I ought, let this attone. [*Going to stab herself.*
> (II. IV. pp. 143–4)

Almahide is here initiated into sexual desire. The initiation complete, Lyndaraxa immediately takes over her destiny, condemning her to star in the Vivarambla spectacle. Almahide's involvement in Lyndaraxa's final puppet-show, then, is no less appropriate than Almanzor's: for both, the period of overt subservience to Lyndaraxa is the climax of an extended period of veiled affinity; for both, moreover, the overt subservience immediately succeeds the seduction attempt and the collapse of the artificial, bookish codes with which the lovers had hoped to stifle the Lyndaraxa within the mind.

The preliminaries to the trial by combat provide the most explicit evidence of the inefficacy of Almahide's sexual code, for her insubstantial values are now, for the first time, measured against the immutable principles of Christianity. Instructing Almahide (as the Ghost had instructed Almanzor), Esperanza dismisses her code as a mere shadow in the face of Christian truth:

> Leave then that shaddow, and for succor fly
> To him we serve, the Christians Deity.
> Virtue's no god, nor has she power divine
> But he protects it who did first enjoyn.
> Trust then in him, and from his grace; implore
> Faith to believe what rightly we adore.   (II. V. p. 149)

Almahide's career is thus, at last, clearly equated with the overtly hallucinatory careers of Almanzor and his like; Almahide herself, we recall, had reproved Almanzor for entertaining daydreams "Empty as shadows" (II. II. p. 114).

Almahide's principles are shadowy and insubstantial because they have no foundation in nature. Her relationship with Almanzor is based on a code of literary conventions that remain obstinately literary, unable to transmute or animate living flesh. Similarly, her conception of marital ethics takes account only of external actions, so that she mistakes outward observance of duty for whole-hearted inner compliance, telling Boabdelin that she has given him both "person" and "mind" (II. I. p. 101) when in fact she has only given her person. In her relationships both with lover and husband, then, she has confused shadow and substance, believing her identity to be comprehended in a set of empty, exterior rituals that in no way answer to her true nature. Her début as stage manager of the Zambra was thus the prelude to a career of unconscious theatre and masquerade, paralleling the conscious dramaturgy of Lyndaraxa and finally, in the trial by combat, becoming absorbed into it. That Almahide, a heroine of chaste and Platonic aspiration, should have been acted by Nell Gwyn is, perhaps, not wholly inappropriate: the apparent disparity between actress and role merely magnifies the disparity between Almahide's true nature and the trite theatrical part which she mistakes for her real personality.

Esperanza moves Almahide to take Christianity on approval, to barter faith for divine protection:

> Thou Pow'r unknown, if I have err'd forgive:
> My infancy was taught what I believe.
> But if the Christians truely worship thee,
> Let me thy godhead in thy succour see:
> So shall thy Justice in my safety shine,
> And all my dayes, which thou shalt add, be thine.   (II. V. p. 149)

This rather tentative and shallow response, however, produces no immediate release from illusion, and subsequent events provide further evidence of Almahide's sexual perplexity and self-deception. Immediately before the tournament, for example, she professes continuing love for her husband:

> What not one tender look, one passing word;
> Farewel, my much unkind, but still lov'd Lord! . . .
> And, to forget me, may you soon adore
> Some happier maid (yet none could love you more.)   (II. V. p. 150)

These words of simple and selfless adoration are quite out of keeping with what we have seen of the bewildered and tangled state of Almahide's emotions. Furthermore, they are contradicted immediately after the combat, when Almahide tells Boabdelin that, though she once loved him, her love is now dead:

> Could you, . . .
> Unheard, condemn, and suffer me to goe

To death, and yet no common pity show! . . .
Though *Almahide* still lives, your wife is dead:
And, with her, dies a Love so pure and true,
It could be kill'd by nothing but by you.   (II. V. p. 153)

The *volte-face* is psychologically realistic, but none the less a *volte-face* for that,
since Almahide has no grievance against Boabdelin that she did not have
when she avowed her continuing love. Indeed, the two speeches present
contradictory reactions to the very same conduct, for in the first speech
Boabdelin's pitiless disregard is lovingly regretted and in the second coldly
despised. The second speech, professing the death of a genuine and unalloyed
love, is in turn contradicted when Almahide confesses to Almanzor that she
loves him (II. V. p. 155), since in doing so she avows a passion that existed
before and throughout her marriage. The second speech clashes with the
first, and the third clashes with both, so that even in her great moment of
vindication Almahide remains perplexed by the ambiguity of her sexual
motives. Once again, moreover, echoes of the villainess's circle emphasise
Almahide's failings, the renunciation of Boabdelin recalling Abdelmelech's
renunciation of Lyndaraxa:

   Abdel. You have at last destroy'd, with much adoe:
   That love, which none could have destroy'd but you.   (II. IV. p. 135)

   Almah. And, with her, dies a Love so pure and true,
   It could be kill'd by nothing but by you.   (II. V. p. 153)

   In this portion of the play, indeed, Almahide's cult of appearances reaches
its most extreme and perilous form. Shortly before she confesses her love to
Almanzor, she tells him that she can never see him again, since to do so after
renouncing her husband would harm her reputation (II. V. p. 154).
Paradoxically, however, she feels that the very act of renunciation enables
her to avow her love with honour and security, and she therefore confesses
another reason for banishing her lover: she now recognises the weakness of
her nature and knows that Almanzor's presence might create irresistible
temptations:

   Then, since you needs will all my weakness know,
   I love you; and so well, that you must goe;
   I am so much oblig'd; and have withal,
   A Heart so boundless and so prodigal,
   I dare not trust my self or you, to stay,
   But, like frank gamesters, must forswear the play. . . .
   This, had you stay'd, you never must have known:
   But now you goe, I may with honour own.   (II. V. p. 155)

The dichotomy between external observance and inner inclination could not be greater, the outward act of renunciation coinciding with and sanctioning the disclosure of emotional and physical commitment. But events are to discredit Almahide's belief in the self-sufficiency of the outward gesture, for, although her treatment of Almanzor is designed to invest her conduct with an impenetrable veil of seemliness, her efforts have in practice quite the opposite effect: the successive, conflicting shocks of the decree of banishment and the declaration of love throw Almanzor into an undignified frenzy of lust, provoking him to smother Almahide's hand in kisses and thus to create a misleading tableau which is easily misinterpreted by Boabdelin; the scheme intended to secure Almahide's reputation thus brings it into its greatest danger, so that the devotee of appearances becomes their victim. Nor is the tableau simply and wholly false: although Almahide had looked to appearances to conceal and divert her inclinations, they instead enact the desires that they were intended to hide. Paradoxically, the deceptive spectacle permits Boabdelin to pierce through Almahide's self-deceiving and oversimplified avowals of loyalty and to see beyond doubt the emotional infidelity that alienates her from him. Significantly, his suspicions are no longer clearly at odds with the facts: his speeches may imply gross and unfounded fears of adultery, but in letter they never transgress the bounds of truth:

> Yes, you will spend your life, in Pray'rs for me;
> And yet this hour my hated Rival see.
> She might a Husbands Jealousie forgive;
> But she will onely for *Almanzor* live.   (II. v. p. 154)

> This, this is he for whom thou didst deny
> To share my bed——Let 'em together dye.   (II. v. p. 156)

Indeed, Almahide is saved from her husband's wrath not by her virtue but by the agency of her evil *doppelgänger*, since Boabdelin's vengeance is thwarted only by Lyndaraxa's betrayal of the town; the heroine's code lies in ruins and her dependence on the villainess has taken a new turn.

In their last scene as heroic pagans, then, both Almanzor and Almahide remain untransformed: their careers have merely brought increasing entanglement in old illusions, and they have lived out a long mimicry of the impotent paralysis of Abdalla's dreamer. For Almahide, as for Almanzor, this final scene of unregeneracy ushers in the final stages of Lyndaraxa's ascendancy: established in Almahide's throne, Lyndaraxa has at last completed her theft of Almahide's part, securing the transfer of roles whose prospect had provided the germinal motive for her career of evil. In her last scene, then, Lyndaraxa invests herself with the attributes of both hero and heroine, speaking in Almanzor's voice and wielding Almahide's authority. And, as Lyndaraxa's death symbolises Almanzor's release from error, so it symbolises Almahide's: as soon as Lyndaraxa's body has been carried off, Almahide enters along with Almanzor, prepares for admission to the Christian faith, and divests herself of her old identity by taking the name of Isabella.

At no time, obviously, does Almahide deliberately deceive Boabdelin. Her behaviour does, however, consistently reflect the perplexity and lack of self-knowledge that she (briefly) recognises in her "Silk-worm" soliloquy. Although Boabdelin's gross suspicions are unjust, he misinterprets not unreserved fidelity but an ambiguity of motive so impenetrable that it defeats Almahide herself. For all the injustice of his conclusions, Boabdelin is, ironically, right to suspect the expressions of unruffled devotion with which his wife seeks to soothe him: if his cynical suspicions are exaggerated, so are her idealistic self-vindications. This intricate interplay of self-deception reaches its climax in the final quarrel, where Boabdelin's speeches both reflect his illusions of cuckoldom and define accurately realities which Almahide fails to recognise. Almahide has naïvely cast herself in a stereotyped and conventional Platonic role (such as that of Atossa in William Cartwright's *The Royall Slave*), imagining that she can accommodate both husband and lover in an ideal and harmonious conjunction.[21] Such feats, however, are not for creatures of flesh and blood, and Almahide is of different and more human stuff than are Atossa and her like. As Dryden had already suggested in his portrayals of Acacis and Zempoalla, heroic and villainous characters differ not in the nature of their passions but in their attitudes towards them. Lyndaraxa overshadows Almahide's life as much as Almanzor's; she is the obverse side of the heroic coin.

IV. THE HEROIC WORLD

Love and heroism are chimerical and destructive ideals, bewitching their adherents with infinite dreams but betraying them into impotence and self-destruction. Almanzor aspires to a divine control of destiny and even to the mastery of time itself: learning of Almahide's engagement to Boabdelin, he becomes tantalised by the illusion that fate and time can be reversed by physical constraint, demanding the "book of fate" in order to "tear out the journal" of the betrothal day (I. III. p. 55); in the seduction attempt he revives his war against time, believing that to surrender to the senses is to attain a timeless stasis, to expand a single night to "a whole life" (II. IV. p. 143); and, banished from Almahide's presence, he attempts to inflate an ephemeral kiss into "A day—a year—an age—for ever" (II. V. p. 156). But his assaults on time dwindle at once into obvious futility, and his claims to omnipotence, discredited by two physical defeats (I. I. p. 33; I. V. p. 80), have ultimately to be abandoned in his submission to his father. Moreover, the vanity of his boasts is betrayed by the absurdity of their formulation, which is due to the deficiency not of Dryden's taste but of Almanzor's understanding. An example is provided by the naïve literalisation of metaphor which permits the hero to arrogate control over Abdalla's fortunes:

> If I would kill thee now, thy fate's so low
> That I must stoop 'ere I can give the blow.
> But mine is fix'd so far above thy Crown,
> That all thy men
> Pil'd on thy back can never pull it down. (I. III. p. 58)

Almanzor's fate is exalted—so exalted that Abdalla and his men couldn't touch it even if they all stood on one another's shoulders. Moreover, Almanzor makes no clear distinction between the elevation of his fate and his own physical stature: he must "stoop" in order to reach Abdalla's grovelling destiny. Aware only of the material cravings of his half-formed personality, he can neither form abstract ideas nor distinguish between the self and an outside reality; infant-like, he must trivialise the abstract into the tangible, the non-ego into the ego.

As always, moreover, the divine dreams of passion covertly advance the dreamers' destruction, and Dryden again principally exemplifies the fatality of passion with his characteristic blending of sexuality and death. In Lyndaraxa's great speech of bloodlust (I. III. p. 52), the object of sexual obsession stands revealed as the priestess of death, providing a conjunction of Eros and Thanatos that each character to some degree recreates. In this single speech, Lyndaraxa stamps her personality on both the great ideals of the heroic world: love and honour, death-tainted eroticism and inhumanly destructive heroism, are both hereafter her property. Even Ozmyn experiences the affinity of death and love, foreseeing a coital pleasure in death by Benzayda's sword ("Then, easie Death will slide with pleasure in" [I. IV. p. 69]). Ozmyn's erotic desire for death is ennobled into an altruistic carelessness of life, but in other characters the death wish remains unregenerately sexual. Boabdelin sees death as an inevitable and supremely appropriate price for three days of sexual ecstasy, imaging copulation as an orgasmic spending[22] and draining of life:

> I should not be of love or life bereft;
> All should be spent before; and nothing left. (II. III. p. 118)

Almanzor, similarly, wishes to sleep with Almahide even though he imagines death to be an immediate, inseparable, and, indeed, appropriate consequence; for him, as for Boabdelin, copulation exhausts life;

> No; from my joyes I to my death would run;
> And think the business of my life well done. (II. IV. p. 142)

Almahide too, though without pleasure, sees that coition must be followed
by the final intimacy of shared death:

> If I could yield; (but think not that I will:)
> You and my self, I in revenge, should kill.
> For I should hate us both, when it were done:
> And would not to the shame of life be wonn.   (II. IV. p. 143)

Soon afterwards, as her Platonic defences fail, she finds that her passions leave
her only the alternatives of adultery and suicide (II. IV. pp. 143−4). In their
period of greatest subservience to Lyndaraxa's spirit, then, both Almanzor
and Almahide experience the affinity of love and death, diversely recreating
the conjunction of opposites that is archetypally embodied in the villainess:
heroic love brings not transcendence of the flesh but bondage to mortality.

This bondage is illustrated still more amply in the aftermath of the
seduction attempt. In Lyndaraxa's pageant of death in the Vivarambla both
Boabdelin and Zulema seek to destroy the object of their passion, while
Almahide reaps the fruit of the mistrust that her equivocal sexual behaviour
has sown in her husband's mind: bound to the stake so that "Flames" may
"be condemned to fire" (II. IV. p. 147), carnality to the death which is its
twin, she is brought face to face with the annihilation to which passion tends.
Although Almanzor's strength rescues her from danger, her misguided
ideals immediately renew the peril of imminent death and bring her career of
Platonic make-believe to its dénouement; her code is powerless to avert the
death that it has invited, and she is saved only because her danger is
swallowed up in the doomed, meteoric triumph of her evil *alter ego*.
Almahide is truly rescued only when Lyndaraxa herself falls victim to the
fatal eroticism that she has for so long manipulated: stabbing his mistress and
sharing her death, Abdelmelech brings coition and death to their fullest and
final identification; the force of envenomed passion is spent, and Almahide
and Almanzor are free.

In fact, the characters' apparently boundless dreams themselves become
prisons: inhabiting a world of fantasy, lost in dreams of omnipotence, the
characters insulate themselves with hallucinations and refuse all knowledge
of self and the world. The triumph of fantasy is accentuated by the extensive
pattern of dream and mirage images, whose focal point is the song of the
Zambra dance (I. III. pp. 50−1). The nocturnal emission here celebrated
represents, as King has noted (p. 64), a fulfilment in fantasy of desires which
life itself fails to satisfy; the idyllic vision produced by mundane urges
parallels the god-like dreams produced by the material impulses of passion.
King has not, however, noted the extent to which the song is anticipated
and echoed throughout the play. Abdalla, Almanzor, Abenamar, and
Abdelmelech are all depicted as the prisoners of dream, illusion, or magical
imposture, their captivity emphasised by the images of impotent immobility
that repeatedly accompany those of illusion: Abdalla compares himself to a

dreamer frozen in a terrifying paralysis (I, III. p. 47); Almanzor is "numm'd, and fix'd" by the "Lethargy" of love (I. III. p. 54), and later views love as an enchantment binding the reason (II. III. p. 128); Boabdelin describes love as "a Magick which the Lover tyes" (I. V. p. 82); Almahide, rebuking Almanzor's commitment to "dream", rebukes also his impotence of will (I. V. p. 84); and later, renewing her reproaches, she reworks Abdalla's simile of the dreamer's helpless immobility:

'Tis but the raging Calenture of Love.
Like a distracted Passenger you stand,
And see, in Seas, imaginary Land,
Cool Groves, and Flow'ry Meads, and while you think
To walk, plunge in, and wonder that you sink.   (II. II. p. 114)

Rebuked by the Ghost but obstinately persisting in forbidden courses, Almanzor justifies himself in a deterministic soliloquy, attributing all his actions to the divine puppeteer and concluding that the mind itself is merely an invisible dungeon:

O Heaven, how dark a Riddle's thy Decree,
Which bounds our Wills, yet seems to leave 'em free!
Since thy fore-knowledge cannot be in vain,
Our choice must be what thou did'st first ordain:
Thus, like a Captive in an Isle confin'd,
Man walks at large, a Pris'ner of the Mind:
Wills all his Crimes, while Heav'n th' Indictment draws;
And, pleading guilty, justifies the laws.   (II. IV. p. 141)

Almanzor mistakes his gaoler, but his imprisonment is genuine enough: rejecting reality and retreating to the imagined autonomy of their desires, the passionate dreamers are all "Pris'ners of the Mind", enslaved to the self and insulated within autistic fantasies; Almahide, lost in her "own Webb of thought" (II. I. p. 103), is also a prisoner of the mind, wrapping herself in theatrical make-believe as her fellows wrap themselves in dream. Dreaming and play-acting are, in fact, parallel manifestations of the prevailing spirit of illusion: they meet in the Zambra dance and they have a single patroness in Lyndaraxa, who masters Granada by the purveyance of dreams and the implementation of overtly theatrical designs. The heroic world is Lyndaraxa's kingdom, and her ultimate enthronement over it is fitting. Her kingdom, however, is as imaginary and insubstantial as her final reign. Lost in egocentric fantasies, the Granadines inhabit a counterfeit world of simulacra and fictions; they are marionettes who mistake the tug of their strings for the free motion of the will, their theatrical *mise-en-scène* for a primary and self-sufficient reality. Only with the death of the puppet-mistress and the triumph of Christianity are the survivors released from their prison of art.

6 *Aureng-Zebe*

In the prologue to *Aureng-Zebe* (1675) Dryden shows that he was beginning to feel constrained by the forms that had hitherto satisfied him, and expresses a prophetic admiration for Shakespeare's "Godlike *Romans*".[1] Although the disenchantment of the prologue embraces *Aureng-Zebe* itself, many critics have felt that the play marks a considerable new departure in Dryden's dramaturgy; and, in many ways, it does. Its innovation does not, however, lie in the creation of a new kind of protagonist. Although Aureng-Zebe is different from his predecessors, he is still of the same genus, the differences between him and them being no greater than those between the contrasting heroes of any single romance: *Cleopatra*, for example, affords heroes of both Almanzor's and Aureng-Zebe's type, a choleric Artaban and a patient Ariobarzanes (see Appendix, pp. 166—7). Indeed, Aureng-Zebe is in many ways comparable to the hero of a romance that Dryden had used extensively in his earlier plays: Madeleine de Scudéry's *Le Grand Cyrus*.[2] Aureng-Zebe is "by no strong passion sway'd, / Except his Love" (I. 102—3); Cyrus, similarly, is at one crisis "neither moved with one Passion or other, but keeps a *medium* between both, since he saw his love was not concerned in it, and that was the only thing that could move him either to joy or sorrow" (I. ii. 80[1]). The similarities between Aureng-Zebe and Cyrus are, however, of a fairly broad and general nature. Occasionally, Dryden does borrow a specific incident from Cyrus' career: in refusing to secure his safety and happiness by means of rebellion (II. 21—30), for example, Aureng-Zebe imitates one of Cyrus' greatest feats of self-sacrifice (III. i. 5—7)—though, as usual, Dryden derives the ideal gesture from egocentric calculation. Minute and extended debts to romance seem, however, to be far fewer than in earlier plays, and the reduced debt to the particulars of romance is a symptom of the new course that Dryden was pursuing.

In *Aureng-Zebe* Dryden chiefly breaks from his earlier works by attempting to free his drama from close and parasitic dependence on the ephemera of contemporary literature. Literary allusion remains an important part of his technique, Aureng-Zebe acting the part not only of Cyrus but of Seneca's Hippolytus and Molière's Alceste,[3] but the allusions are now peripheral parts of a largely self-sufficient fabric, enriching the meaning of the drama but no longer acting as its primary vehicle. When Almanzor and Almahide pursue lives of theatrical illusion, they do so by casting themselves in roles from French romance and from Caroline and Orreryan drama, with the result that Dryden creates a conflict between the capacities of his characters and the expectations fostered by the characters of other authors: Almahide's fantasies are intelligible and plausible because we know that such fantasies were purveyed by the works of Cartwright, Davenant, and Orrery, but there is nothing *within the play* to promote and sustain her misconceptions. In *Aureng-Zebe*, as in *The Conquest of Granada*, self-deceiving characters retreat from reality into lives of theatrical illusion, but now Dryden places the sources of illusion within the play itself, making the theatrical fantasy a natural compensation for the characters' weakness and frustration: for the rage of the old at seeing the young usurp their lost strength and beauty; for the inability of the egoist to value or comprehend existences independent of his own; and for the bewilderment of the inflexible perfectionist faced with an obstinately imperfect reality.

I. REBELLION AGAINST TIME AND SLAVERY TO CHANGE

In *Aureng-Zebe*, as in the earlier heroic plays, capricious and mutable mortals seek vainly to elude human imperfection and sublunary change: once again the goals are heroic magnificence, transcendence of time, and the absolute freedom of the gods; but, once again, Dryden dismisses heroic dreams and asserts his characteristic belief in the weakness and volatility of man's nature—a belief that finds its most explicit and familiar formulation in the play's Dedication:

> As I am a Man, I must be changeable: and sometimes the gravest of us all are so, even upon ridiculous accidents. Our minds are perpetually wrought on by the temperament of our Bodies, which makes me suspect: they are nearer alli'd, than either our Philosophers or School-Divines will allow them to be. I have observ'd, says *Montaign*, that when the Body is out of Order, its Companion is seldom at his ease. An ill Dream, or a Cloudy day, has power to change this wretched Creature, who is so proud of a reasonable Soul, and make him think what he thought not yesterday.[4]

None of the ageing characters can come to terms with the passing of time. Nourmahal—old enough to have an adult son and to have married the Emperor in his prime—devotes her entrance speech to illusions of unchanged youth:

> My eyes are still the same, each glance, each grace,
> Keep their first lustre, and maintain their place;
> Not second yet to any other face.   (II. 209–11)

Her rebellion against change continues with her pursuit of Aureng-Zebe. When she declares her passion, she describes the hero as a physical replica of the young Emperor she had once loved, so that her advances to her stepson

become an attempt to reverse time and re-enact her own lost youth. In the
empty, theatrical pretence of her rejuvenation she falls into play-acting of
the most literal kind, assuming the role of Seneca's Phaedra (cf. *Hippolytus*
646–58):

> I am not chang'd; I love my Husband still;
> But love him as he was, when youthful grace,
> And the first down began to shade his face:
> That Image does my Virgin-flames renew,
> And all your Father shines more bright in you.   (IV. 148–52)

Similarly, in seeking to supplant Indamora in Aureng-Zebe's affections she
tries to steal the role of one whom she sees as an embodiment of her former
self:

> Some Angel copi'd, while I slept, each grace,
> And molded ev'ry feature from my face. . . .
> Heav'n did, by me, the outward model build:
> Its inward work, the Soul, with rubbish fill'd. . . .
> The Gods have poorly robb'd my Virgin bloom,
> And what I am, by what I was, o'rcome.   (V. 265–6, 280–1, 284–5)

Nor can the Emperor come to terms with change: he loses himself in
memories of his glorious past (II. 395–405) and pursues in age the youthful
pleasures that he had neglected in his prime (III. 157–65, IV. 340–52); and,
like his wife, he attempts to take over the role of a lover (Aureng-Zebe) who
seems to embody his own young self. Both he and Nourmahal are mocked
by ever-present images of their irrevocable youth, incarnated in alien and
inaccessible identities; attempting to lay claim to their lost selves, they
achieve only an empty, theatrical mimicry that leaves their natures
obstinately unchanged.

Arimant's infatuation with Indamora duplicates and parodies the
Emperor's, for the old Governor is more overtly comic and enervated than
his master and carries theatrical role-stealing to extremes: failing to usurp
Aureng-Zebe's role in love, he instead usurps it in death, when he actually
impersonates the hero (V. 488–98), playing Patroclus to Aureng-Zebe's
Achilles. Indeed, he lives vicariously throughout the play: when he declares
his love to Indamora, she reacts by asserting that his will has passed out of his
control, becoming a mere projection and extension of her own (II. 103–7);
when the Emperor overhears his protestations of love, Indamora only saves
his life by pretending that he was making love on his ruler's behalf (II.
133–7); forced into the unwanted role of surrogate for the Emperor, he is
then, self-defeatingly, forced by love to act as agent for two further rivals
(Aureng-Zebe and Morat [III. 1–71, IV. 218–23]); and, finally, he gains his
only moment of glory in the guise of another.

As in the earlier plays, the flight from time springs from the supremacy of passion, which deludes the characters with prospects of divine freedom even as it binds them to the world of change. In every respect, the lives of the aged are lives of unwitting theatre, of fantasy that must always be frustrated by reality; and the lives of the young, as we shall see, are no less ruled by illusion. The Emperor is most vociferous in his aspirations to divinity and freedom, expressing a libertine contempt for all restraints upon the will (II. 292–5) and regarding passion as the way to apotheosis: "there's a God-like liberty in Love," he declares (II. 295). Similarly, he desires the irresponsible freedom of Epicurus' gods (III. 184–7) and believes himself to be the Creator of his subjects, having in passion a divine prerogative denied to his mortal creatures:

Did he, my Slave, presume to look so high?
That crawling Insect, who from Mud began,
Warm'd by my Beams, and kindl'd into Man?
Durst he, who does but for my pleasure live,
Intrench on Love, my great Prerogative?   (II. 125–9)

The Emperor's aspirations are parodied by those of the ridiculous Arimant, who also asserts the boundlessness of the passions, finds apotheosis in their indulgence, and longs for a libertine existence: "wishes," he tells Indamora when declaring his love, "are not bounded with things possible" (II. 52–3); when praised by the heroine, he becomes "a God" (II. 82); and, when rebuffed, resolves to "live by Sense a glorious Brute" (III. 46). Nourmahal too longs for divine freedom: when she loses herself in erotic fantasy, the dream of sexual abandonment is also one of apotheosis (IV. 98–115); and, in seeking to turn the fantasy into reality, she too abjures the restraints of civilisation, longing for a primitive state of absolute liberty and claiming that "Promiscuous Love is Nature's general Law" (IV. 132).

Her dreams and passions are shared by her son, Morat, who of the young characters most obviously inherits the vices and illusions of the old. He too deifies himself, believing that he is "in Fate's place", dictating "her Decrees" (IV. 179). Similarly, he can see Fate only as the instrument of his desires: Fate, he asserts, decreed that he and Indamora should be lovers; and Fate has reserved for his hand the privilege of killing Aureng-Zebe:

As Heav'n did to your eyes and form Divine,
Submit the Fate of all th' Imperial Line;
So was it order'd by its wise Decree,
That you should find 'em all compris'd in me.   (III. 511–14)

Morat. My Brother too may live.
Indamora.   He may?
Morat.   He must:
I kill'd him not: and a less Fate's unjust.   (V. 37–8)

As always, however, the passions fail to confer divinity. At worst, they bring bondage and death; at best, the caprice anatomised in the Dedication. In their brief moments of sober reflection, both the Emperor and Nourmahal realise that love has enslaved their wills (II. 457—61, III. 372—3). Moreover, the life of passion once more proves to be a life of self-destruction, for love and death again enter into their inevitable and indissoluble conjunction—a conjunction that is reflected in the many images of deathly embraces, and in the images that equate love with war. The play's second speech depicts the Indus and Ganges, "Each . . . winding, as he runs,/ His bloudy arms about his slaughter'd Sons" (I. 15—16); the third reveals that the destructive civil war has been provoked by "curs'd Cabals of Women" (I. 19). These two passages set the scene for what is to come. The rivers' bloody embraces are echoed in Nourmahal's desire to stifle Aureng-Zebe in her arms (III. 336), in her fear that he may lie "in Death's cold arms" (V. 243), in Morat's "Trees, beneath whose arms 'tis death to sleep" (IV. 361), and in Melesinda's "Nor grudge my cold embraces in the Grave" (V. 363). Similarly, the fatal cabals of women are recalled in images that merge or equate love and war: Aureng-Zebe has "cultivated Love with Bloud" (I. 370), and the Emperor regards the element of warfare in love as a potent aphrodisiac:

> *Indamora.* Force never yet a generous Heart did gain:
> We yield on parley, but are storm'd in vain. . . .
> *Emperor.* No; 'tis resistance that inflames desire:
> Sharpens the Darts of Love, and blows his Fire.   (II. 161—2, 165—6)

To the Emperor, similarly, Indamora is a fort to be guarded (IV. 357—8), to Morat "an Empire" for which "none but Kings should fight" (III. 490). And Nourmahal describes her subjugation by love as "A bloudy Conquest" (III. 374), and reveals that her marriage to the Emperor brought him a realm that he had long sought to gain by war (II. 336—7).

Nourmahal experiences the fatal capacities of eroticism most intensely and obsessively, for throughout the play death and coition are linked—even interchangeable—in her mind:

> I take the Omen, let him die by me.
> He stifl'd in my arms shall lose his breath:
> And Life it self shall envious be of Death.   (III. 335—7)

> And why this niceness to that pleasure shown,
> Where Nature sums up all her joys in one;
> Gives all she can, and labouring still to give,
> Makes it so great, we can but taste and live:
> So fills the Senses, that the Soul seems fled,
> And thought it self does, for the time, lie dead?   (IV. 119—24)

I beg my death, if you can Love deny.
> *Offering him a Dagger.*   (IV. 157)

This Cup [of poison], a cure for both our ills has brought:
You need not fear a Philtre in the Draught.   (IV. 162 – 3)

The Drudge had quench'd my flames, and then had di'd.   (V. 250)

When all anachronistic thoughts of *Tristan und Isolde* have been banished, Dryden's own love-death images still permit us to wonder whether the "Philtre" and the poison are as antithetical as they seem. Our doubts are justified at Nourmahal's death by poison, when the burning dissolution of her body becomes in itself an erotic frenzy; her death symbolises and exposes the manner of her life:

I burn, I more than burn; I am all fire: . . .
Ha, ha! how my old Husband crackles there!
Keep him down, keep him down, turn him about:
I know him; he'll but whiz, and strait go out. . . .
See, see! there's *Aureng-Zebe* too takes his part:
But he blows all his fire into my heart.   (V. 640, 647 – 9, 656 – 7)

Instead of quenching her flames and dying (v. 250), Aureng-Zebe appears in Nourmahal's delirium to be feeding the holocaust that destroys her; although she tries to project the deadliness of her passion on to others—even at the end, she refuses to "come near" herself and tries to engulf the Emperor in her flames (v. 642, 645)—she cannot ultimately elude its consequences.

The furnace of Nourmahal's death comes immediately after Melesinda's departure for her "better Nuptials" (v. 619) upon the funeral pyre. For Melesinda, the flames of love and of death are indivisible:

My love was such, it needed no return;
But could, though he suppli'd no fuel, burn.
Rich in it self, like Elemental fire,
Whose pureness does no Aliment require.
In vain you would bereave me of my Lord:
For I will die: die is too base a word;
I'll seek his breast, and kindling by his side,
Adorn'd with flames, I'll mount a glorious Bride.   (v. 627 – 34)

Melesinda's and Nourmahal's deaths are, of course, vastly different, even in the nature of their flames: Melesinda's, as Richard Morton observes,[5] require "no Aliment", whereas Nourmahal's have "constantly to seize for fuel". The contrast, however, is not simply that of the admirable against the base. Melesinda's death is futile, deplored by all who witness it; and, as

Nourmahal's death is marked by delirium, so Melesinda's is marked by illusion, by an inability to recognise that Morat rejected her even in death: "He's mine; and I can lose him now no more," she persuades herself (v. 622). The close juxtaposition of the two deluded deaths by fire implies that the noblest and basest of earthly loves—Platonism and lust, smokeless and demonic flames—are alike the servants of mortality. The loves that come between these extremes share their single goal. Like Nourmahal, Morat had sought divinity in passion; but, in the end, he too is driven by love to death, willingly sustaining a mortal wound in order to see Indamora once again (v. 327). And Arimant, the most pathetic of the would-be gods, is similarly impelled to a fatal consummation of his desires, usurping in death the role that he had failed to usurp in love.

Every death in the play is portrayed as a consummation of lust or love. At the end, only three characters survive: the Emperor, the hero, and the heroine. The Emperor has triumphantly surmounted the passion that destroyed so many of his household, but Aureng-Zebe's triumph is far more equivocal. He can take little credit for the happy ending, since he and Indamora have been reconciled—have, indeed, survived—not because of his inflexible idealism but in spite of it. Nor does the ending promise a future of flawless bliss. Aureng-Zebe's relationship with Indamora has been one of bickering suspicion, of quarrel, reconciliation, and further quarrel, and the ending gives no assurance that the last reconciliation will be any more stable than its predecessors; the ending of *Aureng-Zebe* is as inconclusive as that of *Le Nozze di Figaro*. Aureng-Zebe's career, like that of Nourmahal and her kind, has been one of self-deception and unstable passion. But, whereas the passions that animate Nourmahal burn themselves into extinction, those of Aureng-Zebe reach only an equivocal and precarious quiescence; unlike Lyndaraxa's death, Nourmahal's does not exorcise the illusions of her heroic counterpart.

II. INDAMORA AND AURENG-ZEBE

Like their fellows, the hero and heroine live lives of histrionic self-deception, assuming roles ill suited to the frailties of human nature: whereas the aged claim a divine immutability that is tragically belied by human decay and mortality, the young hero and heroine, less calamitously, profess a heroic idealism that is persistently discredited and defeated by human imperfection. Before looking at the lovers in relation to one another, I would like to consider those occasions on which Indamora is seen apart from Aureng-Zebe, for her character appears in its most interesting light when her conduct is not constrained by the presence of her idealistic and demanding partner.

Indamora's early behaviour does not invite us to expect a Cassandra or Mandana, a heroine of unshakeable and ethereal decorum, since her initial trials neither demand nor elicit moral dignity: beset with the attentions of troublesome, senile lovers, she handles her admirers with a worldly and witty aplomb worthy of Lady Constance or Jacinta, playing upon Arimant's ridiculous ineffectuality with skilful self-assurance and deflating even the more menacing Emperor with a retort of cruel wit:

> *Emperor.* You may be pleas'd your Politiques to spare:
> I'm old enough, and can my self take care.
> *Indamora.* Advice from me was, I confess, too bold:
> Y'are old enough; it may be, Sir, too old.   (II. 193—6).

So designedly comic is Dryden's portrayal of unheroic love that Indamora's oppressor becomes at one point a twin to—of all people—Woodly in Shadwell's *Epsom-Wells*:

> *Emperor.* I, with less pain, a Prostitute could bear,
> Than the shrill sound of Virtue, virtue hear.   (II. 261—2)

> *Woodly.* A Pox on her troublesom Vertue, would to Heaven she were a Whore, I should know then what to do with her.[6]

And, as we shall see, Indamora's heroic lover is similarly to be drawn by allusion into the realms of comedy.

Later and more exacting trials fail to add to Indamora's dignity, and she never attains the celestial perfection of her namesake, the heroine of Davenant's Platonic masque *The Temple of Love*. On two occasions she is faced in her lover's absence with an opportunity for heroism, and on both occasions heroism (fortunately) eludes her. She first enters the sphere of potentially heroic and tragic experience when Morat offers her the choice between betraying Aureng-Zebe's love and sacrificing his life, but her initial response to her new trial gives no hint of incipient sublimity:

> If, Sir, I seem not discompos'd with rage,
> Feed not your fancy with a false presage.
> Farther to press your Courtship is but vain:
> A cold refusal carries more disdain.
> Unsetled Virtue stormy may appear;
> Honour, like mine, serenely is severe.
> To scorn your person, and reject your Crown,
> Disorder not my face into a frown.   *Turns from him.*
>
> (III. 515—22)

The ponderous manipulation and elucidation of facial expression is self-defeating, destructive of the impression that Indamora wishes to create, for she too patently wants to have the best of two worlds, to cultivate an unfrowning, Olympian serenity while pedantically ensuring that Morat feels the full voltage of the non-existent frown; her serene rejection of her unwanted lover is not an instinctive display of heroic composure but a carefully contrived façade. And the remainder of the encounter reveals a clear disparity between heroic façade and human nature: as Morat departs to order Aureng-Zebe's death, Indamora continues her pose of inflexible rectitude, declaring, "With my own death I would his life redeem; / But, less than Honour, both our Lives esteem" (III. 528–9); but the heroic mood instantly gives way to flustered recognition of the cost of intransigence, and Indamora decides that Morat must not leave "in this fury" (III. 531). And so she undertakes the very course that she has just proudly repudiated, gaining her lover a reprieve by flattering Morat's hopes (IV. 530–5).[7]

The disparity between Indamora's heroic boasts and human capacities reappears in the fifth act, where the emptiness of her death-before-dishonour stand becomes still more obvious. Despite her earlier protestations, she displays remarkable cowardice when her life is finally in danger (V. 205–325):[8] when the time for heroism presents itself, "Without my *Aureng-Zebe* I cannot live" (III. 449) dwindles into "Without my *Aureng-Zebe* I *would* not live" (V. 321; second italics added), and she runs timorously from Nourmahal's dagger. Although she does eventually steel herself to die, her renewed resolution only creates another unideal complication, for the courage wanting at the loss of Aureng-Zebe is ultimately aroused by the loss of Morat. Indeed, Indamora's final encounter with Morat throws the most revealing light on the complex frailties of her character—frailties that she must disguise and suppress when the presence of her lover forces her to seek conformity with his unrealistic expectations.

As Dryden implies in the play's Dedication (Summers, IV. 85), Morat's death scene is modelled on that of the King of Assyria in *Le Grand Cyrus* (IX. i. 6–7). But, whereas Mandana treats Cyrus' rival only with a decorous compassion, Indamora permits herself a quite surprising warmth:

> *Morat.* In sign that I die yours, reward my love,
> And seal my Pasport to the Bless'd above.
> > *Kissing her hand.*
> *Indamora.* Oh stay; or take me with you when you go:
> There's nothing now worth living for below. . . .
> > Oh dismal day!
> Fate, thou hast ravish'd my last hope away.   (V. 429–32, 437–8)

This is a subtle and realistic touch. Aureng-Zebe is believed dead; Morat, whom Indamora has successfully struggled to reform, has just saved her life and now lies dying in her arms; and, in her imagined bereavement, she feels a sudden access of emotion for the man with whose spiritual state she has been so closely involved. There is nothing cynical or mocking in Dryden's treatment of her: Indamora's is, he tells us, "*a practicable Virtue, mix'd with the frailties and imperfections of humane life*" (Summers, IV. 85), and her reaction is eminently human and worthy of sympathy. But, after seeing her in this light, we cannot wholly assent to the strait-laced, oversimplified professions of fidelity with which she seeks to soothe the outraged Aureng-Zebe:

Leave off your forc'd respect
And show your rage in its most furious form:
I'm arm'd with innocence to brave the Storm. . . .
Your alter'd Brother di'd in my defence.
Those tears you saw, that tenderness I show'd,
Were just effects of grief and gratitude.   (v. 461–3, 507–9)

Here a romance heroine is speaking, uttering superficial sentiments that fail to represent the complex, imperfect, but attractive behaviour we have just witnessed. As the play draws to its close, the hero's inflexible, inhuman demands force Indamora to retreat once more into the false confinement of romance stereotype.

For all the rigidity of his demands, Aureng-Zebe is far more extensively flawed than his mistress, outdoing her both in heroic play-acting and human imperfection. He is another of Dryden's naïve idealists, blind to his own frailties but always ready to magnify and deplore the slightest hint of frailty in others. His naïveté, self-righteousness, and manifest imperfection are most elaborately demonstrated in his three quarrels with Indamora, and I shall begin by discussing these, since they will enable me at once to commence examination of the hero and complete that of the heroine, studying her conduct in those scenes when she is under observation by her lover; for the three quarrels are the only three occasions in the play on which the lovers appear together.

When Aureng-Zebe returns from battle in the first act, he finds Indamora reserved and discouraging—because, we know, the Emperor has threatened to kill both lovers should his own passion for the heroine be disclosed or thwarted (I. 284–93). But for Aureng-Zebe there is only one possible explanation of his mistress's demeanour: she has betrayed him. Unlike Indamora, he does not appreciate the intricacy of the problems posed by real life: the slightest departure from his simple, ideal preconceptions can only indicate total depravity, and a single, trivial word—"Perhaps" (I. 384–5)— is sufficient to inspire a frenzy of vituperative jealousy. His excessive suspicion is emphasised and burlesqued by the hyperbole of his reaction, by his absurdly contrived paradoxes (the lines read like a parody of the Hastings Elegy), and by the incongruous glibness of the verse that clothes the mountainous utterances:

Nature her self is chang'd to punish me:
Virtue turn'd Vice, and Faith Inconstancy.   (I. 390–1)

If a mistress frowns, the universe totters; Aureng-Zebe rivals Morat in the egocentricity of his world-picture.

His suspicion of Indamora reappears in Act IV, after he learns that she has saved his life by playing on Morat's infatuation with her. Once again he fails to understand the unheroic compromises enforced by the dilemmas of mundane existence, and once again he can only conclude that Indamora is false. So violent is his suspicion that he can pervert the most innocent of her protestations into sure tokens of guilt, believing the mere fact that she enquires the name of her alleged lover to be conclusively damning:

> *Indamora.* Who told you this?
> *Aureng-Zebe.*   Are you so lost to shame?
> *Morat,. Morat, Morat:* You love the name
> So well, your ev'ry question ends in that;
> You force me still to answer you, *Morat.*   (IV. 433−6)

His mistrust reaches the height of arrogance when, still convinced of Indamora's guilt, he offers to believe her if she will deceitfully profess her innocence:

> Speak; answer. I would fain yet think you true:
> Lie; and I'll not believe my self, but you.
> Tell me you love; I'll pardon the deceit,
> And, to be fool'd, my self assist the cheat.   (IV. 465−8)

This is unsurpassable egocentricity. For Aureng-Zebe, Indamora's depravity is beyond doubt, and any future show of innocence must come not from her own, negligible, resources but from his: her innocence is henceforth to be on loan from him. In itself, this outburst seriously compromises Aureng-Zebe's claim to be regarded as an ideal and exemplary hero, and his claim is compromised still more when we consider the source of the speech: in this quarrel Dryden echoes the fourth act quarrel between Alceste and Célimène in Molière's *Le Misanthrope*,[9] and here the borrowing is particularly close, for in offering to deceive himself into trust Aureng-Zebe does what Alceste has done before him:

> Efforcez-vous ici de paroître fidèle,
> Et je m'efforcerai, moi, de vous croire telle.   (IV. iii. 1389−90)

The allusion is illuminating, for Aureng-Zebe *is* very like Alceste: both are inflexible idealists who cannot understand the compromises exacted by an obstinately unideal reality; but, in one important respect, Aureng-Zebe is even more limited than Alceste, for his rigid self-righteousness blinds him not only to the ethical muddles of life but to the grave flaws of his own character.[10]

The chief flaw revealed in this quarrel and its successor is an explosive irrationality wholly incompatible with Aureng-Zebe's pose of temperate virtue. His irrationality is clearly evident in his suspicion, which distorts and perverts the most innocent of Indamora's words; but it is also, more interestingly, evident in his conversion from suspicion to trust, for the conversion, just though it is, is wholly illogical in character, prompted by causes as arbitrary as the ill dream and cloudy day of the Dedication. When Aureng-Zebe repeats his offer to believe Indamora's lies, she explodes in rage and indignation; her reasoning and explanation have merely provided him with fresh fuel for suspicion, but now the mere fact of her rage effects the transformation that all her explanations have failed to secure, Aureng-Zebe changing his mind not because the truth is revealed to him—the crucial speech is, in fact, a pack of lies—but merely because he has lost the initiative in the quarrel:

> *Indamora.* I'm not concern'd to have my truth believ'd.
> You would be cozin'd! would assist the cheat!
> But I'm too plain to joyn in the deceit:
> I'm pleas'd you think me false——
> And, whatsoe'r my Letter did pretend,
> I made this meeting for no other end.
> *Aureng-Zebe.* Kill me not quite, with this indifference:
> When you are guiltless, boast not an offence.   (IV. 474–81)

Ironically, Aureng-Zebe only starts to accept Indamora's innocence when she falsely asserts her guilt; he trusts her only when she begins to lie.

A fresh bout of suspicion follows, but it is finally quenched, just as irrationally, by a still more intimidating speech from Indamora:

> *Indamora.* Now you shall know what cause you have to rage;
> But to increase your fury, not asswage:
> I found the way your Brother's heart to move,
> Yet promis'd not the least return of Love.
> His Pride, and Brutal fierceness I abhor;
> But scorn your mean suspitions of me more.
> I ow'd my Honour and my Fame this care:
> Know what your folly lost you, and despair.
> > *Turning from him.*
> *Aureng-Zebe.* Too cruelly your innocence you tell
> Show Heav'n, and damn me to the pit of Hell.
> Now I believe you.   (IV. 501–11)

Two lines of Indamora's speech are devoted to explanation of her actions; six to scornful rejection of Aureng-Zebe. The scorn is clearly what persuades him, since it is the only feature that distinguishes this explanation from those he had disbelieved or perverted; for there is no new proof or corroboration to make this new account more credible than its predecessors. Submissive explanations are met with scorn, scornful explanations with submission. And the submissive explanations were the true ones. Here, once more, Indamora browbeats Aureng-Zebe into docility with a speech that is less than veracious: that she promised not the least return of love is more true in letter than in spirit, since she did "flatter" Morat's hopes (III. 554), and her eyes carried the hints that she feared to put into words (III. 537–9); her account is true only by a technicality.[11] The dispute is thus resolved not by the force of reason but by that of unthinking passion, and the two speeches that win Aureng-Zebe's assent are the two that least deserve it.

The impulsive, unthinking nature of the hero's conversion is startlingly confirmed by the wild outburst of lust that motivates his decisive declaration of love. Here the mask of amorous idealism well and truly slips, and Aureng-Zebe reveals a spontaneous, instinctual self wholly at odds with the pose of romance perfection that he habitually assumes, for his orgasmic ravings would have appalled not only Cyrus but any of Cyrus' less principled but nevertheless decorous rivals:

> Love mounts, and rowls about my stormy mind,
> Like Fire, that's born by a tempestuous Wind.
> Oh, I could stifle you, with eager haste!
> Devour your kisses with my hungry taste!
> Rush on you! eat you! . . .
> Invade you, till my conscious Limbs presage
> Torrents of joy, which all their banks o'rflow!   (IV. 533–7, 540–1)

Indeed, this speech suggests that Aureng-Zebe's true affinities may be less with Cyrus than with Nourmahal: his fire imagery anticipates the blazing lust of her death, and his desire to stifle and eat Indamora echoes the excesses of her voracious and destructive passion.[12] To be sure, the spirit of Scudéry is soon reinstated; but, after the vivid realities of doubt and lust, the trite catchphrases of heroic love reborn seem empty and histrionic:

> *Indamora.* My life!
> *Aureng-Zebe.*   My Soul!
> *Indamora.*   My all that Heav'n can give!
> Death's life with you; without you, death to live.   (IV. 547–8)

Should we doubt the intentional banality of these effusions, we have only to consider subsequent events: Indamora's cowardice shows that life without Aureng-Zebe is still life, and death with him still death.[13]

Indamora has not betrayed Aureng-Zebe, and she deserves his love and respect. But the renewal of trust, deserved as it is, is achieved by a devious pattern of irrationality and misunderstanding in which Dryden shows a psychological subtlety for which he has received too little credit. And he here departs markedly from the unimaginative conventions of romance, wherein the hero's jealousy is regularly cured by a simple process of rational explanation. For example, Cyrus catches sight of Mandana, remains unseen himself, sees her smile, and is outraged, because he thinks that she thinks he is dead (x. iii. 192–3). Despair and jeremiads follow. But jealousy is cured by sweet reason when Cyrus discovers that Mandana knew him to be alive, and was in fact smiling through joy at his survival (x. iii. 218). Dryden's characters are far less tractable, and far truer to life.[14]

The fifth act quarrel follows lines very similar to those of its predecessor. Seeing Indamora comfort and mourn the dying Morat, Aureng-Zebe immediately assumes that he has been rejected and once more falls into fierce jealousy, rejecting all his mistress's careful and lengthy self-justifications (v. 461–545). Again, however, Indamora's anger does in an instant what all her painstaking explanations had failed to do: as soon as she takes the initiative in the quarrel by breaking off the liaison, she silences her lover's tirades of repudiation, leaving him deflated if not yet converted (v. 547–51). Once again, moreover, Dryden emphasises the irrationality of the change by linking it to an access of sexual desire that recalls the lusts of the baser characters. In the previous quarrel, Aureng-Zebe had wished both to mistrust Indamora and to favour her with an illusory innocence of his own creation (iv. 465–73); here, somewhat similarly, he wishes to copulate with her in a state of unreasoning appetite that will extinguish knowledge of her baseness:

> Now you distract me more: shall then the day,
> Which views my Triumph, see our love's decay? . . .
> What though I am not lov'd?
> Reason's nice taste does our delights destroy:
> Brutes are more bless'd, who grosly feed on joy.   (v. 550–1, 554–6)

All that Indamora has to do to recover his trust, however, is to stride off the stage (v. 563): faced with this overwhelming argument, Aureng-Zebe can only conclude that "She's guiltless" (v. 566). Once again, therefore, the process of conversion is by no means a process of reason. And once again Aureng-Zebe's renewed trust is at the same time merited and inaccurate: Indamora's intense grief for Morat is one of the play's most subtle surprises, and its tones exceed those of mere friendship; her conduct was understandable and venial, but it is ill represented by the romance clichés that Aureng-Zebe ultimately accepts for the truth. When he renews his faith in his mistress, he renews his faith in an idealised fiction that has little to do with the real human being.

Aureng-Zebe quarrels with Indamora every time that he meets her, and the quarrels reveal much that is to his discredit. His misguided perfectionism leads to cruel and intolerant misinterpretation of his mistress's motives, and to an inability to recognise the intricacy of the problems posed by a baffling and imperfect world. Yet he himself conspicuously fails to embody the ideal, revealing himself as an erratic, irrational, and even sensual character. In both quarrels he moves from suspicion to trust in a wholly arbitrary fashion, and in both the change of attitude is linked with a bout of lust that recalls the passions of Nourmahal. Play-acting is not confined to the aged and base: in attempting to steal the identities of their younger counterparts, the Emperor, Nourmahal, and Arimant are most obviously assuming false, theatrical roles from which they are disqualified by nature; but Aureng-Zebe, capricious and even lustful in his spontaneous moments, is just as unfitted for the roles of ideal lover and inflexible hero that he self-consciously tries to sustain. From the beginning of the play to the end, his life is a life of theatre, dedicated to the cultivation of simple, conventional roles that in no way answer to the complex frailties of his character.

The contrast between self-conscious heroism and spontaneous imperfection first appears at the end of Act I. When Arimant orders the arrest of Indamora, Aureng-Zebe leaps forward to "rescue her, or die" (I. 450), only to be stopped in his tracks by her reproaches. Here we can admire neither Aureng-Zebe's instinctive virtue—his instinct is to rebel, and someone else has to do his thinking for him—nor his successful conquest of natural impulse, for the change is too facile, too exclusively an attempt to cut a fine figure in the world, to command respect: Indamora's admonishment appeals not to Aureng-Zebe's moral sense—the intrinsic immorality of rebellion is not mentioned—but to his eagerness for praise and his interests as a lover, and his reply confirms that these are indeed his sole concerns:

> *Indamora.* Hold, my dear Love! if so much pow'r there lies,
> As once you own'd, in *Indamora's* Eyes,
> Lose not the Honour you have early wonn;
> But stand the blameless pattern of a Son.
> My love your claim inviolate secures:
> 'Tis writ in Fate, I can be onely yours.
> My suff'rings for you make your heart my due:
> Be worthy me, as I am worthy you. . . .
>   *Aureng-Zebe.* I to a Son's and Lover's praise aspire:
> And must fulfil the parts which both require.   (I. 453–60, 465–6)

The hero quite explicitly adjusts his natural behaviour to fit the requirements of an externally formulated role; indeed, by speaking of the "parts" that he is to fulfil he inadvertently characterises his chosen roles in theatrical terms.[15] From the very start, then, we are shown a disparity between Aureng-Zebe's spontaneous impulses and the part which he endeavours to act: when Arimant seizes Indamora, the hero responds as any normal human being would, becoming aggressive; but, when Indamora reminds him of the role he is meant to be sustaining, he hastily represses natural impulse, assuming the guise of the ideal son. He does attempt to slur over the gap between performance and pretension, asserting that his "Virtue was surpris'd into a

Crime" (I. 462), but this excuse provides no real extenuation since the speciously personified process does not, in fact, describe an intelligible psychological reaction: like Hobbes's "*round Quadrangle*" (*Lev.* I. v. p. 113), this is a vacant verbal formula, answering to no reality because it involves a contradiction; for virtue cannot without absurdity be said to commit a crime. By making his virtue the subject of the guilty predicate, Aureng-Zebe provides not self-justification but syntactic legerdemain: his virtue was not, the syntax suggests, a blatant second thought; it was immanent even in his indiscretion.

The irony of this episode is oblique, raising doubts about the hero's conduct but not inviting downright disapprobation: he does the right thing, but does not seem to do it in quite the right manner. Our doubts are at this point hesitant and tentative, but they are to be increasingly confirmed as the play proceeds. At the beginning of Act II, for example, Aureng-Zebe reveals a clear contrast between pretension and motive. Hearing of his wrongs, the army rallies to his support, offering to redress his grievances by force. At first, Aureng-Zebe does all that is expected of an ideal hero: refusing the conspirators' aid, he repudiates rebellion in an exemplary and self-sacrificing speech. But then, characteristically, Dryden adds a human touch to the display of flawless idealism, for Aureng-Zebe adds, in an aside, the view that his interests can be satisfactorily served by loyalty:

> Let them who truly would appear my friends,
> Employ their Swords, like mine, for noble ends.
> No more: remember you have bravely done:
> Shall Treason end, what Loyalty begun?
> I own no wrongs; some grievance I confess,
> But Kings, like Gods, at their own time redress.
> (*Aside*) Yet, some becoming boldness I may use:
> I've well deserv'd, nor will he now refuse.
> I'll strike my Fortunes with him at a heat:
> And give him not the leisure to forget.   (II. 21−30)

Kings do not, after all, "at their own time redress" (l. 26), for Aureng-Zebe plans to dun his father without delay, "And give him not the leisure to forget" (l. 30); the private intention flatly contradicts the public boast.

In this incident Dryden reverts to his old practice of borrowing and modifying romance material, and as usual the function of the modification is to transform the ideal into the human. After Cyrus has been unjustly imprisoned and sentenced to death by Ciaxares, the army rebels in order to save him (III. i. 5−6); like Aureng-Zebe, Cyrus refuses to accept the rebels' aid, but unlike Aureng-Zebe he permits himself no calculation concerning personal advantage, urging the troops to remember "that reverend respect" which they owe unto their king (III. i. 7), threatening to resist their rebellion with his own sword, and vowing to kill himself should they continue to seek his safety by sinful means. Predictably, Cyrus' exemplary behaviour impresses Ciaxares and brings about a reconciliation (III. i. 7–10), with the result that the hero has served his own ends without planning to do so; Aureng-Zebe, by contrast, accompanies his idealistic actions with careful calculations about personal gain, and gets his calculations wrong. There is, of course, nothing reprehensible about his desire to secure his own just deserts; but there is a clear disparity between his heroic professions and human motives.

The disparity continues in the third act. By the end of the second, Aureng-Zebe's plans have proved to be naïvely over-optimistic, for his virtue has not met with an automatic and instantaneous reward, he has been supplanted in the Emperor's favour by Morat, and he is in grave danger of death. Nevertheless, in Act III he confronts his newly elevated brother with serene indifference, claiming to prefer his own unrewarded innocence to Morat's prosperous guilt:

> With all th'assurance Innocence can bring,
> Fearless without, because secure within,
> Arm'd with my courage, unconcern'd I see
> This pomp; a shame to you, a pride to me.
> Shame is but where with wickedness 'tis joyn'd;
> And while no baseness in this breast I find,
> I have not lost the birth-right of my mind.   (III. 202–8)

He then proposes to Morat that they join in an alliance to secure their father from all future danger, ostentatiously drawing attention to the disinterestedness of his proposals:

> If Acts like mine,
> So far from int'rest, profit, or design,
> Can show my heart, by those I would be known.   (III. 244–6)

This is all very impressive. But the audience knows better. Aureng-Zebe's private reaction to Morat's elevation had not been indifference to the triumph of vice and contentment with the birthright of innocence; on the contrary, he had been volubly piqued at the unprofitability of virtue:

> How vain is Virtue which directs our ways
> Through certain danger to uncertain praise!
> Barren, and aery name! thee Fortune flies. . . .
> Virtue is nice to take what's not her own;
> And, while she long consults, the Prize is gone.
>
>   (II. 502–4, 512–13)

Similarly, his "Acts . . . / So far from int'rest, profit, or design" are, in fact, nothing of the kind: they are part of a stratagem to save his life:

> I know my fortune in extremes does lie:
> The Sons of *Indostan* must Reign, or die.
> That desperate hazard Courage does create,
> As he plays frankly, who has least Estate; . . .
> I neither would Usurp, nor tamely die. . . .
> Somewhat I have resolv'd ——
> *Morat*, perhaps, has Honour in his breast:
> And, in extremes, bold Counsels are the best.
> Like Emp'ric Remedies, they last are tri'd;
> And by th'event condemn'd, or justifi'd.
>
> (II. 538—41, 547, 550—4)

What Aureng-Zebe proposes here is pragmatic improvisation in a desperate attempt to save his life, and the intentions and spirit of this speech give a very hollow ring to the high-minded sententiousness of his subsequent encounter with the Emperor and Morat. His concern for his safety and legitimate interests is in no way discreditable; what is becoming increasingly discreditable is his pious pretence to an idealism that he simply does not possess.

His heroic make-believe becomes still more blatantly false in the fourth act. At the beginning of that act, we find him awaiting execution, anatomising his fear of death and pondering the music that has incongruously been provided for him (IV. 1—8). As soon as Nourmahal enters, however, he decides that the occasion calls for a show of Stoicism. When, therefore, she explains her provision of the music (IV. 9—14), he brazenly asserts that he did not even hear it, having been lost in contemplative fortitude. The second claim is somewhat exaggerated, the first a downright lie:

> I ask not for what end your Pomp's design'd;
> Whether t'insult, or to compose my mind:
> *I mark'd it not;*
> But, knowing Death would soon th'Assault begin,
> Stood firm collected in my Strength within:
> To guard that breach did all my Forces guide,
> *And left unmann'd the quiet Senses side.* (IV. 15—21; italics added)

This piece of flagrant pretence is soon followed by play-acting of the most obvious and literal kind. Nourmahal, sustained by histrionic illusions of youth, courts her stepson in a fittingly theatrical manner, repeating the words of Seneca's Phaedra; but, in doing so, she is only following Aureng-Zebe's lead, for he has already addressed her with the words of Seneca's Hippolytus (IV. 127—30; *Hippolytus* 671—85). Hero and villainess, Virtue

and Vice, here occupy the same theatrical realm. Aureng-Zebe's play-acting
continues at the end of the act, when he reproaches Indamora with the words
of Molière's Alceste. His theatrical standing has, however, diminished very
rapidly, for he is no longer the principled idealist of tragedy but the obstinate
precisian of comedy.

His cultivation of the false façade continues to the end. When he sees
Indamora nursing Morat and concludes that she is false, his immediate
impulse is to hide his true feelings behind an "outward show":

> Thou shalt not break yet heart, nor shall she know
> My inward torments, by my outward show;
> To let her see my weakness were too base;
> Dissembled Quiet sit upon my face: . . .
> The specious Tow'r no ruine shall disclose,
> Till down, at once, the mighty Fabrick goes.   (v. 419–22, 427–8)

The nature of the man, however, is too weak to sustain the part of the hero,
and austere resolution soon gives way to comic petulance. Nevertheless,
when his jealousy has driven Indamora away and seemingly alienated her for
ever, he once more opts for a show of inflexibility. As soon as Indamora has
left, he formulates the response required of heroic natures: "Great Souls long
struggle ere they own a crime," he declares (v. 569). Immediately, however,
we see the disparity between the formula and the man:

> I'll call her now; sure, if she loves, she'll stay;
> Linger at least, or not go far away.
> > *Looks to the door, and returns.*   (v. 571–2)

The "struggle" of Aureng-Zebe's soul is brief indeed, and the second line
reveals not a sternly unbending hero but an adolescent pathetically eager for
the least sign of favour. Nevertheless, he remains hampered by his code,
repenting his "foolish pride" (v. 574) but lacking the resolution or humility
to initiate a reconciliation. He lacks, in fact, the resolution to leave the
theatrical stage which is both the locale and the symbol of his existence: he
goes to the limits of the stage set and looks out of the door—but then he
comes back, remaining trapped in his theatrical world.

The quarrel is patched up not by Aureng-Zebe, who is thunderstruck and
bereft of ideas, but by the Emperor, who leads Indamora back and resigns
her to his son, creating an ending utterly different from the standard endings
of romance: when Cyrus and his like at last gain their mistresses' hands, they
have negotiated an immense obstacle course designed to demonstrate their
conformity to a rigidly ideal code of heroic and amorous practice; Aureng-
Zebe, by contrast, is united with Indamora *despite* his code of idealism, for his
unrealistic perfectionism has turned every meeting with her into a quarrel,
led to a serious estrangement, and left him proudly impotent, unable to find

any means to undo the damage that he has caused. His marriage does not show virtue rewarded but cantankerousness unpunished—and, I suspect, unconquered.

Throughout the play, then, Aureng-Zebe assumes idealistic poses that both miscalculate the intricacies of life and ignore the weaknesses of his own nature. These weaknesses remain to be considered.

Like all Dryden's fake paragons, Aureng-Zebe is a character of unruly and indomitable appetite. He aspires "to a Son's and Lover's praise" (I. 465), yet his conduct as a son is repeatedly allayed with pragmatic and worldly calculation, and his conduct as a lover is disconcertingly similar to that of Nourmahal: his inflexible romantic idealism shares with her lust the capacity to consume and destroy its object; and, when the mask of idealism slips, the fiery and convulsive lusts that he expresses anticipate the fiery convulsions of her final ravings.

The destructive capacities of Aureng-Zebe's love appear very early in the play. In his second speech to Indamora he claims that he has "cultivated Love with Bloud" (I. 370), and the love–death image soon acquires an ominous appropriateness. When Indamora, fearing for her lover's life, refuses to explain the reasons for her reserve, Aureng-Zebe urges her to reveal her secret, accepting and even rejoicing in the possibility that disclosure may destroy them both. As Nourmahal equates copulation with death (IV. 119–24), so Aureng-Zebe equates death with copulation:

Speak, Madam, by (if that be yet an Oath)
Your Love, I'm pleas'd we should be ruin'd both.
Both is a sound of joy.
In Death's dark Bow'rs our Bridals we will keep:
And his cold hand
Shall draw the Curtain when we go to sleep.　　(I. 424–9)

This first quarrel sets a pattern which the two later quarrels are to follow, since in both quarrels Aureng-Zebe's grievance is that Indamora has saved one of their lives by unheroic compromise: in Act IV he rages at her for not permitting him to die with joy and honour, and in Act V berates her for daring to survive his reported death (V. 513–15). The Act V quarrel thus creates an absurd paradox: had Aureng-Zebe returned from reputed death to find that Indamora had needlessly thrown away her life, he would have found a mistress eminently worthy of his love; but the fact that she has, like him, survived renders her contemptible. Alive, she is beneath consideration; dead, she would have made an excellent wife. This paradox demonstrates the distance between the hero's love code and the realities of life: had his code been satisfied, neither he nor his mistress would have been alive at the end of the play, for both owe their lives to her unheroic weakness; Aureng-Zebe's love, like that of his fellows, is one that naturally demands fruition in death, and had his demands been met the play would have ended with the same tragic misunderstanding as that which concludes *Romeo and Juliet*.

The fatal potential of the hero's love is emphasised by the organisation of the final act, which stresses the kinship between his passion and the lethal desires of his more tragic associates. The finale of the play consists of a sequence of love-deaths, with fatal passion claiming its successive victims: Morat receives his mortal wound, Arimant's death is announced, Melesinda departs for her self-immolation, and Nourmahal's lusts burn themselves into extinction. Within this sequence, placed between Morat's death and Melesinda's, comes Aureng-Zebe's quarrel with Indamora, provoked by her failure to follow the code soon to be upheld by Melesinda. The quarrel is placed fittingly in the final sequence, a love-death *manqué* among accomplished love-deaths, and its placing lays strong emphasis on the hero's want of credit for the happy ending: not only do Indamora and Aureng-Zebe find reconciliation and marriage in spite of Aureng-Zebe's hindrance; their very survival owes nothing to his efforts, for, had his idealistic expectations been indulged, both he and his mistress would have figured in the pageant of fatal love which they interrupt. The play demonstrates not the glory but the bankruptcy of romance idealism.

Aureng-Zebe's conduct as a son is no less human and imperfect than his conduct as a lover, for, despite his high-minded protestations, he shares with his less pretentious fellows an unremitting, and wholly natural, concern with self-interest. Solyman prepares us very early in the play for the universal and often disingenuous pursuit of gain:

> The little Courtiers, who ne'r come to know
> The depth of Factions, as in Mazes go,
> Where Int'rests meet and cross so oft, that they
> With too much care are wilder'd in their way.   (I. 63—6)

Dryden is at first careful to create circumstances in which there is an unavoidable coincidence between Aureng-Zebe's virtue and interest: he is not the eldest son, assured of the succession under all eventualities and free to act disinterestedly; instead, he is a younger son, doomed by custom to die with his father but elevated by virtue to the succession. Before his entrance, indeed, his inducements to virtue are heavily emphasised:

> *Solyman.* Two vast Rewards may well his courage move,
> A Parent's Blessing, and a Mistris Love.
> If he succeed, his recompence, we hear,
> Must be the Captive Queen of *Cassimere*.   (I. 110—13)

Arimant still more emphatically prepares us for a hero keenly aware of his own interests, since he not only reveals that Aureng-Zebe has a reputation for ambition but concedes its truth, justifying ambition as *prudent self-interest*; significantly, moreover, he removes the hero's quest for fame from the realms of romance idealism, treating this too as a species of self-interest and equating it with the hope for solid recompense:

> He aims at Fame, but Fame from serving you.
> 'Tis said, Ambition in his breast does rage:
> Who would not be the *Hero* of an Age?
> All grant him prudent: prudence interest weighs,
> And interest bids him seek your love and praise.
> I know you grateful; When he march'd from hence,
> You bad him hope an ample recompence:
> He conquer'd in that hope; and from your hands,
> His Love, the precious pledge he left, demands.   (I. 220—8)

The pursuit of glory and the pursuit of tangible reward are comparable expressions of man's worldly self-concern, and Aureng-Zebe is to be happy only when he can combine both modes of expression; indeed, as we have seen, his proud choice of martyred glory repeatedly dwindles into the sneaking hope that glory will bring profit in its train. He does not exalt the self by transcending its frailer desires, as do Corneille's Auguste, Sophonisbe, and their fellows; he is, in fact, not sublimely but mundanely egocentric.

Solyman's and Arimant's assessments of Aureng-Zebe do not encourage us to expect a character animated by a selfless love of virtue. Nor do we find one. As soon as Aureng-Zebe meets in the Emperor's evasiveness the first obstacle to his ambitions, he expresses marked chagrin at the fact that his exertions have brought him only the unprofitable honour of filial virtue:

> Why did my Arms in Battel prosp'rous prove,
> To gain the barren praise of Filial love?   (I. 348—9)

His desire to profit by virtue continues in Act II. For all the impressive self-denial with which he dissuades his supporters from rebellion, he in reality believes that loyalty will advance his interests with perfect adequacy (II. 21—30); despite initial setbacks, he still thinks that virtue is guaranteed to reap profit: "I've well deserv'd, nor will he now refuse" (II. 28), he argues to himself. And, when he discovers that virtue really may be its own sole reward, his mortification is not that of a man who loves righteousness for itself:

> How vain is Virtue which directs our ways
> Through certain danger to uncertain praise!
> Barren, and aery name! thee Fortune flies;
> With thy lean Train, the Pious and the Wise.
> Heav'n takes thee at thy word, without regard;
> And lets thee poorly be thy own reward.
> The World is made for the bold impious man;

Who stops at nothing, seizes all he can.
Justice to merit does weak aid afford;
She trusts her Ballance, and neglects her Sword.
Virtue is nice to take what's not her own;
And, while she long consults, the Prize is gone.   (II. 502—13)

The "lean Train, the Pious and the Wise" betrays an attitude similar to that of Zulema's "Vertue . . . with her lean holy face" (*CG* I. II. p. 43), and Aureng-Zebe's palpable regret at his "nice" scruples over taking another's property is extremely revealing. In fact, he continues to reject rebellion not out of horror for the act itself but, once more, out of a concern to preserve his name.

The covert vein of self-interest continues in Act III, where Aureng-Zebe attempts to secure his safety with acts misleadingly advertised as being without "int'rest, profit, or design" (III. 245). This stratagem to make virtue profitable, however, is no more successful than its predecessors, and in Act IV Aureng-Zebe loses all faith in the utility of virtue and, with it, all desire for continued life: his famous monologue brands life as a cheat because it fails to deliver the expected rewards (IV. 33—44). His optimism is briefly restored by Nourmahal's kindness, which he grotesquely misinterprets as that of an angel descended to reward suffering virtue (IV. 64—5). The truth, however, soon sinks in and, faced with the additional bewilderment of seeing vice unpunished, Aureng-Zebe echoes Hippolytus' perplexity at the seeming abdication of divine order; appropriately seized by the histrionic fit, he reviles Heaven for failing to observe poetic justice:

Heav'ns! can you this, without just vengeance, hear?
When will you thunder, if it now be clear?
Yet her alone let not your Thunder seize:
I, too, deserve to die, because I please.   (IV. 127—30)

His subsequent quarrel with Indamora is a continuation of his quarrel with Heaven. He had trusted in a Heaven that favoured virtue with instant and tangible reward, and he had pursued virtue in the hope of obtaining its rewards. Now all his schemes for securing interest by virtue have failed, and he owes his survival not to the triumph of righteousness but to a troublesome compromise between good and evil. His mind rebels against the devious procedures of mundane life, and, although he ultimately forgives Indamora, he does so not because he recognises and accepts what she has done but because a fit of passion alters his judgement, inducing him to accept a somewhat beautified version of the truth. Yet Indamora's pragmatism secures for him the opportunity that his own schemes had failed to obtain: that of making virtue profitable. Reprieved by Indamora's manipulation of Morat and released from prison by her manipulation of Arimant, he is alive and present in the royal chamber because of her actions; and so, when the Emperor enters the chamber deploring Morat's rebellion, he catches sight of Aureng-Zebe and repents his baseness (IV. 560—71). Virtue and interest are at last allied, and Aureng-Zebe recovers from his suicidal despair:

My Father's kind; and, Madam, you forgive:
Were Heav'n so pleas'd, I now could wish to live.   (IV. 607—8)

At the end of Act IV Aureng-Zebe, despite himself, acquires the opportunity to profit by virtue; in Act V he all but throws the profits away. The rewards of Son and Lover await him: he has regained his father's favour, and his mistress has survived the final tumult; once more, however, he cannot stomach the unideal means by which his rewards have been secured, and, instead of rejoicing in Indamora's survival, he rages at her for not being dead. His ravings rightly alienate her, with the result that the expected progression from virtue triumphant to virtue rewarded is abruptly and significantly interrupted. The final union of Indamora and Aureng-Zebe is the immediate result not of the hero's self-interested achievements but of the Emperor's self-sacrificing redress of the hero's blunders. To the end, Aureng-Zebe's idealistic designs go astray and have to be rectified by those with more knowledge of the world.

Aureng-Zebe, then, does not portray the triumph and reward of a disinterested and virtuous hero. Aureng-Zebe follows virtue in the belief that it will bring him both praise and rewards of a more solid kind; and he is distinctly piqued when he seems likely to receive praise alone. Although he opts for loyalty at the ends of the first and second acts, he does so solely in order to sustain his reputation, and in the latter episode he explicitly disclaims any sense of the intrinsic value of virtue, declaring it to be "vain" and a "Barren, and aery name" (II. 502, 504). His desire to sustain his reputation leads him into clear and repeated pretence, and his desire to make virtue profitable produces only a series of naïve and quickly frustrated stratagems. Ultimately, all his rewards are secured by pragmatic compromises that run counter to his plans.

The reader may object that Aureng-Zebe's motives are being judged by alien and irrelevant standards; that the example of Corneille forbids us to mistrust a hero who makes glory the principle of his action. Corneille's heroes, however, are not piqued when glory is their sole reward; they do not indulge in Aureng-Zebe's disingenuous play-acting; and they do not reveal a bathetic gap between pretension and reality. Reputation cannot survive as a self-sufficient ideal when it is repeatedly associated with unheroic pretence. Moreover, the obsession with reputation, and the cultivation of a reputation that exceeds performance, are integral parts of a far larger distortion of the relationships between appearance and reality, reflection and original. To this we must now turn.

III. THROUGH THE LOOKING-GLASS

The theatrical world which the Indians inhabit is one in which all our
everyday epistemological assumptions are reversed: dream becomes fact and
fact dream; language acquires the attributes of the reality that it describes,
reality the aery insubstantiality of language; and the solid, three-dimensional
world of corporeal forms is perceived as a two-dimensional world of
bodiless surfaces.

The epistemological maze is at its most intricate in the scene in which
Morat, the Emperor, and Melesinda debate Morat's infatuation with
Indamora. "Fame's loud voice proclaims your Lord unkind," observes the
Emperor to Melesinda (IV. 299), provoking Morat to a rejoinder whose
proper significance is not immediately apparent: he relegates fame to a paltry
world of empty façades and claims that he occupies a higher and more
substantial level of reality:

> Let Fame be busie where she has to do:
> Tell of fought Fields, and every pompous Show.
> Those Tales are fit to fill the People's ears;
> Monarchs, unquestion'd, move in higher Spheres.   (IV. 300−3)

Truth, in Morat's topsy-turvy terminology, belongs only to a world of
inane show; the nature of the higher Sphere that transcends truth is not,
however, yet obvious. Soon, however, Morat clarifies matters:

> You'll please to leave me judge of what I do,
> And not examine by the outward show.
> Your usage of my Mother might be good:
> I judg'd it not. . . .
> If your own Actions on your Will you ground,
> Mine shall hereafter know no other bound.
> What meant you when you call'd me to a Throne?
> Was it to please me with a Name alone?   (IV. 312−15; 322−5)

For Morat the will alone is real, all outside its compass an empty wraith, an
accident without substance. In demanding that the Emperor should not
judge "by the outward show", Morat is asking that he should not pass moral
judgements, for these dwell only on the surface of things, ignoring the
essential principle of the will; similarly, he assumes that power allied to
virtue rather than desire is an empty and inane show, "a Name alone". In
both cases moral realities are seen as baseless and tenuous mirages, vanishing
before the triumphant actuality of the will.

Seeing the triumph of will over morality as the triumph of reality over
illusion, Morat arrives at the corollary that a man who has lost his virility—

and therefore has no will left to indulge—can only achieve a counterfeit existence, subsisting on the memories of lost desires:

> If you have liv'd, take thankfully the past:
> Make, as you can, the sweet remembrance last.
> If you have not enjoy'd what Youth could give,
> But life sunk through you like a leaky Sieve,
> Accuse your self you liv'd not while you might. (IV. 344—8)

And, since the Emperor can only live a sham existence, Morat is obliged to take over Indamora in order to create a show of dynastic virility that will hide the reality of his father's less than real existence:

> I've now resolv'd to fill your useless place; ⎫
> I'll take that Post to cover your disgrace, ⎬
> And love her, for the honour of my Race. ⎭ (IV. 350—2)

Moral restraints have been dismissed as matters of baseless appearance, and now the need to sustain appearances acquires the binding force of morality; reality and illusion have changed places.

In attempting to transpose reality and illusion by a triumphant act of the will, Morat is typical of his milieu. All characters attribute to life only the emptiness of hallucination and dream, and, conversely, endow their own empty imaginings with adamantine substance. The Emperor dismisses Nourmahal's just suspicions as "Dreams" (II. 222), but he in turn, rightly suspicious of Arimant's designs on Indamora, is quickly persuaded to see truth as fiction, an independent, rival suit as a bloodless reflection and enactment of his own (II. 114—54). Here, the actual acquires the attributes of the imaginary. In trying to seduce Aureng-Zebe, on the other hand, Nourmahal proceeds by reciting and attempting to actualise an erotic dream (IV. 98—115); and Aureng-Zebe, wrongly thinking Indamora false, wishes to be deluded into thinking her true (IV. 465—8)—and only does begin to believe in her when she starts to lie. Indeed, a dream-like transformation of the real is the essence of heroic love, and characterises it from the outset:

> *Indamora.* Love is an aery good Opinion makes:
> Which he who onely thinks he has, partakes.
> Seen by a strong Imagination's Beam,
> That tricks and dresses up the gaudy Dream.
> Presented so, with rapture 'tis enjoy'd:
> Rais'd by high Fancy, and by low destroy'd.
> *Aureng-Zebe.* If Love be Vision, mine has all the fire
> Which, in first Dreams, young Prophets does inspire:
> I dream, in you, our promis'd Paradise:

An Age's tumult of continu'd bliss.
But you have still your happiness in doubt:
Or else 'tis past, and you have dream't it out.   (I. 372 – 83)

Neither character realises the eventual implications of the imagery: Indamora's derogation of love is enforced by circumstances, and Aureng-Zebe reverses the significance of her imagery, turning the dream into a prophetic intimation of an overwhelming reality. But Indamora speaks the truth without knowing it, and Aureng-Zebe, thinking that he celebrates the magnitude of his love, unintentionally images its illusiveness. The true significance of these images appears at once, for in his next speech Aureng-Zebe falls into a fit of jealous delusion and throughout the play suspiciously misinterprets Indamora's behaviour. The lovers' relationship is one of illusion and theatrical pretence, and the sense of illusion culminates in their final encounter, which is portrayed as that of two people meeting in each other's dreams: "do I dream?" asks Aureng-Zebe (V. 413), only to find his question reciprocated in Indamora's "does my willing mind delude my eyes?" (V. 440). The imagery is fitting, for even at the end Aureng-Zebe places his faith not in the real Indamora but in an idealised fiction prettified into conformity with his romantic expectations. The love of hero and heroine is in truth a "gaudy Dream" (I. 375), a further subordination of the actual to the willed.

Repeated metaphors of pomp emphasise the transposition of illusion and reality, the usurpation of exterior surface upon essential substance, and it is characteristic of Dryden's labyrinthine embroilment of truth and fiction that the attacks on the specious surfaces of pomp are often themselves attempts to create a baseless fabric of deception. The Emperor, trying to conceal his own infidelity, lampoons Nourmahal's "pompous chastity" (II. 259), which is later emphatically exposed as a mere façade. Aureng-Zebe, dressing his own motives in a rather flattering light, treats the "pomp" of Morat's elevation (III. 205) with an indifference that he had certainly not felt in private, and later affects to have overlooked the "Pomp" (IV. 8, 15) provided for him in the death cell, once more creating on his own part an ostentatious and deceptive display. Similarly, Morat outfaces Nourmahal's rage at Aureng-Zebe's reprieve by dismissing her and women generally as creatures of empty, enervating "pomp" (IV. 202)—and thereby covers up the fact that he is himself a woman's pawn, acting under Indamora's influence. Inveighing against a world of empty forms, both hero and villains mimic the vacant charades that they affect to despise.[16]

Attributing solid existence to a world of dream, illusion, and empty forms, the characters pass off the actualities of earthly existence as things of inane and vacant show. Nourmahal, for example, trusts pathetically in her imaginary youth and beauty; but, when she sees in Indamora the reality to which she pretends, she dismisses her as a hollow exterior, a disembodied surface:

Heav'n did, by me, the outward model build:
Its inward work, the Soul, with rubbish fill'd.
Yet, Oh! th'imperfect Piece moves more delight;
'Tis gilded o'r with Youth, to catch the sight.   (v. 280–3)

Mistaking the play-acting of their own lives for reality, the characters regard the lives—even the bodies—of others as pieces of empty mimicry, seeing their fellows only as imperfect, histrionic copies of the self. In doing so, they reveal the near-solipsism that results from the cult of the will: desire becomes indistinguishable from reality, and the will seems to be the pivot of the universe; the solipsist imagines a world derived from himself even in its physical forms, believing that he alone has full and independent existence, and that his fellows are not autonomous creatures but imperfect, semi-existent replicas of the self. Such is the attitude of Morat, for whom the will alone is reality, anything alien to it an illusion.

The denial of others' existence, indeed, often proceeds explicitly from the deification of the will. In a single speech, for example, Morat dismisses his father as a bodiless image ("An Emperor and Lover, but in show" [III. 509]), identifies his will with Heaven's, and claims that he embodies in compendium the identities of all his family:

As Heav'n did to your eyes and form Divine,
Submit the Fate of all th'Imperial Line;
So was it order'd by its wise Decree,
That you should find 'em all compris'd in me.   (III. 511–14)

Later, similarly, he treats his elder brothers as poor first drafts of himself, asserts that he will take over Aureng-Zebe's identity, and assumes that Heaven's will is a reflection of his own:

Morat. My Elder Brothers my fore-runners came;
Rough-draughts of Nature, ill-design'd, and lame:
Blown off, like Blossoms, never made to bear;
Till I came, finish'd; her last labour'd care. . . .
My Brother too may live.
   Indamora.   He may?
   Morat.   He must:
I kill'd him not: and a less Fate's unjust.
Heav'n owes it me, that I may fill his room;
A Phœnix-Lover, rising from his Tomb.
In whom you'll lose your sorrows for the dead;
More warm, more fierce, and fitter for your bed.   (v. 29–32, 37–42)

Nourmahal, likewise, sees Indamora as a hollow replica of her own complete form (v. 280–3) and Morat as a reincarnation of her own identity, and once again combines the self-oriented view of others with an inability to separate divine and personal will: if the gods could not guard Morat as being in their image, she exclaims, "They ought to have respected him as mine" (v. 347). In their solipsistic illusions, the characters even claim to exercise the sun's power, to sustain the cosmos with their vivifying heat[17]—though, as usual, the divine fancies are fulfilled only in death, in the fiery hallucinations of Nourmahal's suicide.

When Aureng-Zebe, blind to Indamora's innocence, invests her with a fantasy innocence of his own creation, he in essence imitates the conduct of those who see independent characters as the creatures of their own minds. Moreover, he too regards his fellows as mere exteriors, as human surface lacking human dimension, sparing only the Emperor from his contempt. In one of his fits of anger, for example, he anticipates Nourmahal's dismissal of Indamora as a beautiful exterior filled with rubbish:

Ah Sex, invented first to damn Mankind!
Nature took care to dress you up for sin:
Adorn'd, without; unfinish'd left, within. . . .
Greatness, and Noise, and Show are your delight;
Yet wise men love you, in their own despight.			(IV. 490−2, 497−8)

Morat comes in for similar abuse:

When thou wert form'd, Heav'n did a Man begin;
But the brute Soul, by chance, was shuffl'd in.			(III. 304−5)

And Nourmahal too is excluded from the ranks of humanity, being furiously exorcised to a land of untenanted human exteriors, a "barbarous Climate" "Which onely Brutes in humane form does yield" (IV. 136, 137).

Characters such as Nourmahal, Morat, and Aureng-Zebe see themselves as the sole exemplars of positive existence in a world of shadowy and insubstantial half-men. In their willingness to deny the reality of their fellows, as in their willingness to take fact for dream, morality for fiction, they perceive the solid forms of reality as the baseless figments of illusion; and, seeing reality as illusion, they see the theatrical roles of spurious divinity and impossible heroism as unquestionable reality. The transposition of truth and illusion reflected in the pomp imagery is all-pervasive.

The transposition of shadow and substance is also reflected in the contradictory values that are attached to the single idea of the "name".[18] Asserting the supremacy of the will over moral fictions, characters use the "name" as a type of the pre-eminently insubstantial: Morat sees power hampered by morality as "a Name alone" (IV. 325); forbidden by custom from intercourse with her stepson, Nourmahal feels herself "made wretched onely by a name" (III. 365); Dianet sees Aureng-Zebe's commitment to loyalty as commitment to a mere "word" (II. 536); and Aureng-Zebe himself can dismiss virtue as a "Barren, and aery name" (II. 504). But, while moral realities are relegated to the realm of insubstantial and aery names, names themselves acquire a concrete and substantial value, so that image and reality once again change places: Indamora repeated her lover's name "as a charm" "And printed kisses on it" (IV. 401, 403), giving the name a material and tactile reality, as Aureng-Zebe in turn does when he believes that the mere sound of Morat's name moves Indamora to orgasmic ecstasy:

> *Indamora.*   has he a name?
> *Aureng-Zebe.* You would be told; you glory in your shame:
> There's Music in the Sound; and, to provoke
> Your pleasure more, by me it must be spoke.
> Then, then it ravishes, when your pleas'd ear
> The sound does from a wretched Rival hear.
> *Morat*'s the name your heart leaps up to meet.
> While *Aureng-Zebe* lies dying at your feet.   (IV. 425–32)

The antithesis that concludes Aureng-Zebe's speech is particularly revealing, for its balance assumes that the name of Morat and the person of Aureng-Zebe are equivalent in nature, and its contrast is one of physical position: Aureng-Zebe is flat on the ground, whereas "Morat" is evidently a few feet above it, since Indamora's heart has to leap up to meet him.

More generally, names are interchangeable with the objects or states to which they refer:

> *Asaph.* The name of Father hateful to him grows.   (I. 88)

> *Arimant.* A Guardian's Title I must own with shame:
> But should be prouder of another Name.   (II. 47–8)

> *Aureng-Zebe.* Even death's become to me no dreadful name.
>   (II. 490)

> *Emperor.* For *Aureng-Zebe* a hated name is grown.   (III. 147)[19]

The characters' misconceptions about language reflect their misconceptions about life: as theatrical image supplants the reality that it imitates, so linguistic symbol supplants the reality that it expresses. Towards the end of the play, indeed, the two transpositions are combined: in usurping Aureng-Zebe's role, Arimant usurps his "name" (V. 493), and the death of the false Aureng-Zebe is depicted as a silencing of the hero's name:

> *Asaph.* His Souldiers, where he fought, his name reveal'd:
> In thickest crouds, still *Aureng-Zebe* did sound: ⎫
> The vaulted Roofs did *Aureng-Zebe* rebound,   ⎬
> Till late, and in his fall, the name was drown'd. ⎭   (V. 139–42)

The cult of the immaterial name has become one with the cult of the
insubstantial image.

One of the chief meanings of "name" is that of "reputation", and in
Aureng-Zebe the pursuit of reputation is not a sublime quest for *gloire* but a
further manifestation of the all-pervasive confusion between sign and
substance, involving both the substitution of theatre for life (as in Aureng-
Zebe's play-acting) and the substitution of language for reality. As the word
acquires the attributes of the object, so fame—the "name"—becomes
interchangeable with the person. The Emperor, for example, characterises
his old age as the decay not of his body but of his reputation, lamenting that
his "Stock of Fame is lavish'd and decay'd" (IV. 383), and in like fashion
Nourmahal wishes on the Emperor not death itself but a loss of reputation
that takes the form of physical death: "May your sick Fame still languish, till
it die" (II. 317). Aureng-Zebe's obsession with fame is similarly akin to
obsession with the seeming tangibility of the mere word, so that his quest for
fame entails a double confusion of baseless show with substantial truth: his
career of theatre assumes the character of life itself, while the living forms of
Morat, Nourmahal, and Indamora seem to be hollow and less than real; and,
as show and substance change place, so do word and reality. Even when he
opts for a course of self-denial, Aureng-Zebe is actuated not by a sense of
moral principle but by a desire to preserve his reputation, and he invariably
tries to magnify the reputability of his actions by means of clear pretence. At
the end of Act II, for example, when his first scheme for self-advancement has
failed, he concludes in disappointment that virtue is a worthless puff of air, a
"Barren, and aery name" (II. 504). Nevertheless, he decides that there remain
compelling considerations that forbid rebellion: "I'll not", he declares,
"betray the glory of my *name*" (II. 529; italics added). The inconsistency is
blatant and significant: for Aureng-Zebe, as for Morat and Nourmahal,
moral principles are mere names and evanescent sounds; but names, on the
other hand, have a compelling force and substance. In revering fame rather
than virtue, Aureng-Zebe is cultivating the word at the expense of the
reality; and he confirms his commitment to the insubstantial when his
determination to preserve the glory of his name leads to the disingenuous
self-righteousness of his Act III encounter with the Emperor and Morat.

The incongruity of Aureng-Zebe's position is at once emphasised by
Dianet:

> The points of Honour Poets may produce;
> Trappings of life, for Ornament, not Use:
> Honour, which onely does the name advance,
> Is the meer raving madness of Romance.
> Pleas'd with a word, you may sit tamely down;
> And see your younger Brother force the Crown   (II. 532—7)

Aureng-Zebe's arcane distinction between aery and substantial names is confounded when his first definition is turned against his second, for in asserting the insubstantiality of honour Dianet duplicates Aureng-Zebe's assertion of the insubstantiality of virtue. At first glance, Dianet may appear to be the anti-romantic heretic, the plain man whose imagination cannot grasp the ideal for which the superhuman hero strives (though a hero volubly disenchanted with virtue is scarcely a man of praeternatural idealism). But, in fact, Dianet's charges are confirmed by the hero's habitual conduct, for Aureng-Zebe's code is one of externals, of fictions and theatrical poses, and such is the code that Dianet satirises: the "points of Honour", he claims, belong to a fictional rather than a real world, being the property of "Poets" and the subjects of "Romance"; they are "Trappings" and "Ornament"; and the prize that they bring is a mere word. Dianet's conclusion—that Aureng-Zebe should usurp the throne—is not that of Dryden, who sanctions the worldly pragmatism of an Indamora rather than the brute violence of an unregenerate Morat. But the speech does push to its logical conclusion Aureng-Zebe's proposition that virtue is a "Barren, and aery name", and in doing so lays bare the inadequacies and incongruities of his cult of fame; for Dianet is at once opposing him and confronting him with the consequences of his beliefs. And Aureng-Zebe's life is, as Dianet's speech suggests, one of contradictions: he wants the reputation of virtue without its inconveniences, and he wants the benefits due only to compromise without the embarrassment of compromise itself. In pursuing fame, as in pursuing ideal love, Aureng-Zebe is chasing an illusion, and his romance creed is fittingly ineffectual, repeatedly failing where Indamora's unideal and at times comic pragmatism succeeds.

Aureng-Zebe, then, is neither an exemplary hero nor even a near-paragon with just sufficient flaws to make him human. On the contrary, Dryden once again creates a hero strikingly akin in mentality and achievement to his villainous counterparts. Aureng-Zebe's inflexibly idealistic love is as destructive as Nourmahal's unbridled lust, and at times gives way to a sensuality disconcertingly similar to hers. In pursuing heroic perfection, he disguises human frailty with histrionic pretence no less than do the villainous and aged in their quest for divine immutability. Caught up in theatrical make-believe, he shares the villains' transposition of reality and illusion: he too denounces the empty pomp of others while himself sustaining a disingenuous façade; he too dismisses others as hollow puppets while believing blindly in the reality of his own histrionics; and he too reverses the functions of sign and substance, treating moral realities as mere names and mere names as things of supreme value. His devotion to reputation, the quality that seems most to align him with the heroes of Cornelian drama, is in fact testimony to his involvement in the perceptual and linguistic errors of the villains. Dryden has come a long way from the crude parallels between Montezuma and Zempoalla, but the foundation of his design remains the same.

Postscript: The Later Dryden

Dryden's heroic plays have been seen both as a sterile aberration in dramatic history and as something of an anomaly in his own career, an immature digression from his true poetic and intellectual calling.[1] I hope I have shown that, in Dryden's hands, the heroic play is neither eccentric nor unworkable as a dramatic form, and that his last two contributions to the genre are really very good indeed. I hope it is also implicitly clear that, in moving from the heroic play to other things, Dryden in no way repudiated the substance of what he had so far written. While I would not argue that the whole Dryden corpus exists in embryo in *The Indian Queen*, I suggest that a surprising amount does: the quest for permanence, in particular, remained an inexhaustibly rich topic, and the limitations of heroism continued to fascinate Dryden throughout his career, as *Cleomenes* (1692) and *Fables Ancient and Modern* (1700) reveal.

Although *All for Love* (1677) is often considered to abandon the heroic model, it in fact merely presents it in another guise. Of course, Dryden dispensed both with rhyme and with the labyrinthine contrivance of the heroic play, renouncing multilayered counterpoint and the intricate genesis of dilemma from dilemma. The emphasis is now upon an individual faced with successive, separate choices, and only when Alexas' final schemes entangle love, friendship, and honour in rivalry and misunderstanding is there any extended reminiscence of earlier plot types; the amorous embroilments of heroic drama survive only in the contrivances of a cowardly eunuch. Nevertheless, *All for Love* retains the central concerns of the heroic plays, once again destroying histrionic shows of divinity with the triumph of human frailty and sublunary change. If Dryden abandoned the form of the heroic play, he did so not because he had lost interest in its subjects but because he was looking for more satisfactory ways to realise old preoccupations. For the chief innovation of *All for Love* lies in its new approach to a favourite procedure: that of writing a play about theatrical illusion.

In every tragedy from *Tyrannick Love* to *All for Love* Dryden produced an examination of dramatic illusion, emphasising the fictitiousness of stage representation and using the theatrical medium as a symbol of his characters' deluded lives;[2] the plays work by drawing attention to their own artifice, uncovering and examining their own processes. However good this procedure may be as the basis for a play, it is rather limited as the basis for a dramatic style, but Dryden evidently found difficulty in moving beyond his first conceptions, and his eventual abandonment of the well-tried formula marked the end of his career as a productive and important tragedian. In *The Conquest of Granada* he had created his life of theatre within theatre by the simple expedient of having his characters act out roles from the works of others. In the next two tragedies, however, he sought to reduce the parasitic nature of his drama: his world of art within art was no longer to be derived, ready-made, from external sources; instead, he attempted to produce a work which generated within itself and from its own resources a secondary, distorted and spurious, work. But, in doing so, he drove himself into a dead end from which he never fully escaped.

In *Aureng-Zebe* the realm of spurious fiction becomes more integral to the play, less parasitically dependent on external sources, than it had hitherto been, and *All for Love* continues—but does not complete—the process initiated in *Aureng-Zebe*. For the most part, Dryden now creates his design of art within art from inside the play, with little dependence on the pygmy writers who had sustained him in *The Conquest of Granada*. Nevertheless, a play concerned with Antony and Cleopatra necessarily unfolds amidst memories of other versions and other interpretations, and Dryden took up the bow of Ulysses precisely because it had been tried so often, finding in the divided and often contradictory tradition the framework of allusion that had formerly been provided by the works of Scudéry and La Calprenède.[3] Such a procedure does not lend itself to successful repetition, and *All for Love* freed Dryden from the limitations of earlier work without providing a pattern for future development. In another respect, too, he transcended the parasitic form of *The Conquest of Granada* by means of an unrepeatable, and indeed desperate, measure: hitherto, he had sought to create a primary work which generated within itself a secondary, quite distinct, species of art, differing from the parent work as false from true, dream from reality; but in *All for Love* he simply jettisoned the primary work, making the "reality" outside his characters' histrionic fantasies an invisible and imponderable force. In the description of the Nile floods that opens the play, Serapion depicts a world in which familiar rules have suddenly been suspended, a world governed by anomalous and mysterious forces of flux and mutability, and such is the world that Dryden evokes throughout *All for Love*. Although the play depicts a decisive struggle for control of the earth, neither the earth nor the enemy army acquire a clear and palpable reality; for the characters blind themselves to the concrete, infinitely various particulars of a vast and hostile world, acknowledging its existence only in instinctive fear of intangible, all-embracing forces of change and conflict. They are threatened, for example, not by an army hastening from Tarentum to Toryne[4] but by "a Storm/Just breaking on [their] heads" (I. 43–4); by an army seen as an impalpable agent of change and turmoil. External threats to the secluded dream-world of Alexandria are few and unseen: the conquering army of Octavius waits to take over the earth but remains an invisible force of uncertain nature, and the one external event that does impinge on the characters' existence—the desertion of the navy—is arbitrary and unconnected with the preceding action; for hitherto we have seen little except the dramaturgic illusions which the characters have substituted for an obscure and menacing reality.

Throughout the play Octavius remains in the wings, waiting to receive the world. Dryden presents us with a dramatic vacuum surrounding the human vacuum of Antony, a man without qualities whose character at first changes with each successive claim that is made on it. The action of the play is created solely by the dramaturgy of its characters, for the play is a battle for Antony's identity, and each of Antony's associates is a would-be dramatist, striving to shape the hero's erratic personality so as to suit a design for the mastery of change. But each of the dramatists, whether the celebrant of soldierly austerity, political pragmatism, or marital decorum, seeks to shape his protagonist according to a narrow and circumscribed view of life that fails to grasp the full complexity of human experience. And so, in the end, the dramatic designs go calamitously astray: Antony fails to act the roles contrived for him, and with the desertion of the navy the dramatists are crushed by a reality beyond their control and powers of prediction. The tragedy of *All for Love* springs from the same source as the comedy of the heroic plays: from the disparity between heroic art and mortal life.

After *All for Love*, however, Dryden produced only one more significant tragedy, and that after twelve years had elapsed. Other interests were certainly drawing him away from the theatre, but we cannot attribute the dearth of good tragedies solely to pressure of other work, since he did not make a decisive break with the theatre until after *Albion and Albanius* (1685), and when financial hardship forced him to turn dramatist again he produced five more plays. In all, he wrote—or had a hand in—five tragedies after *All for Love*, but four are disappointing, and only *Don Sebastian* is entirely his work. It is tempting to believe that he had written himself into a dead end. In *All for Love* he had brilliantly freed his old procedures from their old limitations, but *All for Love* marks the end of one dramaturgic phase without pointing the way to another, and his next two tragedies, *Oedipus* (1678) and *Troilus and Cressida* (1679) show a simpler, far less inventive use of past traditions. Dryden's portions of *Oedipus*—Acts I and III—do tantalise us with unfulfilled promise, portraying a world from which all familiar physical and moral order has vanished: the Theban plague, moving through the scale of existence in the order observed by God in the Creation,[5] threatens to reduce the world to its primal chaos; the forces of chaos are incarnated in the deformed and shapeless Creon, a figure descended not only from Shakespeare's Richard III but from Milton's Death; and the suspension of physical order is complemented by a disintegration of perceptible moral order, manifested in the terrible enigma of Oedipus, at once usurper and legitimate ruler, and equally guilty (though equally free of guilty intent) in both roles. For his very legitimacy—his descent from Lajus—itself taints him, adding to unwitting regicide the crime of unwitting incest. Lee, however, does not develop Dryden's hints, and the play degenerates into a gratuitous bloodbath after the fashion of *Nero*.

Shakespeare's *Troilus and Cressida* provided Dryden with highly congenial material, portraying heroic aspiration as a mixture of sordid sham and tragic illusion. In adapting Shakespeare's bleak account of the heroic life, Dryden did add characteristic touches of his own: as in *All for Love*, for example, he identifies the heroic and the child-like, making the infant Astyanax responsible for Hector's chivalric challenge to the Greek champions;[6] and, by altering the character of Cressida, he creates an irony consistent with that of earlier works, showing the capacity of sham grandeur to destroy ordinary decency. For Cressida is destroyed alike by the unprincipled scheming of Calchas and Ulysses and by the simple idealism of Troilus, an Aureng-Zebe who is not spared the consequences of his inflexible expectations. But *Troilus* is by its nature a work of secondary importance: it provides an intelligent reinterpretation of an older masterpiece, but Dryden's contribution is necessarily a subsidiary one, and his innovations merely introduce motifs that he had exploited more fully elsewhere. Far from deriving new energy from his Shakespearean experiment, he merely produced a minor postscript to the heroic plays.

Dryden displayed far more originality when he returned to tragicomedy in *The Spanish Fryar* (1680). In celebrating the triumph of legitimacy, the play obviously contributes to the Exclusion controversy, but its deliberate moral untidiness makes it poor propaganda and it is by no means a simple exercise in Filmerism. For all its topicality, in fact, it is primarily concerned with issues that had preoccupied Dryden ever since *The Indian Queen*. Torrismond is another military wonder-worker participating in a struggle between rebellious passion and political obligation, though the stark, simple conflict between Montezuma and the Ynca is now transformed into an intricate psychological conflict within the hero, rebellious passion showing itself in his love for the usurping queen, political obligation in his duty as heir to the rightful and apparently murdered monarch. Once again, heroic idealism proves powerless in an appetitive world: the spirit of Montezuma quickly cedes to the spirit of Friar Dominic, whose casuistic defence of appetite and self-interest infects the whole kingdom, entangling the duties of kin and political loyalty and producing Gordian knots that the hero and his circle are powerless to untie. In the end, Right triumphs only because it happens to be in the villain's interest.

The achievements of the heroic plays and *All for Love* were, however, chiefly consolidated not in the plays of 1678–85 but in *MacFlecknoe* (1678), *Absalom and Achitophel* (1681), and *The Hind and the Panther* (1687), works which return to the problem that had haunted and baffled the would-be demi-gods of the heroic plays: that of finding permanence in a transient world. "All humane things are subject to decay"—the first line of *MacFlecknoe*—announces a theme that is to run through all three poems, for dunces, conspirators, and schismatics are alike the slaves of mutability, lost in unthinking appetite to the extinction of their diviner part and unable to forge anything that will outlast their brute life-cycles of copulation and death. But in each work Dryden shows how the mind and spirit of man can triumph over the mortality of his body—with art, with a civilisation whose stable continuity transcends the mortality of its members, and, finally, with a church immortal as an institution and immortal in its membership. In *Absalom* and *The Hind*, moreover, Dryden portrays the contrast between the slaves and the conquerors of change as one between fallen and unregenerate man, again developing a preoccupation already present in *The Indian Emperour*: rebels and sects perpetuate the corruption of Adam's seed, whereas Charles and Rome, both recipients of the divine Logos, in turn provide partial and complete restoration of the lost Eden. In seeing political order as a bulwark against mutability, *Absalom and Achitophel* is consistent with the political poems that Dryden wrote even before embarking on the heroic plays. *To My Lord Chancellor* (1662), for example, celebrates the very kinds of permanence that were to prove illusory in *The Indian Emperour*, associating Clarendon with imperishable fertility ("perpetual Spring" [136]) and with the transcendence of mutability, Fate, Fortune, and time (123–56). Dryden is a Virgilian from the start: in his work, as in the *Aeneid*, individualistic belligerence fails to master Fate, and the cycles of change are tamed only when the hero subordinates self to the cause of history.

After the great political and religious poems, Dryden twice returned to heroic tragedy. *Cleomenes* (1692), his last tragedy, is a dignified but insubstantial play treating the familiar topic of heroic impotence. The spirit of Almanzor is recreated twice, once in the ambitious prattlings of the hero's young, ineffectual child, once in the futile memories of the hero himself, now doomed to passivity, baffled and destroyed by an effete and unheroic society. Rather like Odysseus in the *Odyssey*, he seems the last survivor of an extinct species, stranded in a menacing and malignant Phaeacia. But the heroism and intrigues are standard stuff, and the play really belongs to the class of Crowne's *The Ambitious Statesman*. Far more impressive is *Don Sebastian* (1689), which, like Crowne's unsuccessful *Darius* of the previous year, revives and transforms the aims of the heroic play, providing a new examination of heroic illusion. *Don Sebastian* is not, however, merely a resurrection of the heroic play. Rather, it is a synthesis and consummation of all Dryden's previous work, for it also contains his most original and brilliant interlinking of tragedy and comedy, and combines the concerns of the sixties and seventies with those of the eighties, exposing the futility of heroic pride in a world vitiated by Adam's sin.

Once again, Dryden proceeds by drawing the villainous and heroic into ever closer affinity. His chief villain, the Emperor Muley-Moluch, is Unregenerate Man personified, an heir to Lucifer in his rebellious, self-deifying pride: according to his will the force of divine *fiat*, he scorns both earthly and heavenly power, having dethroned a lawful monarch and even proposing to rewrite the Koran into conformity with his desires (III. i. 65–

74). Despite his obvious and archetypal evil, however, he creates a pattern to which the hero and heroine increasingly conform. Almeyda does at first dissociate herself from him, as a human being repudiating a monster, but her protestations from the start carry little weight: she is, she admits, of Muley-Moluch's family; and the father whose realm she seeks to recover was not a legitimate king but the villain's fellow buccaneer, ousted from his stolen throne by his former accomplice (I. i. 428–73). From the outset, Dryden hints that his heroine's cause and heritage are tainted; and, though they wrap themselves in dreams of heroic excellence, Sebastian and Almeyda follow the same course as their antagonist, idolising the senses and seeing the will of Heaven in the image of their own ambitions and sexual desires. But the terrible revelations of Act v force the heroic self-deceivers to abandon illusions of perfection and acknowledge inherited pollution and guilt; to outgrow their cosy sanctification of heroic love and face a divinity intractable to human desire and inexorable in crushing the will. The unintentional incest does not cast a fortuitous blight on two otherwise perfect lives; inherited guilt is the lot of all humanity, and the incest is a particular form of a common curse, confirming and symbolising a guilt that has been copiously apparent before the final disclosures. In *Don Sebastian* Dryden developed the view that he had briefly set forth in *The State of Innocence*: that heroic idealism is fallen corruption in disguise.

If Sebastian and Almeyda are the descendants of earlier heroes and heroines, Antonio is the descendant of earlier precariously reformed rakes such as Celadon and Palamede, pursuing his seemingly innocuous concupiscence in the pseudo-Eden of the Mufti's garden. Dryden places side by side the worlds of heroic tragedy and sexual comedy, showing them to provide divergent interpretations of a single subject: the consequences of the Fall. The demanding and terrible God of Act v destroys the false security of the comic life no less than the false perfection of the heroic, but Antonio and Morayma remain untouched by the concluding revelations: whereas Sebastian and Almeyda, seeing the heroic world disintegrate, move forward to grasp the new and terrible reality, the comic characters cannot follow them, remaining fossilised in their dead world of comic fantasy, their cheerfully irresponsible marriage covenant overshadowed by the same fearful judgement on sexual sin as has thwarted the aspirations of heroic love. In the two plots of *Don Sebastian*, with their parallel studies of fallen man, Dryden asserts what critics have often denied: that heroic tragedy and ribald comedy are populated by beings of a common nature and ancestry; for Sebastian and Almeyda outgrow their affinity with Antonio only when they leave the realm of heroic drama.

Appendix: Some Sources and Analogues

THE INDIAN QUEEN

Artaban

Artaban, the model of the young Montezuma and part-model of Almanzor, is the greatest of the many superhuman warriors in La Calprenède's *Cleopatra*. He is "a man that drag'd victory after him" (III. iii. 281), an invincible superman: in one battle, for example, "as if the destinies had secretly lodg'd a fatality in his Sword to all that opposed him, he carried it to no part of the fight, where it did not cut down Enemies in heaps, and change the Fortune of both parties, with a prodigious promptitude" (III. iv. 324). Because of his invincible prowess, he is regarded as "a person whom the Gods had raised above mortality" (III. iii. 282), and is at one point hailed as "*that* Artaban, *whose sublime Reputation fills the Universe, who gains so many Battels, who unthrones Kings, overthrows Monarchies, and makes Empires depend on the point of his Sword*" (VII. iv. 96).

Like Montezuma and Almanzor, he is of obscure birth, but like them is proudly choleric and sustained by an inner persuasion that he deserves the highest honours (v. i. 458–9, 471, XII. ii. 169). Under the name of Britomarus, he starts his career at the Æthiopian court (I. iii. 71), but, falling in love with the Princess Candace, is banished after a duel with a rival (I. iii. 79, v. i. 463–4). He then goes to Armenia (v. i. 465), where he proves invaluable in the war against the Medes (p. 466), eventually defeating their champion in single combat (p. 467). His suit to the Armenian Princess is disdained because of his humble birth (pp. 478–9). His sojourn, however, is terminated not by his over-ambitious love but by the perfidy of King Artaxus, who, having promised Britomarus any favour he asks, immediately revokes his word when the hero requests the freedom of two prisoners captured by his own hand (p. 482). Britomarus' response is that of Dryden's heroes: asserting that he is no subject of Artaxus and therefore owes him no allegiance, he claims that the right of capture makes the prisoners his alone (p. 482). Unmoved, Artaxus beheads the prisoners (p. 483), and Britomarus goes over to the Medes, changing his name to Artaban to avoid identification as a former foe (III. iii. 267).

Although the Medes have just suffered a series of massive defeats at the hands of the Parthians, the arrival of Artaban immediately and decisively turns the tables (pp. 267–8), and the Parthian Queen and the Princess Elisa are soon his prisoners (p. 269). When Tigranes, the Median King, confesses that he owes his crown to Artaban and offers to grant any boon the hero asks, Artaban requests the freedom of the Queen and of the Princess, with whom he has fallen in love (p. 273). Tigranes himself, however, falls in love with Elisa, and eventually claims, like Dryden's Hobbist monarchs, that he is not bound by his promise: "It was only to you . . . that I passed my promise, and the knowledge of your self and me, will not let you be ignorant, that I have power to revoke it when I please" (p. 277). Artaban retorts to Tigranes, as he had to Artaxus, that he is not his subject and therefore owes him no obedience; as a result, he is banished (pp. 277–8 [erroneously numbered 276]).

Predictably, Artaban transfers his allegiance to the Parthians and brings victory with him, freeing the Queen and Princess, restoring King Phraates' kingdom to him, and conquering the greater part of Tigranes' (III. 281–91; iv. 292–8). Phraates eventually makes the inevitable unlimited offer, couched in terms very similar to those of the Ynca's offer in *The Indian Queen*: "I can never think the authority truly mine, till you have a share of it. . . . 'tis true, I possess nothing that is not below your merit, but I pretend to go as far in requital, as the dearest and most precious things I have in the world will carry me" (III. iv. 299). On this occasion, Artaban's princess returns his affection, and he therefore asks for her hand; as a result, Phraates throws him into prison, offers Tigranes marriage with Elisa, and sends him Artaban as a wedding present (pp. 305–20). The convoy bearing the lovers to Media is, however, attacked by pirates, and the hero and heroine are separated and plunged into further adventures (pp. 322–8).

After they are reunited they find another obstacle to their happiness in the Emperor Augustus. Augustus' friend Agrippa falls in love with Elisa (VI. ii. 611–14), and, although he himself competes with Artaban in a spirit of scrupulous magnanimity worthy of an Orrery hero (e.g., X. i. 190, XI. ii. 57, 66), the Emperor proves unprincipled and tyrannical in his attempts to further his friend's love. At length, however, Agrippa learns of Augustus' devious efforts on his behalf and selflessly resigns Elisa to Artaban (XII. iv. 248–9). Artaban's final triumph is enhanced by the revelation that he is of a birth commensurate with his self-esteem. At first, it seems that he is to be accorded the royal birth conventionally reserved for heroes of obscure birth, for, when the throne of Parthia is vacated by the death of Phraates, Artaban is declared to be a member of the Arsacid dynasty and heir to the vacant throne (XII. ii. 166–7). Although Artaban himself disproves the story of his royal lineage, he is persuaded to acquiesce in the fiction and accept the throne (XII. iii. 174). But then his true identity is revealed, and he is shown to be of blood even more illustrious than that of kings; for his true father was Pompey the Great, "Master to Kings, and the terrour of all the Powers in the Universe" (XII. iii. 191). In order to retain the Parthian crown, however,

Artaban decides to suppress his true identity and persist in his fictitious one (XII. iii. 197), with the result that he can enjoy the best of both worlds, wielding royal power and silently cherishing the glory of blood that is more than royal.

"I had rather see / You dead, than kind to any thing but me"

(IV. i. 65 – 6)

At the beginning of Act IV of *The Indian Queen* Montezuma and Orazia are each threatened by the villainous rival and protected by the villainous lover, whereupon the hero and heroine urge each other to die rather than favour the villainous lover. This scene is modelled on an incident in *Cassandra*, in which Oroondates and Statira/Cassandra are similarly the captives of their villainous rivals, Perdiccas and Roxana. Roxana attempts to blackmail Oroondates into love by threatening the death of Cassandra, and Perdiccas tries to compel Cassandra's affection by threatening the death of Oroondates. Oroondates is from the outset resolutely self-sacrificing, whereas Cassandra is at first more imperfect and possessive. Oroondates would die many times for the sake of Cassandra, but he cannot demand the like show of devotion from her, though he at first cannot go so far as to urge that she marry Perdiccas:

> . . . If I had a thousand lives to lose, I would give them up all to the rage of my enemies, rather than bestow a moment of them upon other thoughts than those of living and dying for you: but I dare not demand a like proof of your affection, as well because I have not deserved it, as because, if we ought to fear our enemies threats, it would be fatal to you: Peradventure I shall never obtain from the care I have of your safety, so much forgetfulness of mine own, as to advise you to love Perdiccas; . . . but neither can I perswade you to love this miserable man, since by Roxana's threats, your destruction is tied to the affection you shall express to him. (v. iv. 41).

Cassandra cannot at first equal Oroondates' spirit of resignation, but she admits far more frankly than Orazia that her destructive possessiveness is an "imperfection": "I acknowledge my imperfection, and confess I love you not with so unconcern'd an affection, as to look upon you with more contentment in the arms of Roxana, than in the arms of death: I wish the same eye shall behold Oroondates dead, and Oroondates inconstant, and I consent in fine either that he live for none but me, or that he cease to live by my example" (v. v. 41).

The dilemma reaches its climax when, as in *The Indian Queen*, each villainous lover simultaneously threatens the life of the heroic rival and protects the loved one from the violence of the other villain (v. v. 46 – 8).

Now, neither Oroondates nor Cassandra has the heart to urge the other to die: "they both were absolutely resolved to die, and the love of their own lives was not capable to touch them, but neither could consent to the loss of what they loved. . . . My fair Queen, said [Oroondates], you for the safety of your life may follow those waies that displease you least, but I for the preservation of mine, will never cease to love you. My dear Prince, answered the Queen, you shall live, if you can live without me, but I am firmly resolved to die for you, and yet I do not desire you should live for Roxana" (p. 47). Finally, Oroondates decides to die, but begs Cassandra to live and to trust that Providence will spare her from marriage to Perdiccas (p. 47). The lovers are, however, spared by the arrival of more villains and the outbreak of fighting between the supporters of Perdiccas and Roxana.

Oroondates' selflessness is equalled by that of his friend Arsaces/ Artaxerxes, who declares that he would rather resign his beloved Berenice to his rival, Arsacomes, than to death (IV. v. 37). In *Cleopatra* Coriolanus and the heroine are similarly prepared to sacrifice their own interests to save the life of the beloved. Cleopatra is loved by the evil Tiberius, who declares that he will kill Coriolanus if the heroine continues to reject his love (XII. ii. 176). Cleopatra places the choice in Coriolanus' hands, telling him that she will do anything to save his life if he so desires: "I am to offer you the choice of either losing your life, or quitting your pretensions to *Cleopatra*. . . . Advise me, *Coriolanus*, what I ought to do in this extremity, to preserve a life which is much dearer to me then my own. . . . If life be dearer to you then *Cleopatra*, to save it, I will bestow my self, not only on *Tiberius*, but on the most cruel Monster in the world: and if you prefer me before your life, I shall satisfie you, That mine is not so dear to me as that I would preserve it, and not acquit my self of what I owe your affection" (XII. iii. 202). Coriolanus decides to die, but says that he would gladly resign Cleopatra to Tiberius in order to save her life: "I tell you, That were the preservation of your life in dispute, and that you were put to a choice of either death, or a marriage with *Tiberius*, I would conjure you to marry him, as rather inclin'd to see you wedded to my Rival, then lose a life to which I ought to Sacrifice all considerations" (p. 202). Cleopatra then resolves to die with Coriolanus; unlike Montezuma and Orazia, however, Coriolanus does not welcome his loved one's suicidal loyalty but urges her not to make his death more terrible by adding hers to it (p. 203). The lovers are, however, saved by the intervention of Marcellus, Coriolanus' friend and magnanimous rival.

English and French drama afford parallel examples of self-denying magnanimity. In Davenant's *Love and Honour* Prospero wishes to die in order to save his loved one's life and ensure her happiness with his rival (III. p. 148), and in Corneille's *Héraclius* Martian urges Pulchérie to save her life by marrying the hero (I. iv. 341 – 2). In Quinault's libretto for Lully's *Alceste* (1674) Admète is prepared to resign Alceste to Alcide if he delivers her from death (III. pp. 176 – 7, in *Théatre de Quinault* [Paris, 1778], IV); but, when he has performed his task, Alcide is so moved by the spouses' grief at parting that he returns Alceste to Admète (IV. p. 193). Many of Dryden's most attractive later characters—Alibech, Valeria, and Benzayda—are prepared to renounce their loved ones in order to preserve them.

Olympia, another character in *Cleopatra*, faces a dilemma similar to that of the heroine but reacts differently, refusing to save her lover's life by committing incest with her brother (VII. ii. 36). She does so, however, because she believes that betrayal would torment her lover more than death. Orazia, by contrast, thinks only of herself, and in doing so conspicuously fails to practise the altruism she had preached.

THE INDIAN EMPEROUR

Magnanimity between Enemy Commanders

The magnanimity with which Cortez and Guyomar treat each other is generically similar to that displayed by Cyrus and the King of Pontus—enemies in war and rivals in love—in the early part of *Le Grand Cyrus*. When Cyrus sees the King beset in battle by twenty men, he dismisses the twenty and offers him single combat; the King, however, refuses, generously unwilling to fight a man who has saved his life (I. ii. 78 [2]), and soon repays Cyrus by warning him that forty Pontian soldiers have contrived a plot against his life, planning to attack him *en masse* in the next battle (p. 80 [2]). To ensure that no one falls accidental victim to the conspirators, Cyrus sends a message to the enemy army describing the armour that he will be wearing in the next battle (p. 81); and, in the battle, he defeats the conspirators (pp. 85–6), rescues the King of Pontus when he is attacked by sixteen men (p. 86), and subsequently liberates the chief conspirator, requesting the King of Pontus to spare his life (p. 89). Although he warned Cyrus of the conspiracy, the King still fears that he may be suspected of complicity in it, and he therefore publishes an order that no weapon except the sword be used against Cyrus (p. 90); when Cyrus learns of the order, however, he responds by releasing all the prisoners he has taken and disguising himself so as to avoid favoured treatment (p. 91). The King is ultimately taken prisoner (II. i. 15), but despite their rivalry in love Cyrus secures for him peace and liberty on advantageous terms (II. i. 43–9).

Cortez and Orbellan

In portraying the rivalry of Cortez and Orbellan for the hand of Cydaria, Dryden again turned to *Cassandra*, selecting, rearranging, and conflating some incidents from the account of Arsaces' and Arsacomes' rivalry for the hand of Berenice (sister of Oroondates). Arsaces (in reality Artaxerxes,

Prince of Persia) is captured in battle by the Scythians (IV. ii. 111 – 12), falls in
love with Berenice, daughter of the Scythian king (p. 115), and earns the
love of the daughter and the favour of the father, though he prudently
refrains from publishing his true identity. The king, however, has recently
remarried, and his wife is urging that her step-brother, Arsacomes, should
marry Berenice (I..v. 116 – 17)—as Almeria urges that Orbellan be allowed
to marry Cydaria. When Arsaces' true identity is eventually discovered he is
thrown into prison, but escapes (IV. iii. 158, iv. 6). He then makes his way to
the army, where Arsacomes is in command, and fights a duel with his rival
(IV. iv. 6 – 23); Dryden conflates this episode with a later one in portraying
Cortez' duel with Orbellan. When Arsacomes is incapacitated by a wound,
Arsaces unhesitatingly spares him: "I had time enough to have slain
Arsacomes, if I had had a minde to it," he tells the audience of his life-story;
"but how great Interest soever I had in his death, I was not able to give it him,
being he was no longer in a condition to defend himself" (p. 23). The army
then rallies to Arsaces' support, continuing in its loyalty even when he
reveals his true identity (p. 24). Arsaces gives further proof of his
magnanimity by procuring medical aid for Arsacomes, and refuses even to
serve his own interests by keeping his rival prisoner and thus preventing his
marriage to Berenice: "How great interest soever I had to keep him, I
scorn'd to make use of that advantage which I held from fortune, and since
he had escaped my sword, I believ'd my self oblig'd in honour, to restore
him a liberty, which he had lost onely by the defection of his army" (p. 26).
He then liberates Arsacomes in the full knowledge that he is probably
ensuring his rival's triumph: "I know I give my self death, in giving you
liberty, and that you will make no other use of it then to deprive me of that
Princesse, who is the cause of all our differences; but that knowledge is not
able to alter my design: go see Berenice again when you please, but
remember that a generous man ought to win her affection rather by his
services, then by her fathers authority, and that the recompense you owe to
what I now do for you, is not to suffer Berenice to be forc'd" (p. 26). He then
deliberately *retards* the advance of the army towards the city of Issedon, "not
being willing to flye to extremities against the father of Berenice, and
Oroondates" (p. 26). While he is magnanimously delaying hostilities,
however, the king and Arsacomes send two assassins to the army, who steal
into Arsaces' tent and try to murder him (pp. 27 – 8); Dryden conflates this
incident with the earlier duel to make the episode of Orbellan's night attack.
Arsaces kills one assassin (p. 28) and later liberates the other (II. v. 30). And,
angered at his opponents' baseness, he marches on Issedon and besieges it
(II. v. 29 – 30). Prince Carthusis, brother of the king and friend of Arsaces, is
captured in the fighting, and when liberated asks Arsaces for a three-day
truce, during which he hopes to persuade the king to permit the lovers to
marry (pp. 30 – 1). At the end of the three days, however, Carthusis writes to
say that he has been unsuccessful and that Berenice is to marry Arsacomes the
next day (p. 32). Arsaces therefore decides to attack the town in order to

prevent the wedding (p. 33), but gives strict orders that no one is to be killed unless he resists (p. 35). The assault is successful, Berenice is rescued, and Arascomes is once more spared: "Arsacomes may live also," Arsaces proclaims, "since I cannot give him his death without advantage" (p. 35). Many more complications and acts of magnanimity, however, are to ensue before the lovers are finally united.

TYRANNICK LOVE

Porphyrius, Berenice, and Maximin

The triangle of Porphyrius, Berenice, and Maximin is based on that of Tyridates, Mariamne, and Herod in *Cleopatra* (parts of whose story also provided Dryden with hints for Part II Act v, of *The Conquest of Granada*). Herod espouses Mariamne, granddaughter of the two kings Hircanus and Aristobulus, and then dispossesses Hircanus and destroys all rightful heirs to the throne (I. i. 8). Mariamne is commanded by her mother and Hircanus to marry Herod, and, though she has "a just resentment against this Cut-throat of her Family," she obeys (p. 8). "But they could never bow her soul to love that Husband," whom she regarded with "aversion and disdain" (p. 9). Yet, had he not murdered her brother, Aristobulus, "she had liv'd in a most admirable moderation with him, and with an excess of virtue done violence upon her inclinations, by induring him, whom Heaven and her Parents had given her for a husband" (p. 9).

Tyridates, younger brother of the King of Parthia, flees to Judaea from his brother's tyranny (p. 7), finds favour with Herod (p. 8), falls in love with Mariamne (p. 9), unluckily excites the love of Salome (p. 12), and by his heroism earns the chief command of Herod's armies (p. 13). At first, Tyridates entertains no "thought that might justly offend" Mariamne, but then starts to hope for her favours and to consider that Herod has no claim on her affections (p. 10). He tells Mariamne that he deplores her condition, but she considers that she cannot lawfully entertain any resentments against her husband, and believes that she is being punished by heaven for her crimes (pp. 11–12). Later, when Tyridates offers to execute any orders she may give against Herod, she declares, "I cannot love him . . . but I must tell you . . . that . . . he is yet my husband; that my apprehensions of his injuries are not more prevalent than the rules of my duty, and that I am not permitted to desire a revenge against him, which Heaven hath reserved for its own appointment" (pp. 16–17). Realising that Tyridates loves her, she pardons his offence but henceforth takes care to talk to him only in company (pp. 17–19); and, by means of her exalted virtue, she raises Tyridates to a like spirit of self-denial: "the knowledge I had of her admirable Vertue, having extinguisht with my hopes a part of those flames her Beauty had kindl'd, I learn'd to think my Passion sufficiently rewarded by the esteem she had of me: Indeed there was never any person lov'd with less interest; and with truth I may say, I loved *Mariamne* for her self alone; nor in all the process of my Passion did I ever consider Tyridates" (p. 19). At length, Mariamne's heart is softened with pity for her lover; "but it was never capable of an impression not conformed to the severe Rules of her Duty" (p. 19).

Despite her virtue, however, Mariamne increasingly excites her husband's jealous suspicion: she enrages him by modestly refusing to kiss him in public (p. 22), and later forbids him his conjugal rights, since she has discovered that whenever he went to battle he left orders that she was not to survive his death (I. ii. 32). Meanwhile, Salome has been inflaming Herod's jealousy, since Tyridates has rejected her advances and turned her love to hate (I. i. 23−4, ii. 29). Herod consequently believes that Mariamne's coldness springs from love for Tyridates, and Tyridates is forced to flee (I. ii. 33−9). Nevertheless, he returns to Jerusalem in disguise, with difficulty gains an interview with Mariamne, and once again offers to free her from Herod (pp. 40−1). She, however, is indignant both that Tyridates should endanger her reputation (p. 14) and that he should offer injury to her husband: "the Crime of *Herod* cannot authorize mine," she tells him: " . . . I am neither permitted by Law Divine or Humane to serve my self of your assistance" (p. 42). She then commands him never to see her again, but feels that the perpetual separation permits her to avow that she is not insensible to his merits: "I have not been so insensible, but if Heaven and my Parents had left me in a condition to make my own choice, and *Tyridates* imbrac'd the true Religion, I had prefer'd him above the rest of Mankind" (p. 42). She then implants a kiss on his forehead—"the greatest and most signal favour I ever received of *Mariamne*", Tyridates tells his listeners (p. 43).

After Tyridates' departure, Herod is at first jealous, but eventually love reasserts itself and he professes penitence. Mariamne "was pacified, as she believed it was her duty to be, and she was reconciled to him as far as the disproportion of their manners, and the memory of the cruel injuries she had received in the death of all their relations, would permit" (v. iv. 552). After further alternations of love and jealousy, however, Herod condemns Mariamne to death (v. iv. 560). Immediately before her execution, she delivers a speech of exemplary virtue: "the repugnance which his cruelties have caused in me either to his manners or person, never inclined me to the least thought of offending against my own honour or the duty of a Wife: . . . As for *Tyridates*, I thank God, I feel no remorse of conscience that can accuse me of the least fault against my Husband, and I had no other thoughts for his person but of acknowledgment and esteem as due to his vertue" (p. 564). She then pardons Herod and Salome, and is beheaded (p. 564); and, when Tyridates hears of her death, he at once expires with grief (p. 566).

THE CONQUEST OF GRANADA

"I cannot stay to ask which cause is best"

Romance heroes regularly give unquestioning assistance to outnumbered or
overmatched opponents, and in doing so sometimes help the wrong side. In
helping an unrecognised underdog, for example, Cyrus unwittingly
protects the King of Assyria as he abducts Mandana (II. i. 75—7).
Nevertheless, there is no moral ambiguity about Cyrus' action: he has a
clear-cut duty to help the oppressed and is not to be blamed if the oppressed
turn out to be wrong-doers. Moreover, the portrayal of his intervention
contrasts markedly with that of Almanzor's: "the generosity of *Artamenes*
not permitting him to see one single man in his presence, assaulted by eleven;
never stood considering what he had to do, but as soon as he saw these
Cavaliers assault a single man, drew his sword, and commanded us to do the
like" (p. 75). Whereas Cyrus does not stay "considering what he had to do",
Almanzor does not stay "to ask which cause is best": by stressing the absence
of moral reflection Dryden implies the desirability of its presence and
confuses what in Scudéry is a perfectly straightforward obligation. For a
monstrously intricate example of this standard situation see *Cleopatra* I. iv.
89—93. For other examples see *Cleopatra* VII. i. 9—11; *Cassandra* I. i. 2, III. v.
47; *Almahide* II. i. 104; *Polexander* II. iv. sig [¶ ¶ ¶3ᵛ]; Suckling, *The
Goblins* I. i. 70.

"I'le set thee free, / That I again may fight and conquer thee"

The closest parallel to Almanzor's action and sentiment is provided by
Cyrus, who "sent back to the King of *Phrygia, Imbas* his Lieutenant General
whom he had defeated, and took prisoner, . . . commanding the Herauld
which was to conduct him to tell that Prince, how gallantly this valiant man
had defended himself; and had given such testimony of a noble soul during
his disgrace, that he would not do him the displeasure to keep him Prisoner
during the Battle; nor deprive himself of that honour to vanquish him the
second time, if good fortune failed not" (II. i. 14). Almanzor and Cyrus both
express the desire for a second conquest. Nevertheless, their speeches are very
different in character: Cyrus is moved by concern and respect for the
general, desiring the return bout in self-effacing terms that do more to
compliment his opponent than to puff his own valour; Almanzor, by
contrast, confines himself to an egocentric assertion of his physical
superiority. Furthermore, whereas Dryden does nothing to dilute or
mitigate the impulsiveness of Almanzor's action, Scudéry provides Cyrus
with a reasoned justification of his—namely, that the return of one prisoner
to the enemy has freed many guards for combat duty on his own side (p. 14).
Dryden transforms a gesture of prudent magnanimity into one of irrational
selfishness.

"Take friendship: or if that too small appear, / Take love which Sisters may to Brothers bear"

In making Almahide save Almanzor by marrying Boabdelin Dryden copies an episode in *Cassandra*, in which Parisatis agrees to marry Hephestion, the favourite of Alexander the Great, on condition that Alexander spares the life of her lover, Lysimachus (II. ii. 221 – 2). Once again, however, the behaviour of the romance hero contrasts instructively with that of Almanzor. Like Almahide, Parisatis offers her dispossessed lover the consolation of sisterly affection—"*the same inclinations I had heretofore for* [my] *dear brother*" (II. ii. 222). Lysimachus, however, proves far more tractable than Almanzor: "I promise you that I will never disobey you while I live. I will lay my neck under *Hephestions* foot if you desire it, and with respect and submission will kiss the very hand that murthers me, if you command me" (p. 223). "Consider a little," he asks the friends to whom he relates his history,

> . . . and withall admire the wonderful change of my humour; see how mild I was grown, and how different from that furious *Lysimachus* who but a few days before ran with his sword drawn into *Hephestions* house. . . . Certainly, when I make reflexion upon this sudden *Metamorphosis*, I cannot sufficiently admire the power of *Parisatis*, whose will had in a moment carried mine from one extremity to the other, nor forbear concluding by this proof, that never man equalled me in the perfection of Love. . . . To devest ones self of the most pressing and most violent thoughts a soul is able to conceive or suffer, to cast off the interests of a mans own life, to establish the repose of his enemy, by the losse of his own, and to pass from an excess of rage, to such submissive resignations, is that which we see in very few persons. (pp. 224 – 5)

Lysimachus completes his metamorphosis by retiring to the country to console himself with the philosophical works of Callisthenes. Here, in the Utopian world of romance, we see a successful example of the conventional transformation through pure affection that Almahide *vainly and self-deceivingly* tries to accomplish in her less simple world.

The Heroine in an Unwanted Marriage: Almahide and Her Romance Counterparts

Like Almahide, romance heroines tend to be less in control of their passions than the heroines of Carlell, Davenant, and Orrery. But they are decidedly less frail than Almahide. The forced marriages in *Cyrus* invariably produce bitter misery, but the heroines differ from Almahide in the honesty with which they appraise their emotions and the prudence with which they direct their lives; they do not strike false and impossible poses. The heroines of

Cassandra are rather more successful at conforming inclination to duty. Parisatis continues to love Lysimachus, but nevertheless conjures up all the fitting wifely emotions for the husband who is forced upon her: she "really lov'd *Hephestion*, as her duty, and the merite of such a husband obliged her" (II. ii. 230). Statira, her sister, has to face a similar conflict. Tricked into believing that her lover, Oroondates, is unfaithful, she marries Alexander the Great, only to make an immediate discovery of Oroondates' innocence (I. v. 139 – 41). Although she vows to banish the unlawful remembrance of Oroondates and to devote her heart solely to Alexander (p. 141), she finds that her first love cannot be vanquished with the anticipated throughness (I. vi. 145 – 6). Nevertheless, she succeeds in loving Alexander as much as she ought (I. vi. 167), retaining for Oroondates an affection that is completely pure (pp. 168 – 9), and throughout her short marriage she manages her emotions, her behaviour, and her lover with faultless propriety and equity. Like Parisatis (and unlike Almahide), moreover, she has considerable success in refining her lover's affections, inspiring Oroondates to declare that Alexander alone deserves her love (p. 160). Almahide's emotions are less malleable and less pure than those of La Calprenède's heroines: she does not develop any love for her husband, and she finally realises that her love for Almanzor carries with it the risk of adultery (II. IV. pp. 143 – 4, V. p. 155). The flaw which sets her quite apart from romance heroines, however, is her sustained and dangerous self-deception. (In Scudéry's *Almahide* the heroine only enters a fake marriage with Boaudilin, so her case is not comparable with that of her Dryden namesake).

AURENG-ZEBE

Ariobarzanes

Ariobarzanes (one of the heroes of *Cleopatra*) is not the direct model of Aureng-Zebe, but he is an excellent example of the *kind* of hero that Aureng-Zebe tries to be, scrupulously and successfully negotiating the dilemmas that prove insoluble in Aureng-Zebe's more realistic world.

Adallas, King of Thrace, is infatuated with his sister, Olympia, and wishes to marry her (VI. i. 586 – 90). But she flees (p. 593) and is shipwrecked on an island (VI. ii. 596), where she meets a young man who turns out to be Ariobarzanes, brother of King Artaxus of Armenia (VI. ii. 597 – 8, VII. i. 4). They fall in love (VI. ii. 598 – 610), but Olympia tells Ariobarzanes that she cannot marry without her brother's consent, and explains the circumstances that make his consent unlikely (VII. i. 5 – 6). Some combatants land on the island, and Ariobarzanes intervenes to bring victory to the underdog, who turns out to be Adallas (pp. 9 – 13). Adallas realises that Ariobarzanes (whom he believes to be called Ariamenes) is his rival (p. 15), and tells Olympia that, although he will never possess her by force, he will prevent anyone else from possessing her (p. 16). He also declares that, since Ariobarzanes has in equal measure done him service and outrage, he will convey him anywhere on earth except Thrace, and will only revenge himself by withholding reward (pp. 17–18). Ariobarzanes is set ashore in Cyprus (p. 19), and the brother and sister head for Thrace, having heard that the Thracians are in revolt (pp. 21–4). They are, however, becalmed in Crete for six weeks, and while there learn that a stranger has inflicted grave defeats on the rebels (p. 25)—a stranger whose name turns out to be Ariamenes (p. 28).

When Adallas returns to Thrace, he disregards Ariobarzanes' great services, imprisons him, and sentences him to death (VII. ii. 33–5), though Olympia refuses to be blackmailed into a sinful marriage by the threat to her lover's life (p. 36). Adallas is, however, captured in battle (p. 38), and the Byzantines proclaim Olympia their Princess (p. 39), whereupon she frees Ariobarzanes and commands him to rescue Adallas (pp. 39–40). Ariobarzanes agrees without hesitation (p. 40), defeats the rebels, and salutes Adallas with "all the Civility and Respect that could be due to him in his better Fortune" (p. 47). Before restoring Adallas to his throne, Ariobarzanes obtains a promise that he can marry Olympia (p. 49); but Adallas at first delays fulfilment of his promise (pp. 51–2), and at length tells Ariobarzanes that he can marry Olympia at once, provided that he is executed the next day (p. 53). Ariobarzanes accepts the proposal, but Olympia will not consent (p. 54). Adallas then says that Ariobarzanes can marry Olympia providing that he goes to Armenia and brings back proof of his identity (p. 55). On the voyage, Ariobarzanes thwarts a murder conspiracy arranged by Adallas (pp. 57–8), but his ship is assailed by pirates (pp. 59–60), with the result that he and Olympia are separated. Hereafter, Adallas fades out of the story, and, after further adventures, the lovers are eventually married (XII. iv. 253).

Notes

CHAPTER 1

1. 332–3, in *Sophoclis Fabulae*, ed. A. C. Pearson, corrected ed. (Oxford, 1928). Translations from foreign languages are my own except where I indicate otherwise.

2. *Doctor Faustus* I. i. 90, in *The Complete Works of Christopher Marlowe*, ed. Fredson Bowers (Cambridge, Eng., 1973), II.

3. The following works assume that Dryden's heroes are intended to invite unmixed admiration: Lewis N. Chase, *The English Heroic Play* (New York, 1903); Cecil V. Deane, *Dramatic Theory and the Rhymed Heroic Play* (London, 1931); Bonamy Dobrée, *Restoration Tragedy 1660–1720* (Oxford, 1929), pp. 13–24; Thomas H. Fujimura, "The Appeal of Dryden's Heroic Plays", *PMLA*, 75 (1960), 37–45; Allardyce Nicoll, *A History of Restoration Drama, 1660–1700* (Cambridge, Eng., 1923), pp. 90–121; B. J. Pendlebury, *Dryden's Heroic Plays: A Study of the Origins* (London, 1923); James Sutherland, *English Literature in the Late Seventeenth Century*, Oxford History of English Literature, 6 (Oxford, 1969), 47–63; John Harold Wilson, *A Preface to Restoration Drama* (Cambridge, Mass., 1968), pp. 67–83. The following argue, with varying emphasis, that some or all of the heroic plays show initially unruly heroes subjected to a process of education: Michael W. Alssid, *Dryden's Rhymed Heroic Tragedies: A Critical Study of the Plays and of Their Place in Dryden's Poetry*, Salzburg Studies in English Literature, Poetic Drama, 7, 2 vols. (Salzburg, 1974); Jean Gagen, "Love and Honor in Dryden's Heroic Plays", *PMLA*, 77 (1962), 208–20; Arthur C. Kirsch, *Dryden's Heroic Drama* (Princeton, 1965); Richard Leslie Larson, *Studies in Dryden's Dramatic Technique: The Use of Scenes Depicting Persuasion and Accusation*, Salzburg Studies in English Literature, Poetic Drama and Poetic Theory, 9 (Salzburg, 1975); Scott C. Osborn, "Heroical Love in Dryden's Heroic Drama", *PMLA*, 73 (1958), 480–90; Eugene M. Waith, *The Herculean Hero in Marlowe, Chapman, Shakespeare and Dryden* (London, 1962), pp. 156–76; *Ideas of Greatness: Heroic Drama in England* (London, 1971), pp. 203–31; John A. Winterbottom, "The Development of the Hero in Dryden's Tragedies", *JEGP*, 52 (1953), 161–73; Selma Assir Zebouni, *Dryden: A Study in Heroic Characterisation*, Louisiana State University Humanities Series, 16 (Baton Rouge, 1965). Michael West believes that Dryden initially celebrated heroism but became increasingly disenchanted with it during his career: "Dryden and the Disintegration of Renaissance Heroic Ideals", *Costerus*, 7 (1973), 193–222. D. W. Jefferson argues that Dryden intended to evoke simultaneous admiration and laughter: "The Significance of Dryden's Heroic Plays", *Proceedings of the Leeds Philosophical and Literary Society*, 5 (1940), 125–39, reprinted in Earl Miner (ed.), *Restoration Dramatists: A Collection of Critical Essays* (Englewood Cliffs, N.J., 1966), pp. 19–35. A similar idea is advanced with some qualification in Landrum Banks, "Dryden's Baroque Drama", in Thomas A. Kirby and William J. Olive (eds.), *Essays in Honor of Esmond Linworth Marilla* (Baton Rouge, 1970), p. 196; Waith, *Ideas of Greatness*, p. 215; "Dryden and the Tradition of Serious Drama", in Earl Miner (ed.), *John Dryden*

(London and Athens, Ohio, 1972), pp. 71–2. Alan S. Fisher argues that Dryden exploited absurd paradox in order to vindicate and exalt Almanzor: "Daring to be Absurd: The Paradoxes of *The Conquest of Granada*", *SP*, 73 (1976), 414–39. The best ironic reading of a heroic play is Robert S. Newman, "Irony and the Problem of Tone in Dryden's *Aureng-Zebe*", *SEL*, 10 (1970), 439–58.

4. Bruce King, *Dryden's Major Plays* (Edinburgh and London, 1966); Anne T. Barbeau, *The Intellectual Design of John Dryden's Heroic Plays* (New Haven and London, 1970). Miss Barbeau too is concerned with the education of the unruly hero.

5. *Aureng-Zebe* IV. 396–543, in L. A. Beaurline and Fredson Bowers (eds.), *John Dryden: Four Tragedies* (Chicago and London, 1967); *Le Misanthrope* IV. iii. 1277–1435, in Molière, *Œuvres complètes*, ed. Robert Jouanny, 2 vols. (Paris, 1962), I.

6. *Tyrannick Love* V. 453–93, in *The Works of John Dryden*, X, eds. Maximillian E. Novak and George Robert Guffey (Berkeley, Los Angeles, and London, 1970). Hereafter cited as California Dryden, X.

7. The 1920s witnessed an inconclusive and unnecessary debate between William S. Clark and Kathleen M. Lynch, Clark asserting the plays to be chiefly derived from romance, Lynch from Platonic drama: Clark, "The Sources of the Restoration Heroic Play", *RES* (O.S.), 4 (1928), 49–63; "The Platonic Element in the Restoration Heroic Play", *PMLA*, 45 (1930), 623–4; Lynch, "Conventions of Platonic Drama in the Heroic Plays of Orrery and Dryden", *PMLA*, 44 (1929), 456–71. For other studies of the debt to romance see Herbert Wynford Hill, *La Calprenède's Romances and the Restoration Drama*, University of Nevada Studies, II. 3 (1910), III. 2 (1911); Leslie Howard Martin, "The Consistency of Dryden's *Aureng-Zebe*", *SP*, 70 (1973), 306–28; Jerome W. Schweitzer, "Dryden's Use of Scudéry's *Almahide*", *MLN*, 54 (1939), 190–2; "Another Note on Dryden's Use of Georges de Scudéry's *Almahide*", *MLN*, 62 (1947), 262–3; for briefer comments on the subject see Deane, *Dramatic Theory and the Rhymed Heroic Play*, pp. 13–15; Waith, "Dryden and the Tradition of Serious Drama", pp. 58–63. For the debt to epic theory and romance see A. E. Parsons, "The English Heroic Play", *MLR*, 33 (1938), 1–14; Pendlebury, *Dryden's Heroic Plays*. For the debt to Platonic literature see Alfred Harbage, *Cavalier Drama. An Historical and Critical Supplement to the Study of the Elizabethan and Restoration Stage* (New York and London, 1936); Kathleen M. Lynch, *The Social Mode of Restoration Comedy* (New York and London, 1926), where the Platonic fashion is traced back to its origins in Honoré d'Urfé's pastoral romance *L'Astrée* (1602–27). For other studies of romance and Platonism, not concerned with the genesis of the heroic play, see Jefferson Butler Fletcher, *The Religion of Beauty in Woman, and Other Essays in Platonic Love in Poetry and Society* (New York, 1911); T. P. Haviland, *The Roman de Longue Haleine on English Soil* (Philadelphia, 1931); Dorothy McDougall, *Madeleine de Scudéry, Her Romantic Life and Death* (London, 1938); Laurens J. Mills, *One Soul in Bodies Twain. Friendship in Tudor Literature and Stuart Drama* (Bloomington, 1937); "The Friendship Theme in Orrery's Plays", *PMLA*, 53 (1938), 795–806; Philip A. Wadsworth, *The Novels of Gomberville* (New Haven and London, 1942). James W. Tupper derives the heroic play from the traditions established by Beaumont and Fletcher: "The Relation of the Heroic Play to the Romances of Beaumont and Fletcher", *PMLA*, 20 (1905), 584–621. In *Dryden's Heroic Drama* Kirsch stresses the influence both of native tradition and Corneille's drama. The ancestry of the heroic plays is well summarised in *The Works of John Dryden*, VIII, ed. John Harrington Smith *et al.* (Berkeley and Los Angeles, 1962), 282–93; the editors, however, assume that Dryden's plays endorse the values that they inherit.

8. "Dryden's *Aureng-Zebe*: Debts to Corneille and Racine", *Revue de Littérature Comparée*, 46 (1972), 5–34. Brooks illustrates creative digestion and transformation rather than close, extensive borrowing. The following works postulate debts to French drama and dramatic theory: Chase, *The English Heroic Play*; Deane, *Dramatic Theory and the Rhymed Heroic Play*; Kirsch, *Dryden's Heroic Drama*; Zebouni, *Dryden: A Study in Heroic Characterisation.*

9. For examples of identity transfer and re-enactment of the past in Corneille see, e.g., *Le Cid* I. i. 37, ii. 103, iii. 212, iv. 265, II. viii. 676, 680, 720–32, III. vi. 1028–30, IV. iii. 1180, v. i. 1499–500; *Cinna* I. iii. 237–40, II. i. 377–94, 427–8, 638, III. ii. 829–44, iv. 1029–31, IV. iii. 1227–8, iv. 1313–14, v. 1347, 1370, vi. 1419–24, v. i. 1527–40, ii. 1589–90, 1595–604; *Rodogune* I. iii. 169–210, II. iv. 713–18, III. iii. 855–62, 884, IV. i. 1159–66, 1185–94, iii. 1339–48, vii. 1487–90, v. iv. 1819–24. Unlike *Rodogune*, *Cinna* concludes with a triumphant release from the past: v. ii. 1605–16, iii. 1731, 1773–4. Citations from Corneille are to *Œuvres complètes*, ed. André Stegmann (Paris, 1963).

10. Gauthier de Costes, Seigneur de La Calprenède, *Cassandra: The Fam'd Romance*, trans. Sir Charles Cotterell (London, 1661), v. v. 34–48. In referring to romances, I for the sake of consistency treat each book as a separate volume, and use the conventions appropriate to works of more than one volume. I summarise the most important romance sources in the Appendix.

11. La Calprenède, *Hymen's Præludia, or Love's Master-Piece. Being that so much admired Romance, entituled Cleopatra*, I, trans. Robert Loveday *et al.* (London, 1665), I. i. 5–44, v, iv. 552–66. For later books of the romance, I use *Hymen's Præludia, or Love's Master-Piece. Being the Six Last Parts of that so much Admired Romance, Intituled, Cleopatra*, trans. J[ohn] C[oles] and I. D. (London, 1663).

12. *The Indian Emperour*, I. ii. 153–61, II. ii. 86–99, in *The Works of John Dryden*, IX, ed. John Loftis and Vinton A. Dearing (Berkeley and Los Angeles, 1966); *Rodogune* III. iv. 979–1047.

13. *All for Love* II. 251–461, in *Four Tragedies*, ed. Beaurline and Bowers; *Cinna* v. i. 1425–561.

14. "Of Heroic Plays: An Essay", prefixed to *The Conquest of Granada*, p. 163, in *"Of Dramatic Poesy" and Other Critical Essays*, ed. George Watson, 2 vols. (London and New York, 1962), I. Hereafter cited as Watson. Dedication of *Aureng-Zebe*, p. 85, in *The Dramatic Works*, ed. Montague Summers (London, 1931–2; rpt. New York, 1968), IV. Hereafter cited as Summers.

15. "The History of Aglatidas and Amestris" narrates a sequence of absurd jealousies and misunderstandings, at the climax of which Amestris punishes her lover and herself by marrying the base and ugly Otanus: *Artamenes or The Grand Cyrus*, trans. F. G. (London, 1653), I. iii. 103–55, III. ii. 85, iii. 147–53, IV. ii. 250–87.

16. In Thomas Killigrew's *Claracilla* (1636; 1660) Philemon loves the heroine, who is the mistress of his friend Melintus. But, Melintus tells Claracilla, "to serve us/In our wishes was all the heaven he aym'd at" (II. sig. [D11]), in *The Prisoners and Claracilla: Two Tragæ-Comedies* [London, 1641]. (When citing Caroline plays, I give the year of the first known performance and of the first known Restoration revival, if any. Dates of Caroline performances are taken from Harbage, *Cavalier Drama*, pp. 260–84; those of Restoration revivals from William van Lennep, Emmett L. Avery, and Arthur H. Scouten (eds.), *The London Stage 1660–1800, Part I: 1660–1700* [Carbondale, Ill., 1965]. I treat 1 January as New Year's Day. Where no Restoration revival is known, I give the date of first publication or republication, if any, after 1650). *Cyrus* does contain a few magnanimous rivals, though their self-denial is never

as perfect and spectacular as that of the ideal lovers who populate the English stage. The King of Cyprus, mistakenly believing his friend to be in love with his mistress, resigns her to him—much to the friend's annoyance and embarrassment (II. iii. 170– 7); the King does, however, eventually marry his loved one (II. iii. 193). Tisander, realising that his friend loves his wife, urges her to be pleasant to him and bequeaths her to him when he dies (III. iii. 173–8). Mazares, one of Mandana's lovers, eventually resolves to assist Cyrus in the search for her and "to love her for her own sake only . . . without any hopes" (v. ii. 114); he subsequently, however, has many bouts of irresolution (e.g. VII. i. 22; iii. 156, 192). Another unsuccessful lover, Tysimenes, does resemble Orrery's heroes and their predecessors in wooing his beloved on his friend's behalf, but he does so unwillingly and inexpertly, and conveys bad news to his friend with more pleasure and conviction than he can muster when the news is good (VIII. iii. 32–3). In *Almahide* Zelebin is even more resentful and mindful of self when employed in the suit of his Prince and unwitting rival, Audalla, though Audalla acts with magnanimous resignation when he realises the true situation: Georges de Scudéry, *Almahide; or the Captive Queen*, trans. John Phillips (London, 1677), III. ii. 11–51.

17. For the image of the smokeless flame see William Cartwright, *The Siege* (1638; collected works pub. 1651) III. vii. 1362–4; William Davenant, *The Siege of Rhodes* (1656; 1661) II. I. p. 313, in *The Dramatic Works of Sir William D'Avenant*, ed. J. Maidment and W. H. Logan (Edinburgh and London, 1872–4), III (hereafter cited as Maidment and Logan); William Habington, "A Dialogue betweene Hope and Feare", in *Castara* (1634), ed. Edward Arber (London, 1870), p. 28; "Detraction Execrated", ll. 25–32, in *The Works of Sir John Suckling: The Non-Dramatic Works*, ed. Thomas Clayton (Oxford, 1971), p. 36. For the image of the unfuelled flame see William Cartwright, *The Royall Slave* (1636) III. iv. 939–51; Suckling, *Aglaura* (1637; 1661) I. v. 18–22, in *The Works of Sir John Suckling: The Plays*, ed. L. A. Beaurline (Oxford, 1971); Suckling, "Love's World", ll. 33–6, in *Non-Dramatic Works*, p. 23.

18. For extended expositions of Platonic ideals see William Cartwright, *The Royall Slave* III. iv. 911–67; *The Siege* III. vii. 1275–407; Davenant, *The Temple of Love* (1635; collected works pub. 1673), in Maidment and Logan, I. 289–305; Walter Mountague, *The Shepheard's Paradise* (1633; London, 1629 [misprint for 1659]) IV. pp. 94–6.

19. Lodowick Carlell, *Arviragus and Philicia* (1636; 1672; London, 1639) I. II. sig. [B7ᵛ].

20. *Argalus and Parthenia* (1638; 1661) II. p. 30, in *The Plays and Poems of Henry Glapthorne* (London, 1874), I. The idea of love surviving disfigurement seems to have been a minor topos: see Habington, "A Dialogue betweene Araphill and Castara", in *Castara*, pp. 71–2; *Cyrus* VIII. ii. 158. For other references to communion of souls see Carlell, *The Deseruing Fauorite* (London, 1629; repub. 1659) v. sig. N3; William Cartwright, *The Lady-Errant* (1637) II. v. 631–2; Davenant, *The Platonic Lovers* (1635) II. p. 42, IV. p. 78, in Maidment and Logan, II; Habington, "To the World. The Perfection of Love", in *Castara*, p. 51; John Hall, "The Lure", ll. 79–80, in George Saintsbury (ed.), *Minor Poets of the Caroline Period*, II, (Oxford, 1906), 195; Katherine Philips, "To my dearest Antenor, on his Parting", ll. 13–24, in Saintsbury (ed), *Minor Caroline Poets* I (1905), 551. For love of or communion with the partner's mind see Carlell, *The Deseruing Fauorite* I. sig. [B3], III. sig. [G4ᵛ], v. sig. N2ᵛ; *The Passionate Lovers* (1638; London, 1655), I. I. p. 16; Habington, "A Dialogue betweene Araphill and Castara", in *Castara*, pp. 71–2; Thomas Killigrew, *Claracilla* III. sig.

[E9]; Orrery, *The Black Prince* (1667) II. iii. 217–26, in *The Dramatic Works of Roger Boyle, Earl of Orrery*, ed. William S. Clark (Cambridge, Mass., 1937), I. For variations on these ideas see William Cartwright, *The Siege* III. vii. 1387–93; Walter Mountague, *The Shepheard's Paradise* III. p. 52. *The Platonic Lovers* and *The Lady-Errant* treat their Platonic themes sceptically.

21. See also *Claracilla* II. sig. [D9]; *The Shepheard's Paradise* I. p. 3.

22. *The Deseruing Fauorite* v. sig. N3ᵛ: "[Love] hath to vs beene iust this day as well as kinde./Rewarding vertuous Loue let none then call him blinde."

23. "To my dearest Antenor, on his Parting", ll. 7–8, in Saintsbury (ed.), *Minor Caroline Poets*, I. 551. See also Carlell, *The Fool Would be a Favourit* (1637; repub. 1657), ed. Allardyce Nicoll (Waltham Saint Lawrence, 1926) v. p. 87; Habington, "To the Right Honourable, the Lord P.", in *Castara*, p. 74. Cf. Aristophanes' speech in Plato, *Symposium* 189c–193e, in *Platonis Opera*, ed. Ioannes Burnet (Oxford, 1901), II.

24. Davenant, *The Fair Favourite* (1638) v. p. 280, in Maidment and Logan, IV; *The Siege* (1629) v. p. 436, *ibid.*; Habington, *The Queen of Arragon* (London, 1640; 1668) v. sigs. I, I2; Orrery, *The Generall* (1664) v. i. 422. Don Sanche in Corneille's *Le Cid* is a similarly good loser (v. vi. 1759–62).

25. *Love and Honour* (1634; 1661) v. p. 184, in Maidment and Logan, III. See also *The Deseruing Fauorite* v. sig. Nᵛ Davenant, *The Rivals* (1664) v. pp. 291–3, in Maidment and Logan, v. In *The Fair Favourite* the Queen's virtue, more gradually and convincingly, diverts the King's love from Eumena to her: see especially v. p. 278.

26. For further examples of the rational redistribution of affections see *The Fool Would be a Favourit* v. pp. 86–7; George Cartwright, *The Heroick Lover, or, The Infanta of Spain* (1650; London, 1661; prob. unacted) v. p. 72; Richard Flecknoe, *Love's Dominion* (unacted; London, 1654) v. pp. 72–9; *Love's Kingdom* (London, 1664) v. p. 79 (this play is an extensively revised version of *Love's Dominion*); *Erminia, or the Chaste Lady* (no known performance; London, 1665) v. pp. 92–3; Edward Howard, *The Womens Conquest* (1670; London, 1671) v. p. 85; Orrery, *Henry the Fifth* (1664) II. i. 356–71; *The Black Prince* v. v. 445–655.

27. *The Royall Slave* III. v. 999–1052; William Peaps, *Love In it's Extasie* (1642[?]; London, 1649) IV. sig. Eᵛ; *Aglaura* IV. iv. 68–85, v. iii. 189–93 (tragi-comic version). The Queen in *The Fair Favourite* strives with pain and difficulty for a similar complaisance (IV. pp. 255, 264–5). A similar kind of altruism is shown by those lovers who declare that the loved one can only remain worthy of them by remaining faithful to a rival, and that to reciprocate their love would be to destroy it: see *Arviragus and Philicia* I. IV. sig. C[11]; *The Deseruing Fauorite* III. sigs. H, [H4]. In *The Passionate Lovers* Prince Clarimant challenges his brother, Agenor, to a duel for jilting a woman they both love (I. v. pp. 80–4).

28. For the lover wooing the rival on behalf of the beloved see *The Fair Favourite* IV. p. 265; *Love's Dominion* I. pp. 6–7, II. p. 20; *Love's Kingdom* I. pp. 10–12, II. pp. 21–2. For other acts of self-denying magnanimity on behalf of the loved one see Davenant, *The Unfortunate Lovers* (1638; 1661) I. pp. 21–2, III. pp. 55–8, in Maidment and Logan, III; *Love and Honour* III. pp. 148–9; *The Siege* v. p. 433; Thomas Killigrew, *Claracilla* II. sig. [D11]; *The Prisoners* (1635; collected plays pub. 1664) IV. sig. Cᵛ; Orrery, *The Black Prince* IV. ii. 414–23, iii. 440–I, v.iv. 305–444, v. 473–89. For the sentiment that to deserve is better than to possess see Orrery, *The Black Prince* I. iv. 484–5, v. ii. 65–6, *The Generall* III. ii. 143–4, *Henry the Fifth* II. i. 152–5, *Mustapha* (1665) III. ii. 401–5, *Tryphon* (1668) III. iv. 518–19. Orrery's heroes echo

Suckling's Brennoralt, who is, however, content with merit as a substitute for possession, not as a condition superior to it (*Brennoralt* [1639; 1661] III. iv. 94 — 8). Corneille's heroes also display self-denying magnanimity: see *Polyeucte* II. v. 634 — 6, IV. iv. 1295 — 313, V — vi. 1353 — 86; *Théodore* IV. v. 1459 — 90, V. iii. 1573 — 601.

29. The definitive study of idealised friendship is Mills, *One Soul* (see above, note 7). See also Mills, "The Friendship Theme in Orrery's Plays" (see above, note 7). For the shared soul idea see Carlell, *Arviragus and Philicia* II. III. sig. [E8ᵛ]; William Cartwright, *The Lady-Errant* II. vi. 681 — 718; Davenant, *The Distresses* (1639) III. p. 313, in Maidment and Logan, IV; *The Platonic Lovers* I. p. 15; Glapthorne, *Argalus and Parthenia* IV. p. 52; Katherine Philips, "A Dialogue of Absence 'twixt Lucasia and Orinda", ll. 5 — 8; "A retir'd Friendship. To Ardelia", 2, in Saintsbury (ed.), *Minor Caroline Poets*, I. 522, 524. *The Distresses*, like *The Platonic Lovers* and *The Lady-Errant*, treats Caroline ideals ironically: the scepticism of Dryden's heroic plays has plenty of precedents. Early dissent from Caroline ideals is also evident in Shirley's *Love's Cruelty* (1631; 1660), which depicts the failure of friendship to cope with the disruptive power of love.

30. According to Mills, *One Soul*, pp. 99 — 105, the motif of the lover wooing the beloved on behalf of a rival originates in Sir Thomas Elyot's tale of Titus and Gisippus: see *The Boke Named the Governour*, ed. H. H. S. Croft (London, 1883), II. II. xii. 132 — 61. For later examples of the motif see Fletcher's *Monsieur Thomas* (c. 1615; 1661) II. iv. pp. 118 — 20, III. i. pp. 121 — 6, V. viii. pp. 171 — 2, in *The Works of Francis Beaumont and John Fletcher*, ed. A. H. Bullen *et al.* (London, 1904 — 12), IV; *The Love-Sick Court* (1640) II. i. pp. 115 — 18, in *The Dramatic Works of Richard Brome* (London, 1873), II; Carlell, *The Deseruing Fauorite* I. sigs. Cᵛ, Eᵛ — E3ᵛ; *The Fool Would be a Favourit* IV. pp. 69 — 70, V. p. 79; George Cartwright, *The Heroick-Lover* II. pp. 15 — 18; Davenant, *The Distresses* V. pp. 361 — 3; Etherege, *The Comical Revenge; or, Love in a Tub* (1664) I. iv. 1 — 23, 51 — 66, in *The Dramatic Works of Sir George Etherege*, ed. H. F. B. Brett-Smith, The Percy Reprints, 6 (Oxford, 1927), I; Habington, *The Queen of Arragon* IV. sig. [G3ᵛ]; William Killigrew, *Love and Friendship* (no known performance) III. p. 29, IV. pp. 32 — 6, in *Four New Playes* (Oxford, 1666). Corneille once again provides parallels: *Rodogune* IV. i. 1237 — 42; *Sertorius* I. ii. 224 — 40. For other acts of magnanimity between rival friends see Carlell, *Arviragus and Philicia* II. I sigs. [E6 — E8ᵛ]; *The Deseruing Fauorite* I. sig. Bᵛ, III. sig. H2ʳ⁻ᵛ; *Osmond the Great Turk, or The Noble Servant* (1637; pub. 1657). ed. Allardyce Nicoll (Waltham Saint Lawrence, 1926) I. pp. 4 — 6, II. pp. 16 — 20; *The Passionate Lovers* I. II. p. 20; Habington, *The Queen of Arragon* V. sigs [H3ʳ⁻ᵛ], 12. The self-sacrificing rival is not an intrinsically absurd figure, as Hans Sachs and the Marschallin demonstrate; what is absurd is the slick facility with which English dramatists turn the magnanimity on.

31. *Henry the Fifth* II. iii. 250 — 355, V. iv. 307 — 406; *Mustapha* III. iii. 395 — 422; *Tryphon* IV. i. 53 — 136.

32. *Tyrannick Love* IV. 230 — 312, V. 1 — 102; *Marriage à la Mode* IV. i. 70 — 97, in *Restoration Comedies*, ed. Dennis Davison (Oxford, 1970).

33. In California Dryden, VIII, v. i. 284 — 5.

34. An exception is provided by the lovers who serve Venus Urania ("The History of Philoxypes and Policrite", *Cyrus* II. iii. 151 — 93).

35. For unhappy rejected lovers see *Cyrus* V. i. 74 (Perinthus), VIII. iii. 41 (Tysimenes), IX. i. 7 (the King of Assyria), IX. iii. 126 — 7 (the King of Pontus). Hermione in *Cassandra* (III. iv. 27) is similarly inconsolable. Artaban's easy changes of heart are possible (and indeed excusable) only because his first two affections had not taken deep root (*Cleopatra* V. ii. 486 — 7). A career of spectacular but comic resilience

is related in Georges de Scudéry's supposedly autobiographical "The History of Abindarrays and Aldoradine" (*Almahide* II. i–ii. 61–194).

36. The marriage of Amestris and Otanus is unhappy (see above, note 15), as is that of Arpasia and Hydaspes (*Cyrus* x. iii. 230).

37. E.g., Memnon and Oxyatres (*Cassandra* v. iii. 68–91), Marcellus (*Cleopatra* II. i. 111), Drusus (*Cleopatra* v. iii. 547), Agrippa (*Cleopatra* XII. iv. 239–49). For examples from *Cyrus* and *Almahide* see above, note 16. *Cassandra* narrates a tragically unsuccessful experiment in complaisant magnanimity: Cleonimus loves Alcione, the wife of his cousin Theander, with an intense but chaste love, and Theander insists that his wife should respond with sisterly affection; but the arrangement ultimately leads to Theander's jealousy and suicide (II. vi. 64–90).

38. *The State of Innocence and Fall of Man* v. p. 460, in Summers, III.

39. Summers, IV. 85; italics reversed.

40. Italics reversed. Cf. "An Apologie of *Raymond Sebond*", pp. 276–85, 323–6.

41. In the Preface to *All for Love* Dryden again distinguishes the realistic frailty of his characters from the impracticable virtue of French heroes and heroines (Watson, I. 224). The Montaignesque sentiments of the *Aureng-Zebe* Dedication are echoed in the "Life of Plutarch" (1683), p. 275, in *The Works of John Dryden*, XVII, ed. Samuel Holt Monk *et al.* (Berkeley, Los Angeles, and London, 1971), and in the Dedication and Preface of *Don Sebastian* (1690; Summers VI. 18; Watson, II. 50). For later interpretation of Achilles as a designedly vitiated character see Preface to *Examen Poeticum* (1693; Watson, II. 166–7); "A Parallel betwixt Painting and Poetry" (1695; II. 185); most important and extensive are the comments in the Dedication of the *Æneis* (1697), pp. 159–60, 167, 179, 183, in *Essays of John Dryden*, ed. W. P. Ker (Oxford, 1900), II.

42. Mary Evelyn's reactions to the play, recorded in a letter written *c.* Jan. 1671, are well known:

Since my last to you I have seen "The Siege of Grenada," a play so full of ideas that the most refined romance I ever read is not to compare with it; love is made so pure, and valour so nice, that one would image it designed for an Utopia rather than our stage. I do not quarrel with the poet, but admire one born in the decline of morality should be able to feign such exact virtue; and as poetic fiction has been instructive in former ages, I wish this the same event in ours. (Cited in Lennep *et al.*, *The London Stage, 1660–1700*, p. 177)

43. *Dryden's Criticism* (Ithaca and London, 1970), p. 14. Hume does, however, change his mind in *The Development of English Drama in the Late Seventeenth Century* (Oxford, 1976), p. 273. Gagen notes Achilles' flaws but believes that Dryden glosses over them ("Love and Honor", p. 214).

44. "Dryden and the Heroic Ideal", p. 9, in Bruce King (ed.), *Dryden's Mind and Art* (Edinburgh, 1969).

45. Waith, *Ideas of Greatness*, p. 4; Alssid, *Dryden's Rhymed Heroic Tragedies*, I. 60–1; Sidney, *An Apology for Poetry*, ed. Geoffrey Shepherd (London, 1965), p. 119; see also pp. 107–8. Waith at once concedes and minimises the flaws of Achilles and Rinaldo (*Herculean Hero*, p. 58).

46. E.g., in Canti x and XI Ruggiero rescues Angelica from a sea monster but— un-Perseus-like—bungles the job of slaying the beast. Carrying the rescued damsel through the air on his hippogryph, he finds that her beauty severely tests his fidelity to his beloved Bradamante and makes an unscheduled stop-over in Brittany, dismount-

ing one steed in the hope of mounting another. In the eagerness of his lust, however, he gets hopelessly tangled while shedding his armour, giving Angelica time to render herself invisible with a magic ring. Throughout the episode there is a comic disparity between the grandiose supernatural apparatus—the divinely sent monster, the flying horse, the magic accoutrements—and the mundane frailties of the characters who move amidst the magnificent trappings; and, in the end, Ruggiero the man is comically defeated by the armour which is the token of Ruggiero the hero. Bradamante, his destined bride, is subjected to a parallel irony when, falsely convinced of her lover's infidelity, she delivers a Didoesque suicide speech and stabs herself—only to find that, in her tragic passion, she has forgotten to remove her armour (XXXII. 37–44). A different kind of irony appears in the deeds of the mad Orlando, whose insane acts of vandalism against shepherds and donkeys parody the more pointless knightly combats in a manner anticipating that of Cervantes. Heroic grandeur is yet more overtly compromised in St John's famous discourse on poetry and patronage (a sardonic reworking of Horace, *Odes* IV. ix), which was to be cited by Dryden in the Dedication of the *Æneis* (Ker, *Essays of John Dryden*, II. 220). St John concludes that the surest way to discover historical truth is to invert epic tradition: "che i Greci rotti, e che Troia vittrice, / e che Penelopea fu meretrice" ("that the Greeks were routed, Troy victorious, and Penelope a whore"; XXXV. 27, in *Orlando Furioso*, ed. Dino Provenzal [Milan, 1955]). Here, in a work which Dryden cites as the starting-point of his heroic plays, is ample precedent for all his heroic comedy and anti-heroic irony.

47. Girolamo Graziani, *Il Conquisto di Granata* (1650). Graziani's version is very different from Dryden's, though the chief Moorish warrior *is* named Almansor and the poem opens with his recall from exile and reconciliation with Baudele. Graziani also wrote an epic entitled *La Cleopatra* (1633). Its chief and probably fortuitous point of contact with *All for Love* is that it ultimately reverses Plutarch's Platonic condemnation of the lovers, as Dryden's Cleopatra attempts to do when she claims the "noble madness" (II. 17) of the *Phaedrus*.

48. For the belief that epic should instruct princes by example see Tasso, *Discourses on the Heroic Poem*, trans. Mariella Cavalchini and Irene Samuel (Oxford, 1973), I. p. 5; Pierre Le Moyne, "Traité du Poëme Héroique", prefixed to *Saint Louys ou la Sainte Couronne Reconquise* (Paris, 1658), sig. a iii^v; William Davenant, Preface to *Gondibert*, p. 13, in *Gondibert*, ed. David F. Gladish (Oxford, 1971); Petrus Mambrunus (Pierre Mambrun), *De Epico Carmine Dissertatio Peripatetica*, pp. 341, 479, in *Opera Poetica. Accessit Dissertatio de Epico Carmine* (Fixae Andecavorum [Flèche], 1661); René Rapin, *Réflexions sur la Poétique d' Aristote*, in *Les Œuvres de Rapin*, 2 vols. (Amsterdam, 1709), II. 124, 163. For the reputation of Achilles in the Renaissance see John M. Steadman, "Achilles and the Renaissance Epic: Moral Criticism and Literary Tradition", in Horst Meller and Hans-Joachim Zimmermann (eds.), *Lebende Antik: Symposion für Rudolf Sühnel* (Berlin, 1967), pp. 139–54; *Milton and the Renaissance Hero* (London, 1967), pp. 1–22.

49. *Platonis Res Publica*, ed. Ioannes Burnet (Oxford, 1902), 489e, 390e, 391a–c.

50. *Poetics*, ed. D. W. Lucas (Oxford, 1968), 15, 1454b. Arguing that tragedians should portray men as better than they really are, Aristotle suggests that the poet who portrays wrathful and apathetic men ("ὀργίλους καὶ ῥᾳθύμους") should nevertheless make such characters decent people ("τοιούτους ὄντας ἐπιεικεῖς ποιεῖν") Then comes some syntactic nonsense containing the name of Achilles: "παράδειγμα σκληρότητος οἷον τὸν Ἀχιλλέα ἀγαθὸν καὶ Ὅμηρος." This may

be an intrusive scholion, or it may garble an illustration of the preceding proposition, to the effect that Homer portrayed Achilles as at once a good man ("ἀγαθὸν") and an exemplar of harshness("παράδειγμα σκληρότητος"), at once ἐπιεικής and ὀργίλος. The crux was interpreted with interesting variations in the sixteenth and seventeenth centuries. Of the two popular emendations (I ignore inconsequential variations of punctuation) the less drastic was as follows: "τοιούτους ὄντας ἐπιεικείας ποιεῖν παράδειγμα ἢ σκληρότητος δεῖ, οἷον τον Ἀχιλλέα ἀγαθὸν καὶ Ὅμηρος"—the poet should create either an exemplar of decency *or* one of harshness, such as Homer creates in the good Achilles. This emendation thus reduces the implication that Achilles' flaws coexist with good qualities. It was adopted in, for example, the complete Aristotle of Erasmus (Basel, 1531), II. 162–3, the edition and Latin translation of Alexander Paccius (Venice, 1536), pp. 13ᵛ–14ʳ, 16ᵛ the Italian translation of Bernardo Segni (Florence, 1549), p. 314, and the commentaries of Francesco Robortello (Florence, 1548), p. 181, Vincentius Madius and Bartholomaeus Lombardus (Venice, 1550), pp. 174–5, and Lodovico Castelvetro (Vienna, 1570), pp. 184ʳ⁻ᵛ. Robortello believes that Achilles is cited as "exemplar . . . absolutum iracundiae", and lessens his goodness still further by translating ἀγαθὸν as *fortem* (brave). Similar translations are offered by Segni and Madius-Lombardus. Another emendation, however, was the following: "τοιούτους ὄντας ἐπιεικείας ποιεῖν παράδειγμα, ἢ σκληρότητος δεῖ, οἷον τον Ἀχιλλέα Ἀγάθων καὶ Ὅμηρος" —in portraying easy-going or irascible characters, the poet should create "either an exemplar of decency or of harshness, such as Agathon and Homer have created in Achilles". With the transformation of ἀγαθὸν into Ἀγάθων, all traces of virtue seem removed from Achilles' character. This reading is adopted in the commentaries of Alessandro Piccolomini (Venice, 1575), pp. 227–8, and Paolo Beni (Padua, 1613), p. 398, in the edition and commentary of Daniel Heinsius (Leyden, 1610), pp. 40, 91, in the Latin translation of Theodore Goulston (London, 1623), pp. 35–6, and in Goulston's edition (Cambridge, 1696), p. 45. Both readings are entertained in the Latin translation and commentary of Antonio Riccoboni (Padua, 1587), pp. 19, 80–1. Piccolomini sees Achilles as an abstract of "iracundia", Beni as an exemplum of vice. Heinsius and Goulston, however, translate this emendation in a way far more favourable to Achilles: the poet should propose to himself an exemplar of decency *rather than* of harshness. This interpretation has the advantage of consistency with Aristotle's preceding proposition; its disadvantage is that it strains the sense of the Greek. Of epic theorists, Trissino, Mambrun, and Le Bossu use the first emendation: Trissino and Mambrun stress Achilles' virtue (though Mambrun elsewhere denounces his cruelty), whereas Le Bossu cites Aristotle to prove that Achilles is morally bad but poetically excellent.

51. *Q. Horati Flacci Opera*, ed. T. E. Page (London, 1910), ll. 120–4.

52. "What is beautiful, what base, what profitable, what not."

53. "The stormy passions of foolish kings and peoples."

54. "How to Study Poetry", pp. 133–41, in *Moralia*, trans. Frank Cole Babbitt, Loeb Classical Library, I (London and Cambridge, Mass., 1927).

55. Beni, *Comparatione* (Padua, 1607), pp. 3–4, 10; Mambrun, *De Cultura Animi*, "Fortitudo", pp. 81–2, in *Opera Poetica*; Rapin, *La Comparaison* (1664), pp. 102–7, 122–4, in *Œuvres*, I. Davenant's disapproval of the Homeric hero is reflected in *Gondibert* itself, in frequent warnings against wrath, ambition, and revenge: e.g., II. iii. 2, viii. 21, 28–46, 58, III. i. 57. Like Tasso and Graziani, Mambrun and Le Moyne wrote epics celebrating defenders of the Christian faith, Mambrun choosing

Constantine for his hero and Le Moyne St Louis. Beni, of course, advocates the Christian warrior-hero.

56. Trissino, *Le Sei Divisioni della Poetica* (1562), p. 105, in *Tutte le Opere di Giovan Giorgio Trissino Gentiluomo Vicentino non più raccolte*, 2 vols. (Verona, 1729), II: Achilles, Trissino argues, is "iracondo, ma amorevole e buono". Mambrun's change of mind is, in fact, merely a change of classical source: his defence of Achilles is (like Trissino's) based on the contentious passage in Aristotle, *Poetics*, 15, 1454b; his condemnation, on Plato, *Republic* IX. 586.

57. *La Gerusalemme Liberata*, ed. Lodovico Magugliani (Milan, 1950), II. 59. "D'ogni Dio sprezzatore" ("contemptuous of every god") is, however, Tasso's addition. The allusion to Horace is obscured in the Edward Fairfax translation, *Jerusalem Delivered*, ed. Roberto Weiss (London, 1962):

> Bold was his heart, and restless was his sprite,
> Fierce, stern, outrageous, keen as sharpen'd brand,
> Scorner of God, scant to himself a friend,
> And prick'd his reason on his weapon's end.

58. "Excess of anger." Fairfax greatly intensifies the tone of condemnation, rendering the phrase as "this fault commit / By hasty wrath, by rash and headstrong ire". In the *Allegory of Jerusalem Delivered* Tasso identified Rinaldo with the irascible power of the soul and wrote that, in his estrangement from the Christian cause, Rinaldo represented "*Anger, not governed by reason*": *Godfrey of Bulloigne, or The Recoverie of Jerusalem*, trans. Edward Fairfax (1600), sig. A4^{r-v}; cited in Waith, *Herculean Hero*, pp. 56–8.

59. (Paris, 1675), III. x. pp. 363–5.

60. See above, note 41.

61. "But this man wants to be above all others, to be king and lord of all."

62. And possibly another pejorative epic allusion. The term is derived from the name of Rodomonte, the cruel and boastful Saracen in *Orlando Furioso*.

CHAPTER 2

1. To avoid unwieldy phrasing, I follow the editors of the California Dryden (VIII. 283) in abbreviating "Howard and Dryden" to "Dryden", though I invoke Dryden's name as seldom as possible. Unlike the California editors, however, I regard Howard as the chief author of the play, being persuaded by H. J. Oliver's arguments in *Sir Robert Howard* (Durham, N.C., 1963), pp. 63–7. The play is properly included in a discussion of Dryden's *œuvre* in that it forms the basis for his subsequent single-handed efforts in the heroic genre. For what the observation is worth, touches anticipating the mature Dryden seem most evident in the last two acts.

2. Barbeau, *Intellectual Design of Dryden's Heroic Plays*, p. 64; Chase, *The English Heroic Play*, p. 103.

3. Miss Barbeau repeatedly identifies normative characters in the heroic plays: see, e.g., pp. 65, 72–4, 84, 86, 101, 113, 119, 124, 125, 127, 136–7. Critics frequently see Acacis and/or Orazia as perfect and exemplary characters: see, e.g., Jean Hagstrum, "Dryden's Grotesque: An Aspect of the Baroque in His Art and Criticism", p. 103, in Miner (ed.), *John Dryden*; Waith, *Ideas of Greatness*, p. 204;

Zebouni, *Dryden*, pp. 12—13. Gagen, "Love and Honor", pp. 213, 220, sees Acacis as exemplary but concedes that Orazia has flaws.

4. Flame images: III. ii. 141—2, 149—50, IV. i. 37—8. Flood images: I. ii. 30—1 (the image is used by Traxalla but reflects on Zempoalla), IV. i. 43—4, 106—8.

5. Storm images: I. i. 61—2, II. iii. 46—7, 62—7, III. i. 19—20, IV. i. 13—14. Flame images: II. i. 45—8, V. i. 56. Water images: II. i. 19—20, 37—40.

6. The messenger has already attributed divine qualities to Montezuma: I. ii. 68, 76.

7. *The State of Innocence* III. p. 439, in Summers, III.

8. Boabdelin similarly identifies orgasm and death, exclaiming, "I should not be of love or life bereft; / All should be spent before; and nothing left" (*CG* II. III. p. 118). That to yield to the flesh was to follow death was, of course, a notion frequently expressed in the Bible and in Christian writing: see, e.g., Romans 6:19—21, 7:5, 8:5—6, 13, Galatians 6:8, Ephesians 4:22, St Augustine, *Confessions*, trans. R. S. Pine-Coffin (Harmondsworth, 1961), II. vi. p. 50, III. xxi. p. 330, xxii. p. 331. Robert South provides a particularly clear statement of the idea in Sermon LVII, p. 280, in *Sermons Preached upon Several Occasions* (Oxford, 1823), VII: "Wicked men are said to *love death*: but can any man make his greatest evil the object of his best desire, which is love? No, assuredly, while he considers it as such, he cannot; but because it is rational from men's choice to infer and argue their love, they may be said therefore truly and properly to love death, because they choose it."

9. The idea is a commonplace, most familiar to us from Pope's *Essay on Man* II. 133—6. Epigram 57 in *The Latin Epigrams of Thomas More*, ed. Leicester Bradner and Charles Arthur Lynch (Chicago, 1953), pp. 37—8, develops the irony with especial force:

> Nugamur, mortemque procul, procul esse putamus,
>   At mediis latet haec abdita uisceribus.
> Scilicet ex illa, qua primum nascimur hora,
>   Prorepunt iuncto uita morsque pede.

("We fool ourselves, and think death is far, far away. But it lies hidden within our innermost being: assuredly, from the very hour of our birth, life and death creep forward with a single step.") The idea was popular from ancient times, occurring, for example, in Seneca, *Hercules Furens*, l. 874, in *Seneca's Tragedies*, trans. Frank Justus Miller, Loeb Classical Library (London and Cambridge, Mass., 1917), I; St Augustine, *Confessions* IV. x. p. 80; *City of God*, ed. David Knowles, trans. Henry Bettenson (Harmondsworth, 1972), XIII. x. pp. 518—19. But, as so often, Dryden need have looked no further than Montaigne: see especially "That to Philosophie [*sic*] is to Learn how to Die" (*Essays* I. xix. 87, 91).

10. See, e.g., Herbert Butterfield, *The Origins of Modern Science*, 2nd edn (London, 1957), pp. 15—17; Giorgio de Santillana, *The Origins of Scientific Thought* (London, 1961), pp. 108—28.

11. Literal storms are attributed to elemental spirits in *Tyrannick Love* IV. 163—6. Lucretius treated natural upheavals—storms, floods, earthquakes, volcanoes—as products of the eternal conflict of earth, air, fire, and water: see *De Rerum Natura*, ed. and trans. Cyril Bailey (Oxford, 1947), I. VI. 96—534, 639—702, 712—37.

12. III. i. 155, IV. i. 35—6, V. i. 66—7.

13. See also I. ii. 52, III. ii. 73, IV. i. 37—8.

14. "Significantly, her life was the forfeiture promised if she failed to keep her

bargain with the 'Great God of Vengeance.' What she thinks of as a free act of courage is in fact a necessary consequence of her commitment to the pursuit of power" (Barbeau, *Intellectual Design of Dryden's Heroic Plays*, p. 68).

15. Jean Gagen recognises that, in this incident and elsewhere, Orazia's love is "as selfish and jealous as that of quite ordinary mortals" ("Love and Honor", p. 213).

16. Acacis' failure to meet the standards of ideal friendship may be gauged by contrasting his speech with one of Katherine Philips' tributes to an ideal friend, "Rosania shadowed whilst Mrs. Mary Awbrey," in Saintsbury (ed.), *Minor Caroline Poets*, I. 536:

> And as the highest element is clear
> From all the tempests which disturb the air;
> So she above the World and its rude noise,
> Above our storms a quiet calm enjoys.   (ll. 51—4)

In seeing love as a passion that eternity will cure, Acacis also departs from Caroline tradition, which envisages an Elysium populated by eternally blissful lovers: see Carlell, *Osmond the Great Turk* v. pp. 57—8; Glapthorne, *Argalus and Parthenia* v. pp. 64—5; Orrery, *The Generall* III. ii. 145—52.

17. For base rivals willing to duel with erstwhile friends see *Cyrus* I. iii. 121—3, VII. i. 71; Carlell, *The Fool Would be a Favourit* IV. pp. 68—9. For less serious treatment of the same motif see Davenant, *The Distresses* IV. pp. 343—5; William Cartwright, *The Lady-Errant* III. ii. 984. The editors of the California Dryden derive the duel episode from the conflict of Memnon and Oxyatres in "The History of Barsina", *Cassandra* v. iii. 68—91, and the combat of Polexander and Phelismond in Marin Le Roy, Sieur de Gomberville, *The History of Polexander*, trans. William Browne (London, 1647), II. iv. Neither seems to me to be really comparable. The initial conflict of Memnon and Oxyatres gives way to magnanimous rivalry similar to that celebrated in Cavalier drama: Memnon resigns Barsina to Oxyatres (p. 85), who responds by resigning her to Memnon (p. 87). Acacis, however, fails to attain such self-denial. I have only read that part of *Polexander* which relates to the combat of the hero and Phelismond, but from this evidence it is clear that their combat, too, differs greatly from that of Acacis and Montezuma. The duel of Polexander and Phelismond is arranged before they meet, and their first meeting creates a bond between them: Polexander sees a single stranger fighting five men, goes to his assistance, and later discovers that he is his destined opponent (sigs. [¶   ¶   ¶3ᵛ—4ᵛ]). They decide, therefore, to postpone any formal friendship until after the combat (sig. ¶   ¶   ¶   ¶2ʳ). Acacis, by contrast, fights Montezuma after their friendship has been cemented.

18. In Carlell's *Osmond the Great Turk*, by contrast, Osmond vows to resign Despina to Melcoshus even in Elysium (v. pp. 57—8).

CHAPTER 3

1. California Dryden, IX. 302. Waith praises Kirsch's analysis, though he concedes that Cortez is at times "dangerously swayed by passion" (*Ideas of Greatness*, pp. 209—10). Winterbottom believes that Guyomar is a perfect character but that Cortez sacrifices honour to passion when he agrees to call of hostilities for Cydaria's sake: see "The Place of Hobbesian Ideas in Dryden's Tragedies", *JEGP*, 57 (1958), 668. The same view is maintained by Zebouni (*Dryden*, pp. 13—14).

2. *De Rerum Natura* v. 772–836.

3. See Chapter 1, note 9.

4. This imagery is analysed in my article "The Significance of *All for Love*", *ELH*, 37 (1970), 540–63. I no longer hold all the views expressed in this article (*All for Love* is clearly not a Pyrrhonistic play), but the discussion of mutability still seems to me to be sound.

5. Loftis (California Dryden, IX. 327) identifies the savage and gentle gods as Huitzilopochtli and Quetzalcoatl, and notes that the historical Cortez' victory was facilitated because the Mexicans interpreted his arrival as the return of Quetzalcoatl to earth. With the benefit of hindsight, Dryden reverses Cortez' divine affiliations.

6. This confinement is best illustrated in the religious beliefs that Montezuma maintains in the torture scene, where he describes the cycles of nature as the unending medium of human existence:

> Thou art deceiv'd: for whensoe're I Dye,
> The Sun my Father bears my Soul on high:
> He lets me down a Beam, and mounted there,
> He draws it back, and pulls me through the Air:
> I in the Eastern parts, and rising Sky,
> You in Heaven's downfal, and the West must lye.   (v. ii. 43–8)

7. *Poetical Works*, ed. Douglas Bush (London, 1966), XI. 423–901, XII. 1–551.

8. *The Poems and Fables of John Dryden*, ed. James Kinsley (London, 1962), ll. 216–19. All citations of Dryden's non-dramatic poems are to this edition. The conspirators are repeatedly associated with imagery of cycle and change: perhaps most memorable is the "revolving Moon" (l. 549) that presides over Zimri's changefulness (ll. 544–68).

9. Mutability is the chief characteristic of the sects, the sense of cyclic repetition being particularly strong in I. 60–1, II. 582–6. For further stress on the linear movement of truth through time see II. 164–7, 355–6.

10. "An Apologie of *Raymond Sebond*" (*Essays*, II. xii. 323).

11. II. ii. 66–72, II. iii. 59–62, 167–72, IV. iv. 153–6, v. ii. 117–18.

12. Cortez is later to use the fever image in his reflections on man's restless desires (IV. i. 111–12).

13. Cortez' attitude is similar to that of the hero of Orrery's *Henry the Fifth*. Though Henry loves Princess Katherine, he refuses to avert war with France by marrying her, believing that he can only merit her by acquiring the glory of conquering her country (II. i. 75–137).

14. Cortez' behaviour contrasts, for example, with Solyman's magnanimity towards the fleeing Rhodians: see *The Siege of Rhodes* II. v. p. 355, in Maidment and Logan, III.

15. See, e.g., *Cassandra* I. iii. 80; *Cleopatra* II. iv. 190; *Cyrus* II. i. 14.

16. In *Orlando Furioso* XLV Ruggiero, as a result of an injudicious oath, fights to enable his rival to possess his mistress. Throughout *Le Grand Cyrus* the hero punctiliously observes his oath to inform the King of Assyria of developments in the search for Mandana, though he fears that to do so is to harm his interests (e.g. II. ii. 97–8). In Orrery's *Tryphon* (1668) Demetrius vows to aid Tryphon in love, only to discover that Tryphon loves his own mistress, Stratonice (III. iv. 385–88). Nevertheless, he scrupulously observes his vow, urging Stratonice to relinquish him and accept Tryphon (IV. i. 29–146).

17. Dryden's episode seems particularly indebted to the episode in *Cleopatra* where Coriolanus is propositioned by Augustus' daughter, Julia (II. ii. 136–8), for in both the interlocutors evasively treat the temptation as a jest: Julia's "You construed my Discourse aright . . . when you apprehended it *raillery*" (p. 137) is clearly echoed in Almeria's "You construed me aright,——I was in Jest" (IV. i. 97). Coriolanus, however, remains firmly unresponsive to temptation. For other examples of the unequivocal rebuff see, e.g., *Cassandra* II. iv. 2–3, v. v. 44; *Cleopatra* v. ii. 514–19; *Cyrus* IX. ii. 122.

18. Kirsch's book seems to me to be particularly vitiated in this respect: repeatedly, he documents Dryden's code of honour from speeches which are rapidly discredited by subsequent dramatic events.

CHAPTER 4

1. In the Preface to *Tyrannick Love* Dryden accounts for "*faults of the writing and contrivance*" by claiming that the play "*was contrived and written in seven weeks*" (California Dryden, X. 111).

2. Alssid's treatment of the heroines (the best so far) provides an exception but is still excessively laudatory. He recognises that Catharine's destructiveness is ironically similar to Maximin's (I. 175) but nevertheless attributes it to an adamantine spiritual integrity, concluding that her "character provides . . . an exemplary instance of the perfect Christian" (p. 180). Similarly, although he recognises Berenice's inability "to dissociate the life of the flesh from the life of the spirit" (p. 187), he considers that her views on Providence are vindicated and that she is both reliable and successful as Porphyrius' spiritual guide (pp. 187–8). Osborn suggests that Dryden, though intending to present Catharine favourably, in fact created a typical case of "religious melancholy" ("Heroical Love", pp. 487, 489).

3. King, *Dryden's Major Plays*, pp. 47–58; Barbeau, *Intellectual Design of Dryden's Heroic Plays*, pp. 17, 77, 94–105; William Myers, *Dryden* (London, 1973), pp. 33–4. The assumption also pervades the commentary in the California Dryden. Despite his reservations about Catharine, Osborn sees Berenice as a perfect character (p. 489). For other interpretations of one or both heroines as exemplary characters see, e.g., Kirsch, *Dryden's Heroic Drama*, pp. 102–6, Lynch, "Conventions of Platonic Drama", p. 462, Winterbottom, "The Place of Hobbesian Ideas", p. 677, Zebouni, *Dryden*, p. 16. Jean Hagstrum is so convinced that Berenice is a "civilized norm" and "an ideal" that he kills her off with "a Christian death of beauty and dignity, in full hope of an unsullied union with her lover in the other world" ("Dryden's Grotesque"), pp. 103–4.

4. Miss Barbeau's citations are to *Patriarcha*, p. 62, and *The Anarchy of a Limited or Mixed Monarchy*, p. 289 (not, as in her footnote, p. 284), in Robert Filmer, "*Patriarcha*" *and Other Political Works*, ed. Peter Laslett, (Oxford, 1949). With greater plausibility, Roper and Myers detect the doctrine of non-resistance to usurpers in Dryden's early panegyrics: Alan Roper, *Dryden's Poetic Kingdoms* (London, 1965), pp. 61–2; Myers, *Dryden*, p. 18.

5. Laslett, "*Patriarcha*" *and Other Political Works*, pp. 33–43, 47–8. Phillip Harth reproves Miss Barbeau for exaggerating Filmer's importance in the sixties and seventies and for viewing him in isolation from other political theorists: "Religion and Politics in Dryden's Poetry and Plays", *MP*, 70 (1973), 241–2.

6. Dedication of *The Duke of Guise*, p. 216, in Summers, v (italics reversed). Cf.

Tillotson, Sermon CXXXVII, "The Wisdom of God in his Providence", pp. 456–7, in *The Works of Dr. John Tillotson* (London, 1820), VI.

7. Jean Bodin, *The Six Bookes of a Commonweale*, trans. Richard Knolles, ed. Kenneth Douglas MacRae (Cambridge, Mass., 1962), II. iv. pp. 218–20.

8. Digges, *The Unlawfulnesse of Subjects taking up Armes against their Soveraigne in what case soever* (Oxford, 1643), sig. N3^v; Bramhall, *The Serpent-Slave; or, A Remedy for the Biting of an Asp* (1643), p. 320, in *The Works of . . . John Bramhall, D. D.*, ed. A. W. H. (Oxford, 1842–5), III; Williams, *Vindiciæ Regum; or, The Grand Rebellion: That is, a Looking-Glasse for Rebels* (Oxford, 1643), sigs. C3^v, H2–I2^v; Hudson, *The Divine Right of Government 1. Naturall, and 2. Politique* (London, 1647), sig. R2^v; Coke, *Elements of Power and Subjection* (1660), sigs. O–[O4^v], [P4^v]–Q, in *A Survey of the Politicks of Mr. Thomas White, Thomas Hobbs and Hugo Grotius. Also Elements of Power & Subjection: or the Causes of Humane, Christian, and Legal Society* (London, 1662); Edward [Hyde], Earl of Clarendon, *A Brief View and Survey of the Dangerous and Pernicious Errors to Church and State in Mr. Hobbes's Book, Entitled "Leviathan"*, 2nd impression (Oxford, 1676), pp. 92–3; Warwick, *A Discourse of Government, as Examined by Reason, Scripture, and Law of the Land* (London 1694 [written 1678]), p. 35. For views closer to those of Filmer see Robert Sanderson, *Lectures on Conscience and Human Law*, trans. Christopher Wordsworth (London, Oxford, and Cambridge, 1877), pp. 134–8. I have been guided in my consultation of Royalist writers by J. H. M. Salmon, *The French Religious Wars in English Political Thought* (Oxford, 1959). This valuable book has been too little used by Dryden scholars. Other plays of the period conclude with the forcible overthrow of usurpers, including Davenant's *Macbeth* (1664), Edward Howard's *The Usurper* (1664), and Dryden's *Marriage à la Mode* (1671?). Davenant, however, stresses that private men should not depose usurpers simply in order to usurp the throne themselves (III. pp. 353–5, in Maidment and Logan, V).

9. *Six Bookes* II. v. p. 221. Roper (*Dryden's Poetic Kingdoms*, p. 66) underestimates the direct acquaintance of Royalist writers with Bodin. For a more reliable assessment see Salmon, *French Religious Wars*, pp. 88–96, 123–46. Specific citations of Bodin can be found, e.g., in the works of Griffith Williams, Peter Heylyn, Roger Coke, and Sir George MacKenzie. Seth Ward's library at Salisbury Cathedral contains the Latin version of Bodin. The evidence for Dryden's acquaintance with his work is, admittedly, sketchy. For what it is worth, I offer the observation that the famous passage against innovation in *Absalom and Achitophel*, ll. 799–810, is strikingly similar in sentiment and imagery to *Six Bookes* IV. iii. pp. 469–70. The constitutional settlement in *Tyrannick Love* is, of course, very un-English, but John M. Wallace has wisely counselled against the search for exact and extended contemporary parallels in works based on historical events: "Dryden and History: A Problem in Allegorical Reading", *ELH*, 36 (1969), 265–90. For Dryden's receptiveness to a variety of constitutional forms see "The Character of Polybius and his Writings" (1693; Watson, II. 69); Dedication of the *Æneis* (Ker, *Essays of John Dryden*, II. 170–1).

10. *Dryden's Major Plays*, p. 155; *Directions for Obedience to Government in Dangerous or Doubtful Times* (Laslett, *"Patriarcha" and Other Works*, pp. 233, 232). King's reference to *The Spanish Fryar* is to IV. ii. p. 61, in the first edition (London, 1681). I use the text in Summers, V, in which the reference for the present passage is to IV. p. 181.

11. As Dryden says she does: "*The part of* Maximin . . . *was designed by me to set off the Character of S.* Catharine" (Preface, p. 110). He makes the same point in "A

Parallel betwixt Painting and Poetry" (Watson, II. 203) and in the same work suggests that *Tyrannick Love* may be at fault in portraying the suffering of a "wholly perfect" character (p. 184). My interpretation of St Catharine's character is, I must confess, more complex than such comments seem to permit. Many critics, however, take a similar latitude with the character of Octavia, who in the Preface to *All for Love* is described in terms very hard to reconcile with the evidence of the play itself (Watson, I. 222).

12. *De Rerum Natura*, ed. and trans. Bailey, I. II. 1—4

> SVAVE mari magno turbantibus aequora ventis,
> e terra magnum alterius spectare laborem;
> non quia vexari quemquamst iucunda voluptas,
> sed quibus ipse malis careas quia cernere suave est.

("Sweet it is, when on the great sea the winds are buffeting the waters, to gaze from the land on another's great struggles; not because it is pleasure or joy that anyone should be distressed, but because it is sweet to perceive from what misfortune you yourself are free" [Bailey's trans.].) In translating this passage in *Sylvæ* (1685) Dryden made two modifications. He gives less emphasis than Lucretius to the scene of suffering (whereas Catharine is more detailed and emphatic than her source). And, whereas Lucretius goes on to say that nothing is, however, more sweet ("sed nil dulcius est" [l. 7]) than the detachment of philosophic wisdom, Dryden adds that the pursuit of *virtue* is "much more sweet" (l. 7) than the preceding pleasures, in effect slighting the joys of wreck-spotting: *The Works of John Dryden*, III, ed. Earl Miner *et al.* (Berkeley and Los Angeles, 1969), 46. In "Translation as Baptism: Dryden's Lucretius", *Arion*, 7 (1968), 576—602, Norman Austin brilliantly argues that Dryden "misrepresented" Lucretius (p. 579) in order to make him "the strongest of Christian apologists from pagan antiquity" (pp. 600—1).

13. Cf. *De Rerum Natura* II. 9—10.

14. See Maren-Sofie Røstvig, *The Happy Man: Studies in the Metamorphosis of a Classical Ideal, Vol I: 1600—1700*, revised edition, Oslo Studies in English, No. 2 (Oslo, 1962), pp. 229—310.

15. Dedication of *Aureng-Zebe*, p. 83.

16. Epistola CCXXVIII, in *Patrologia Latina*, ed. J.-P. Migne, XXXIII (Paris, 1902), cols. 1013—19; *In Joannis Evangelium Tractatus* CXXIV, XV. ii. col. 1511, XXVIII. ii. cols. 1622—3, in *Patrologia Latina*, XXXV (Paris, 1902). In the second and third passages, Augustine notes that flight from persecution is sanctioned by the example of Christ (John 4:1—3, 7:1).

17. Is Dryden playing on the disparity between role and actress, as he quite flagrantly does in the play's extraordinary epilogue? After all, the figure "on a Theater" is both Saint Catharine and (in the first season) Mistress Peg Hughes, soon to be Prince Rupert's paramour and Nell Gwyn's peer in notoriety. For the pairing of the two actresses see, e.g., Tom Brown, *Letters from the Dead to the Living*, pp. 241—5, in *The Works of Thomas Brown, Serious and Comical, in Prose and Verse* (London, 1715), II. Alssid discusses the histrionic aspects of Catharine's career, but believes that her dramaturgy is opposed to Maximin's as true to false (II. 279—81). I am not sure that matters are so simple. In *Microcosmos, The Shape of the Elizabethan Play* (Lexington, 1965), Thomas B. Stroup argues that the theatre imagery in Elizabethan drama expresses the commonplace view of the world as a stage on which the Christian is tested before God, though he also documents uses of theatre imagery to

indicate falsity and self-deception. Dryden's theatre imagery seems to me to be always of the latter kind.

18. *The Rule of Faith* (1666), II. iii—iv. pp. 297—301, IV. ii. pp. 439—40, in *Works*, x. Catharine's arguments are echoed in *Religio Laici* (1682), but are there used to subordinate reason to *scriptural* revelation: see especially ll. 34— 5, 297—300, 368—9. The idea of the few plain rules is also much used by William Chillingworth in *The Religion of Protestants a Safe Way to Salvation* (1638; London, 1664), where it is again applied to Biblical texts: see especially sigs. C2^v—C3, pp. 17—20, 36, 50—4, 74, 77, 82, 91, 93, 98, 115, 123—4, 146. Chillingworth also anticipates Catharine's mistrust of "witty glosses" on "Heav'ns will", denouncing "This presumptuous imposing of the senses of men upon the words of God, the special senses of men upon the general words of God. . . . This Deifying our own interpretations, and Tyrannous inforcing them upon others" (p. 177). Again, however, he is concerned with the obfuscation of clear Biblical testimony.

19. Tillotson voices the Church's traditional suspicion of the active quest for martyrdom in Sermon XCVIII, "The Support of Good Men under their Sufferings for Religion" (*Works*, V. 221). For the Church's traditional position, see the article on "Martyrs" in the *Catholic Encyclopedia*. Corneille's Polyeucte seeks martyrdom actively, but Corneille was at least aware of the tension between the demands of *gloire* and of Christian orthodoxy: in a scene in which Polyeucte and Néarque debate the virtues of instant martyrdom (II. vi. 637—720), Polyeucte inverts arguments advanced by St Augustine in *City of God* I. xxvii. pp. 38—9. For a similar tension, contrast *Théodore* III. iii. 899—916 (especially 911—14) with *City of God* I. xvi—xx. pp. 26—32: Théodore, conscious that she is choosing a course ordinarily forbidden to Christians, seeks death to avoid rape; Augustine provides the most famous prohibition of such escape from defilement.

20. Catharine's image contrasts strikingly with *The Hind and the Panther* I. 128—33:

> Why chuse we then like *Bilanders* to creep ⎫
> Along the coast, and land in view to keep, ⎬
> When safely we may launch into the deep? ⎭
> In the same vessel which our Saviour bore ⎫
> Himself the Pilot, let us leave the shoar, ⎬
> And with a better guide, a better world explore. ⎭

In both cases, the imagery is concerned with religious belief. *The Hind and the Panther* is a dangerous key with which to interpret *Tyrannick Love*, but the contrast of marine enterprise expresses a contrast that could easily have been in Dryden's mind when he created the character of St Catharine: whereas Catharine's image recreates the detachment of the Lucretian spectator when faced with the storm-endangered traveller, Dryden's in *The Hind* recreates Christ's miraculous intervention when his disciples were endangered at sea.

21. *Measure for Measure*, ed. J. W. Lever, The Arden Shakespeare (London, 1965), IV. iv. 63.

22. The most obvious precedent for Catharine's dilemma is in *Measure for Measure*, which was extensively revised by Davenant and staged in 1662 under the title of *The Law against Lovers*; in Davenant's version Isabella's sanctity is archly compromised (*she* thinks up the bedroom trick, though it is never put into practice), and she ends up by marrying the exonerated Angelo, thereby contributing to a

general triumph of fruition over sterility. (Wagner's *Das Liebesverbot* was to complete the decline in her marital prospects by pairing her off with *Lucio*.) The same dilemma is used with simple seriousness by Shirley. In *The Traitor* Sciarrha asks his sister, Amidea, to save his life by sleeping with the Duke of Florence; she refuses, and is killed by her brother (v. i. pp. 171 – 7, in *The Dramatic Works and Poems of James Shirley*, ed. William Gifford [London, 1833]), II. In *Love's Cruelty*, similarly, Eubella is not prepared to ransom her father's life with her virginity (III. iii. p. 234, IV. ii. pp. 247 – 8, in *Dramatic Works*, II). There is, however, another group of stories in which the pious woman elects defilement as the lesser of two evils (i.e. rather than sacrifice to idols), but is spared by divine intervention. Such a story had been dramatised in Corneille's *Théodore*. St Ambrose, in the passage that furnished Corneille with his source, narrates that the saint went unhesitatingly to the brothel with the reflection that a virgin mind is preferable to a virgin body: *De Virginibus*, II. iv. col. 225, in *Patrologia Latina*, XVI (Paris, 1880). Similar tales can be found in the lives of Saints Lucy, Agnes, and Daria in *The Golden Legend*.

23. Catharine's incongruity of motive is noted with somewhat different emphasis in Hagstrum, "Dryden's Grotesque", p. 109.

24. Catharine does not go to the extremes of Hobbes, but the processes she describes are those postulated by Luther when, denying the freedom of the will, he argued that God *did* actively harden Pharaoh's heart. See *The Bondage of the Will*, trans. J. I. Packer and O. R. Johnston (London, 1957), p. 206: "God works evil in us (that is, by means of us) not through God's own fault, but by reason of our own defect. We being evil by nature, and God being good, when He impels us to act by His own acting upon us by the nature of His omnipotence, good though He is in Himself, He cannot but do evil by our evil instrumentality." For contemporary Anglican denials that divine "pow'r controls" the actions of the sinner see John Bramhall's contribution to *The Questions Concerning Liberty, Necessity and Chance*, in *The English Works of Thomas Hobbes of Malmesbury*, ed. Sir William Molesworth (London, 1839 – 45), V (see especially pp. 111, 121 – 4, 133); Robert South, Sermons XIX and XXVIII (Sermons, v. 342 – 61, VI. 59 – 86); Tillotson, Sermons CXIV and CXV (*Works*, V. 509, 519 – 21, 538). South's Sermon XXVIII contains an attack on Hobbes (p. 76).

25. Symeon Metaphrastes, Μαρτυρίον τῆς Ἁγίας ... Αἰκατερίνης, cols. 293 – 6, in *Patrologia Graeca*, ed. J.-P. Migne (Paris, 1891); *Le Martyre de Sainte Catherine* (1649), IV. iv. pp. 61 – 2. The play is anonymous, but has been variously ascribed to D'Aubignac, Desfontaines, and Saint-Germain. The place of publication is not given. For information about the play, see California Dryden, X. 390 – 1.

26. Gordon Bourne, *Pregnancy* (London, 1972), p. 350.

27. Berenice's speech is akin to a piece of clearly premeditated nonsense in the Dryden – Davenant *Tempest* (1667), in which Hippolito and Dorinda naïvely speculate upon the nature of the soul: if his soul had left his body, Hippolito assures Dorinda, "it should have walk'd upon / A Cloud just over you, and peep'd" (v. ii. 23 – 4, in California Dryden, X). As party to this deliberate exercise in absurdity, Dryden could hardly have been blind to the folly of Berenice's utterances.

28. *Don Sebastian* II. i. 553 – 6, in *Four Tragedies*, ed. Beaurline and Bowers.

29. Mandana, e.g., declares, "Since I have put my self into the custody of the Gods, it is my duty to wait upon their pleasures, and submit unto what they shall ordain me" (*Cyrus* II. ii. 130). See also III. iii. 156, X. i. 4.

CHAPTER 5

1. Summers, III, I. II. p. 42.

2. I. I. pp. 34–5, 36–7, I. III. p. 58, I. V. p. 79, II. II. p. 119, II. IV. p. 141. See Barbeau, *Intellectual Design of Dryden's Heroic Plays*, p. 109.

3. "From that law of Nature...there followeth a Third; which is this, *That men performe their Covenants made*: without which, Covenants are in vain, and but Empty words; and the Right of all men to all things remaining, wee are still in the condition of Warre" (*Leviathan*, ed. C. B. MacPherson [Harmondsworth, 1968], pp. 201–2).

4. Kirsch, *Dryden's Heroic Drama*, p. 107. Cf. Waith, "Herculean Hero", pp. 156–8.

5. Alssid, *Dryden's Rhymed Heroic Tragedies*, I. 190–213; Barbeau, *Intellectual Design of Dryden's Heroic Plays*, pp. 18–19, 62, 113–17; Gagen, "Love and Honor", pp. 214–16; Osborn, "Heroical Love", pp. 480, 489; Winterbottom, "The Development of the Hero", pp. 162, 166–72; Zebouni, *Dryden*, pp. 16–18. Kirsch and Waith postulate moral development as well as primitivistic purity. Larson, however, sees Almanzor's development as inconclusive (*Studies in Dryden's Dramatic Technique*, pp. 113–42). I shall on a few occasions in this chapter make points similar to Alssid's, but shall usually reverse the conclusions that he draws from them.

6. King, *Dryden's Major Plays*, pp. 59–81.

7. See, e.g., *Cassandra* I. iii . 80; *Cleopatra* v. i. 481–3; *Cyrus* II. I. 14, VI. iii. 142.

8. Dryden here has in mind Orrery's tiresome and shallow idealisation of friendship. In *The Generall* Clatus asks his friend Memnor to second him in a duel against Lucidor, who is the lover of Memnor's sister. Memnor agrees, but (like Almanzor) refuses to be told the causes of the dispute:

> *Clat.* Butt I'le relate our Quarrell in one word,
> That you may see 'tis worthy of yoᵣ sword....
>   *Mem.* Hold, *Clatus*, pray! for if yoᵣ Quarrell bee
> Well grounded, you're the lesse oblig'd to mee;
> And if an unjust Quarrell you pursue,
> Then I am much the less oblig'd to you.
> The story cannott more my friendshippe binde,
> And you by telling itt may change my minde....
> Knowe freindshipp is a greater tye than blood.
> A sister is a name must not contend
> With the more high and sacred name of freind.

(I. iii. 274–5, 278–83, 293–5)

Memnor's blinkered commitment to friendship is (undesignedly) absurd, but his desire to remain ignorant of his friend's grievance does show a moral unease, a wish to shut his eyes to the possibility of injustice. In brushing aside Abdalla's explanations, by contrast, Almanzor shows a frank and cheerful disregard of ethical issues.

9. Magnanimity to valiant foes is the rule in romances. See, e.g., *Cassandra* I. i. 12–13; *Cyrus* II. i. 16.

10. See Suckling, "Against Fruition [II]", 5–6, in *Non-Dramatic Works*, p. 38; *Aglaura* I. v. 18–22.

11. See Appendix, p. 165.

12. Alssid, *Dryden's Rhymed Heroic Tragedies*, I. 190–213; Osborn, "Heroical Love", pp. 480, 489; Gagen, "Love and Honor", pp. 214–16.

13. Or Owen Tudor, or Delaware, or Demetrius: *The Generall* III. ii. 143 – 4; *Henry the Fifth* II. i. 154 – 5; *The Black Prince* v. ii. 65 – 144; *Tryphon* III. iv. 518 – 19. All these characters are modelled on the hero of Suckling's *Brennoralt* (III. iv. 94 – 98).

14. Summers, v. I. p. 356.

15. In the corresponding passage in Pérez de Hita's *Guerras Civiles de Granada* the Queen's assent to Esperanza's Christian instruction is unconditional: *Las Guerras Civiles; or the Civil Wars of Granada; and The History of the Factions of the Zegries and Abencerrages, Two Noble Families of that City, to the Final Conquest by Ferdinand and Isabella*, trans. Thomas Rodd (London, 1801), pp. 285 – 6. I have checked the relevant parts of Rodd's translation (which is more concise than the original) against the Spanish text in the Paris edition of 1660.

16. Cf. Madeleine de Scudéry's explanation of the war between Cyrus and Croesus: "As love is such an heroique passion as is infinitely above the capacity of the vulgar, so the people of *Sardis* could not believe that Mandana was the reall cause of the Warr; but on the contrary they imagined it to be ambition only which exasperated Cyrus against them" (VI. i. 11). Dryden's moral untidiness has no precedent in Pérez de Hita: there, the virtuous Abencerrages aid Ferdinand's cause and in doing so fulfil a Christian potential they had long possessed (see especially pp. 186, 228, 273, 366); the Zegrys, by contrast, are banished by Ferdinand for their treachery to the Abencerrages (p. 383). In Graziani's *Il Conquisto di Granata* the conflict of Christian and pagan is also one of Heaven and Hell, as in Tasso: St James gives Ferrando a celestial sword (Canto II), Isabella is rapt to Heaven in a vision (XIX), and Granada is repeatedly defended by a guardian demon faintly prophetic of Milton's Satan. In Mariana, however, Ferdinand acts with a certain amount of political pragmatism, and both he and Isabella are given flaws as well as excellences: Juan de Mariana, *The General History of Spain*, trans. Captain John Stevens (London, 1699), Book XXV, pp. 442 – 59 (see especially pp. 458 – 9). *Almahide* deals extensively with the factional unrest in Granada, but Scudéry's original stops before Ferdinand's victory. The final part of the 1677 English translation is the work of the translator, and is much indebted to *The Conquest of Granada*; see Schweitzer, "Dryden's Use of Scudéry's *Almahide*".

17. For a similar unveiling scene see Carlell, *Osmond the Great Turk*, I. pp. 4 – 5. Ianthe approaches Solyman veiled in *The Siege of Rhodes* I. II. p. 269, but inspires him to chaste affection without unveiling.

18. I. IV. p. 72, "Why...ask"; I. v. pp. 82 – 3, "How blest...the place"; p. 85, "You like...my sight".

19. *Love and Honour* v. p. 184; *Henry the Fifth* II. iii. 356 – 71.

20.

> Love, like a Scene, at distance should appear;
> But Marriage views the gross-daub'd Landschape neer....
> When Hearts are loose, thy Chain our bodies tyes;
> Love couples Friends; but Marriage Enemies.

This passage also provides further distortion of lyric, Platonic sentiment, since Boabdelin echoes and perverts John Hall's Platonic arguments against marriage (Saintsbury [ed.], *Minor Caroline Poets*, II. 196):

> We will be friends, our thoughts shall go,
> Without impeachment, to and fro;...

Love's like a landscape, which doth stand
Smooth at a distance, rough at hand.   ("Platonic Love", ll. 5−6, 19−20)

21. *The Royall Slave* III. iv−v. 874−1052.
22. For the "spend" pun see Suckling, "A Candle", l. 9 in *Non-Dramatic Works*, p. 19.

CHAPTER 6

1. Prologue to *Aureng-Zebe*, l. 15, in *Four Tragedies*, ed. Beaurline and Bowers.
2. In "The Consistency of Dryden's *Aureng-Zebe*", Leslie Howard Martin argues that *Aureng-Zebe* is generically akin to Dryden's earlier heroes, and examines Dryden's debt to *Le Grand Cyrus*. He believes, however, that Dryden endorses and perpetuates romance values.
3. In "Dryden's *Aureng-Zebe*: Debts to Corneille and Racine", Harold F. Brooks demonstrates that *Aureng-Zebe* contains many verbal reminiscences of Corneille and Racine. The reminiscences do not, however, amount to sustained allusion. For other studies of influences upon *Aureng-Zebe* see Edward S. LeComte, "*Samson Agonistes* and *Aureng-Zebe*", *Études Anglaises*, 11 (1958), 18−22; William Frost, "*Aureng-Zebe* in context: Dryden, Shakespeare, Milton, and Racine", *JEGP*, 74 (1975), 26−49.
4. Summers, IV. 85−6; italics reversed.
5. "By No Strong Passion Swayed: A Note on John Dryden's *Aureng-Zebe*", *English Studies in Africa*, 1 (1958), 66.
6. *The Works of Thomas Shadwell*, ed. Montague Summers (London, 1927), II. II. p. 131.
7. I here repeat observations made by Robert S. Newman in "Irony and the Problem of Tone in Dryden's *Aureng-Zebe*", p. 456. Newman's article is the best hitherto published on any of Dryden's heroic plays, and has been too little noted in later criticism.
8. Indamora's behaviour contrasts markedly with that of the heroines in *Cassandra*: "Then did these two great Princesses no longer doubt but that the end of their life was come, yet in that fear they did not any thing that misbecame their greatness; and if they made shew of any grief, 'twas only out of a sense wherewith nearness of blood and affection inspired them mutually" (v. vi. 56).
9. *Œuvres complètes*, ed. Jouanny, I. IV. iii. 1277−435. Like Célimène (1365−75), Indamora deflates her lover by scornfully admitting his charges (IV. 501−8); and, like Célimène (ll. 1391−414), she follows up her admission by telling her lover that his ceaseless suspicions are intolerable (ll. 519−28). Aureng-Zebe's speech beginning "Ah Traitress!" (ll. 489−500) is similar in sentiment to Alceste's speech beginning "Ah! traitresse" (ll. 1415−20), since both deal with the helplessness of the rational man before female beauty. And, like Alceste (ll. 1389−90), Aureng-Zebe offers to deceive himself into believing his mistress innocent (ll. 465−8). In addition, there is a general, though not verbally precise, resemblance between the speeches in which Alceste and Aureng-Zebe describe their mistresses as at once beautiful and poisonous (*Mis.* 1317−20; *AZ* 404−9).
10. Alssid argues that "the hero's constancy develops into a fraility [*sic*] which, in time, reveals his tragic 'flaws'—his great despair and his debilitating self-righteousness" (*Dryden's Rhymed Heroic Tragedies*, I. 229). Alssid, however, finds Aureng-Zebe's "constancy" and virtue far more simple and convincing than I do.

11. Interestingly, but probably irrelevantly, the unauthoritative third to sixth quartos make her flirtation with Morat quite explicit, attributing the line "A little yielding may my love advance" (III. 536) not to Morat but to Indamora.

12. The parallel with Nourmahal is noted in Morton, "By No Strong Passion Swayed", pp. 63–4.

13. "My life! My Soul!" forms an ingeniously appropriate transition from lust to romantic banality. Discussing Roman comedy in *Of Dramatic Poesy*, Dryden writes, "but to speak generally, their lovers say little, when they see each other, but *anima mea, vita mea*; ζωὴ καὶ ψυχή as the women in Juvenal's time used to cry out in the fury of their kindness: then indeed to speak sense were an offence" (Watson. I. 42). In Juvenal's Sixth Satire ζωὴ καὶ ψυχή is described as a lascivious phrase, fit for use only under the blankets (ll. 194–6).

14. Obsessive jealousy such as Aureng-Zebe's is considered in *Le Grand Cyrus* to be a grave vice. Asked to name the most unfortunate of four cases of unfortunate love—the absent lover, the lover not loved, the jealous lover, and the bereaved lover (III. i. 17–83)—Martesia awards the palm of suffering to the bereaved lover and has little sympathy with the jealous.

15. Metaphors of actors playing parts are extremely common in Restoration drama: see, e.g., Orrery, *Mustapha* v. v. 294, "His hand then acts the second Tragick part"; *The Black Prince* I. ii. 261, "He suffers not, but plays the Lovers part"; *Tryphon* III. iv. 391, "Oh, why am I Condemn'd to Act this Part?"; Etherege, *The Man of Mode*, ed. W. B. Carnochan, Regents Restoration Drama Series (London, 1967), I. 226–7, "The quarrel being thus happily begun, I am to play my part; confess and justify all my roguery."

16. For other images of pomp see I. 8, III. 72–3, 401, 545–6, 557–8, v. 60.

17. I. 80–1, II. 125, 291, III. 167–9, IV. 94.

18. In her excellent discussion of *All for Love*, Anne Davidson Ferry notes that the play is permeated by "metaphors endowing words with the solidity of objects" (*Milton and the Miltonic Dryden* [Cambridge, Mass., 1968], p. 198). Myers (*Dryden*, pp. 42–3) briefly touches on the interchangeability of language and reality in *Aureng-Zebe*, reaching the incomprehensible conclusion that Dryden "clearly . . . had to move away from a mode which accorded mere names and titles such mastery over reality." Myers evidently believes that the flaws with which a dramatist endows his characters necessarily vitiate the play. The language theme in *Aureng-Zebe* has been more extensively examined by David W. Tarbet, "Reason Dazzled: Perspective and Language in Dryden's *Aureng-Zebe*", *Criticism*, 18 (1976), 256–72. Tarbet, however, believes that Aureng-Zebe is an exemplary character associated with the proper use of language, and sustains his case by an inaccurately selective review of the evidence: for example, he notes Aureng-Zebe's concern for the glory of his "name" (II. 529; p. 262) but fails to mention that Aureng-Zebe dismisses virtue as a "Barren, and aery name" (II. 504).

19. See also I. 306–11, II. 338–41, v. 43–5, 77–8.

POSTSCRIPT

1. Heroic drama in general, of course, has been seen as an aberration in dramatic history. Dryden's heroic plays are quite exceptional in their quality and intelligence, but other heroic plays of the seventies reproduce his concern with the limitations of heroism, and in this respect are consistent with such "post-heroic" plays as John

Crowne's *The Ambitious Statesman* (1679) and *Darius* (1688), Nathaniel Lee's *Lucius Junius Brutus* (1680) and *The Princess of Cleve* (1680?), Thomas Otway's *Venice Preserv'd* (1682), and Thomas Southerne's *Oroonoko* (1695). The following heroic plays are all in some measure critical of heroic ideals (asterisks indicate especially extensive or interesting criticism): John Banks, *The Rival Kings* (1677), *The Destruction of Troy* (1678)*; Crowne, *The History of Charles the Eighth of France* (1671), *The Destruction of Jerusalem* (1677)*; Lee, *Sophonisba* (1675)*, *Gloriana* (1676); Otway, *Don Carlos* (1676)*; Henry Nevil Payne, *The Siege of Constantinople* (1674)*, which contains a pseudo-hero who combines characteristics of Almanzor and Pyrgopolynices; Sir Charles Sedley, *Antony and Cleopatra* (1677).

2. Images of dramaturgy and play-acting are a regular feature of Restoration tragedies and comedies. In plays such as *The Country Wife* and *The Man of Mode* the theatre—like the mask—is a central, controlling metaphor; Horner, for instance, appropriately uses the theatre as the locale for his social début in the guise of a eunuch. In less accomplished comedies and tragedies, the theatrical metaphors tend to be sporadic and undeveloped, but they do suggest a view of dramatic illusion more complex and sophisticated than the doctrine of total surrender peddled in dramatic theory. For examples in some works of the second (or lower) rank see John Caryll, *The English Princess* (London, 1667) II. p. 28, IV. p. 45, V. p. 57; Crowne, *Juliana; or, the Princess of Poland* (1671) III. pp. 63, 67, V. p. 105, *The Dramatic Works of John Crowne*, ed. James Maidment and W. H. Logan (Edinburgh, 1874), I; Lee *Mithridates* (1678) IV. i. 285—6, in *The Works of Nathaniel Lee*, ed. Thomas B. Stroup and Arthur L. Cooke (New Brunswick, N.J., 1955), I; Samuel Pordage, *The Siege of Babylon* (London, 1678) II. p. 19, IV. p. 39, V. p. 56; Thomas Durfey, *A Fond Husband* (London, 1677) I. p. 11, II. pp. 12, 14; Sir Francis Fane, *Love in the Dark* (London, 1675) II. p. 36, IV. p. 69; Edward Ravenscroft, *The Careless Lovers* (London, 1673) III. p. 38 (1); *The Citizen Turn'd Gentleman* (London, 1675) I. p. 9.

3. In "The Jewel of Great Price: Mutability and Constancy in Dryden's *All for Love*", *ELH*, 42 (1975), 38—61, J. Douglas Canfield argues that *All for Love* continues a uniform tradition in which the Antony and Cleopatra story is regularly used to depict the triumph of constancy over mutability. Canfield's account of the tradition is, however, extremely misleading, and contains several serious factual errors. In discussing Cesare de' Cesari's *Cleopatra* (1552), for example, he mistakes the Chorus' praise of Charmion and Iras for praise of Antony and Cleopatra, and bases his interpretation of the play on this elementary mistake (p. 41). I am at present preparing my own account of *All for Love* and its relation to earlier tradition.

4. Shakespeare, *Antony and Cleopatra*, ed. M. R. Ridley, The Arden Shakespeare (London, 1954), III. vii. 21—3.

5. Summers, IV. I. p. 355.

6. Summers, V. II. p. 44.

Index